EDUCATION AS FREEDOM

EDUCATION AS FREEDOM

African American Educational Thought and Activism

EDITED BY
NOEL S. ANDERSON AND HAROON KHAREM

LEXINGTON BOOKS
A Division of Rowman & Littlefield Publishers, Inc.
Lanham • Boulder • New York • Toronto • Plymouth, UK

LEXINGTON BOOKS

A division of Rowman & Littlefield Publishers, Inc.
A wholly owned subsidary of The Rowman & Littlefield Publishing Group, Inc.
4501 Forbes Boulevard, Suite 200, Lanham, MD 20706
www.lexingtonbooks.com

Estover Road, Plymouth PL6 7PY, United Kingdom

British Library Cataloguing in Publication Information Available

Library of Congress Cataloging-in-Publication Data

The hardback edition of this book was previously cataloged by the Library of Congress as
follows:

Education as freedom : African American educational thought and activism / edited by
   Noel S. Anderson and Haroon Kharem.
      p. cm.
   Includes bibliographical references and index.
   1. African Americans—Education—History. 2. African American educators.
   3. Discrimination in education—United States—History. I. Anderson, Noel S., 1970–
   II. Kharem, Haroon.
   LC2741.E35 2009
   371.829'96073—dc22   2008035877

ISBN: 978-0-7391-2068-2 (cloth : alk. paper)
ISBN: 978-0-7391-3260-9 (electronic)
ISBN: 978-0-7391-2069-9 (pbk. : alk. paper)

Printed in the United States of America

♾ ™ The paper used in this publication meets the minimum requirements of American
National Standard for Information Sciences—Permanence of Paper for Printed Library
Materials, ANSI/NISO Z39.48-1992.

This book is dedicated to
Dr. Asa G. Hilliard III
for his pioneering work and for his deep love
affair with people of African ancestry

CONTENTS

Foreword

PAULINE F. BYNOE
BROOKLYN COLLEGE, CITY UNIVERSITY OF NEW YORK

Is there a will to educate all of our children?

—ASA G. HILLIARD III (1991)

A preeminent African American contributor to the knowledge-base of who, what, why, when, where and how to engage the will to educate African Americans. He has left a legacy of considerations in the depth and scope of his work to "connect the dots" about the nation's will to deliver this humane principal to "close achievement gaps" towards education equity and freedom.

—ASA G. HILLIARD III (1933–2007)

I F THE NATIONAL *WILL* IS TO EDUCATE ALL OF OUR CHILDREN, and if Blacks in America are included in "all," then an examination of education as liberation and freedom for Blacks in America is most meaningful here. Over several decades, Dr. Asa G. Hilliard III was a standard-bearer who challenged the nation's will to educate African Americans. He deconstructed education practices in the United States, and regarded African American history as a means to provide real educational opportunities and excellence for children.

Dr. Hilliard posited that the history of race, politics, and economics are the lens through which education is viewed and acted upon in the United States. This history is bound in the 10th Amendment of the U.S. Constitution that requires each state to interpret education policy that emanates from the national level. This same Constitution considered African Americans less than human—equated to an economic value of land and animal. This same Constitution spoke of liberty, equality, freedom, and the pursuit of happiness while promoting injustice.

Over time, how have the assertions of liberty and equality been translated and transformed in the education of African Americans? Asa Hilliard III was our elder who, for several decades, framed and tooled ways to know and accomplish excellence in the education of African Americans: abandoning the race construct related to hegemony, removal of alien and/or invalid curriculum, recognition of culture as a framing context, African American academic excellence without excuse, and the effects of special treatment/services which result in disparate treatment in education (Hilliard, 1998, 1999).

Though his lifework, Dr. Hilliard illustrated how these binding elements impact educational opportunities and outcomes for our children. Among the range of contributions, he was a renowned expert witness in several successful federal landmark cases on assessment equity and a contributor to the development of national assessments for educators and children. Dr. Hilliard was a founding member of the Association for the Study of Classical African Civilizations and produced many multimedia educational materials on African history. He established models for valid assessment and pluralistic curriculum, with a repository of seminal works about African American history, assessment equity, teaching strategies, and public policy.

At best, there is a tacit recognition or mention of a legacy of Black perspectives and strategies on educating Black children in United States. Dr. Hilliard tirelessly sought to illuminate examples of African American effort and excellence in his research and writings on Black education, and in his endless *will* to support and mentor educators and activists who attempt to understand and effectively educate Black children. Subsequently, he has left us a hefty body of work in theory, policy, and practice on how African Americans can achieve optimal educational outcomes for young people.

Education as Freedom: African American Educational Thought and Activism is a keen testament to Dr. Hilliard's work and dedication, his distillation of knowledge, and his deep concern with the well-being and freedom of people of African ancestry. This text is included in that legacy Dr. Hilliard illuminated, a legacy that centers on informing policy and practice, and that continues to push our nation's *will* to educate all of its children.

Works Cited

Hilliard, Asa G., III. 1991. "Do we have the will to educate all children?" *Educational Leadership* 49 (1).

———. 1997. "Teacher education from an African American perspective." In *Critical knowledge for diverse teachers and learners.* Washington, DC: The American Association of Colleges for Teacher Education.

———. 1998. "Cultural pluralism in education." In *Creating the future, perspectives on educational change,* ed. Dee Dickinson. Seattle: New Horizons for Learning.

———. 1999. "What do we need to know now? Race, identity, hegemony, and education." *Rethinking Schools* 24 (2).

Acknowledgments

I WOULD LIKE TO THANK EACH CONTRIBUTOR to *Education as Freedom* for making this text such a rich addition to the discourse and literature on Black education. I want to thank Yusuf Ransome, our graduate researcher and future colleague/scholar. A warm thanks to my colleagues and dear friends at Brooklyn College, New York University, and the University of Pennsylvania. There are too many to name and the support is endless. A shout out to Farai Chideya, Lisette Nieves, Greg Gunn, Year Up–NY, Darlene Burroughs, Vanessa Watson, Aaron Thomas, and the National Urban League family, Dordy Jourdain, Larry and Sharon Patterson, EP, Monty and Carol Ross, and Jackie Simmons for monitoring my progress on the book. Deep gratitude to my family, my mother, Martha, my sisters, Monefa and Kawana, my brothers from another mother, Alec and Dominic. I want to thank, posthumously, Morris and Miriam McDuffie, for being my towering intellectual figures and moral guides. Most importantly I want to thank my love force, wife, Lashan, and son, Avery, for bringing such joy (and humor) to my life.

Noel S. Anderson

I want to give thanks and acknowledge all the African American scholars and educators that worked hard studying to develop a pedagogy that forced a paradigm shift in education. I want to acknowledge Deborah Shanley for her support as the lives and future of the kids in east New York continue to take precedence over my research. I want to especially thank the kids at the Performing Arts and Technology High School (PATHS) and all the kids I visit in the elementary schools in east New York (ENY). They remind me of what all this work is about. A politician once commented that east New York is a "wasteland." Some scholars and educators have wrongfully labeled ENY kids dysfunctional and deficient model learners. Yet, these kids have learned to navigate, deal with stress better than some adults, and survive in spite of a society that has neglected and marginalized them. My experiences with these kids will always provide me with research ideas, as I continue to incorporate African-centered knowledge entwined with Paulo Freire's work of *conscientizacao* into the classroom.

I want to thank Lynda Sarnoff for supporting my "Black Power" class. I want to give thanks to Lottie Almonte for the opportunity to teach her students at PATHS. I also give thanks to my former students Sharleen, Terri, Nate, Brian, and all the students that were in Sankofa who put into practice what they learned, challenged, and demanded the structures of higher education to provide them and those who would follow the opportunity to learn from an African-centered pedagogy.

Haroon Kharem

Introduction: Education as Freedom
African American Educational Thought and Activism

NOEL S. ANDERSON AND HAROON KHAREM

SINCE THE 1954 *Brown v. Board* Supreme Court decision outlawing racial segregation in public education until the current flurry to close the "racial achievement gap" in education highlighted by such controversial federal initiatives as the "No Child Left Behind" Act of 2002, the condition and prescriptions for Black education have been hotly debated. In compelling ways, Blacks continue to be "America's metaphor" (Wright 1957, 108–9), whereas the educational performance of African American[1] students has become the barometer for assessing the condition and future of public education in this country, particularly in urban areas.

Yet in the shadow of the contemporary research spilling from governmental agencies, think tanks, and educational reform organizations that call for more accountability and "new" audit approaches to improving urban public schools or closing the gap between white and Black students, is a rich tradition of African American educational thought and activism. Contrary to popular belief, the wealth of educational ideas and activism emerging from Black communities over decades has centered on utilizing education as an instrument for Black resistance; Black solidarity, social improvement, and political power; and, most of all, freedom. The ideas were not simply parroted from white thinkers and educators or passively borrowed from European models of schooling; nor was the formation of Black educational institutions steered solely by the benevolent interests of white philanthropy. Indeed, African American educational ideas and activism emerged from diverse Black civic, political, and religious communities and organizations and were informed by the complexity of the Black experience in America.

Early Movements in African American Education

Enslaved Africans in the American colonies advocated literacy and numeracy as a method of emancipation. Constitutionally, slaves were classified as "non-persons," as subhuman property, equivalent to livestock.
Yet, absurdly, there were also laws throughout the Union that made both
teaching a slave and a slave learning to read, to write, or do math illegal.
So becoming literate as a slave was not only criminal, it was revolutionary,
in that it enabled an enslaved person to reclaim a sense of humanity in face
of inhumane circumstances and develop skills of resistance and liberation.

In the eighteenth century, African American leaders continued to express a deep concern for the education of their children. On June 25, 1792,
Prince Hall addressed the African Lodge in Charlestown on the education of Black children (Hall 1792) and, subsequently, in 1798 opened the
first all-Black school in his home in Boston. Further, after the Civil War,
Blacks were at the forefront of the movement to establish public schools
and erect institutions of higher learning (Anderson 1988). From that moment on Blacks have struggled to educate their children and fought to
discredit the lies that Blacks were an "indolent and shiftless" race.

Starting with the work of Prince Hall, leading to the pioneering work
of James McCune Smith, John Mercer Langston, Anna Julia Cooper, and
Nannie Burroughs in the nineteenth century, to W. E. B Du Bois, Carter G.
Woodson, Mary Mcloud Bethune at the turn of the twentieth century, to
post–*Brown v. Board* educators such as Mwalimi J. Shujaa, Lisa Delpit, William H. Watkins, and countless others, African American thinkers and educators have argued for a more definitive theoretical framework in the education
of African American children. For instance, Foster (1997) and Kunjufu
(2002) argue for more responsive schools for Black students, highlighting
that over 80 percent of the teaching population today are white middle-class
women and from non–urban areas. In many urban public schools across the
nation, Blacks make up a significant portion of the public school population. However, there is a paucity of African American educational ideas and
history reflected within the curriculum of public schools and teacher training programs, other than scant mention in courses on "urban teaching" or
"multiculturalism" offered in some schools of education.

Learning for Liberation

While educators, teachers, and school administrators grapple with the failure rate of African American children and search for solutions, there exists

a substantive body of past and current scholarship on African American educational ideas that need to be studied by aspiring teachers, specifically, and by those concerned with African American education in general.

Education as Freedom: African American Educational Thought and Activism is a groundbreaking edited text that thematically documents, traces, and reassesses the distinctively African American empirical, methodological, and theoretical contributions to knowledge-making, learning, pedagogy, and schooling from the 1800s until the present day. The nineteenth and twentieth centuries represent a wide-ranging time in history and constitute a dynamic and prolific period of African American educational thought and activism. The varied history of African American thought and activism on education formed from an array of traditional academic disciplines, such as history, sociology, theology, philosophy, and education; from the dramatic, visual, and musical arts; and from grassroots social, political, and religious movements. Put simply, there has never been a monolithic history or movement within "Black education." Just as African Americans represent a diversity of thought, identities, and histories, the moniker "Black education" is an amalgamation of diverse and sometimes controversial ideas on education. In this spirit, *Education as Freedom* brings together essays by scholars across traditional academic disciplines of education, history, philosophy, sociology, psychology, and political science, as well as interdisciplinary fields such American studies, urban, cultural, and postcolonial studies, analyzing the published and unpublished writings, speeches, literary works, the lives of African American educators, thinkers, activists, as well as social and political movements regarding education, past and present. The overarching purpose is to illuminate the power of ideas and actions for the advancement of Black education in the United States and abroad.

Structure of the Book

The book is organized thematically into three parts: (1) "From Bondage to Freedom: Early African American Educational Thought and Activism," (2) "This Skin I'm In: African American Identity and Education," and (3) "Advancing the Race: African American Education and Social Progress." Each part attempts to analyze the ways in which African American thinkers, educators, scholars, and activists have resisted slavery and other forms of oppression through literacy; espoused the purpose and design of schooling during and shortly after Reconstruction; formulated ideas of education under Jim Crow segregation and civil rights struggles; posited

Black Nationalism, Afro-centrism, and multiculturalism; and advanced contemporary ideas about Black education and globalization.

In chapter 1, Haroon Kharem begins part 1, "From Bondage to Freedom: Early African American Educational Thought and Activism," by looking at the pioneering role of scientist and intellectual James McCune Smith in "Medical Doctor, Integrationist, and Black Nationalist: Dr. James McCune Smith and the Dilemma of an Antebellum Intellectual Black Activist." McCune Smith was one of the first abolitionists to challenge, publicly, popular scientific racist assumptions about Black intelligence and capacity for learning in the mid-nineteenth century. Born a slave, McCune was the first Black to garner a medical degree in Scotland, to practice pharmacology and medicine in segregated New York, and to become one of the most vocal Abolitionists and advocates for Black schools.

In chapter 2, Judith King-Calnek in "John Mercer Langston and the Shaping of African American Education in the Nineteenth Century" examines the life's work and ideas of John Mercer Langston, an unrivaled figure who was not only an inspector general of the Freedman's Bureau, but, in the face of Jim Crow, went on to head Howard University and then become a respected congressperson. King-Calnek illuminates Langston's groundbreaking work in not only advancing Black schooling but pushing through legislation that would lay the ground work for compulsory schooling for Blacks in future years.

In chapter 3, Karen Johnson compares the educational ideas and work Anna Julia Cooper and Nannie Burroughs, in "On Classical versus Vocational Training: The Educational Ideals of Anna Julia Cooper and Nannie Helen Burroughs." Contemporaries of W. E. B. Du Bois and Booker T. Washington, these women held passionate and courageous views regarding the roles of classical and industrial training for the advancement of Black people. Johnson artfully explores this discourse as it plays out in the lives of these two Black women.

Part 2, "This Skin I'm In: African American Identity and Education," shifts attention to discourse on the role of education in promoting ideas of self-identity formation as well as Black consciousness. Sabrina Ross, in chapter 4, "Womanist Conceptualizations of African-Centered Critical Multiculturalism: Creating New Possibilities of Thinking about Social Justice," uses a womanist lens to examine the tension between an essentialist African-centered pedagogy and the Eurocentric critical multiculturalism as they relate to Black education. Ross is skeptical of both strands of thought because of what she sees as the power of each to suppress diversity, individuality, and acceptance of the gender, racial, class, and sexual orientation differences prevalent in Black communities. Subsequently, she attempts to find a middle ground that would foster a healthy self-identity and liberatory education for all children.

In chapter 5, Eric Hurley, in "The Performance Gap: Stereotype Threat, Assessment, and the Education of African American Children," traces the trajectory of ideas and research regarding the achievement gap among Black and white students, moving the analysis from Kenneth and Mamie Clarke's "doll test" during the *Brown v. Board* case to the current and popular "stereotype threat" research advanced by Stanford psychologist Claude Steele. Hurley interrogates the ways in which psychology in general, and Black psychologists in particular, have played a role in shaping the educational and racial identity of Black children in research and in the larger American imagination.

In chapter 6, Ojeya Cruz Banks explicates the Afro-Caribbean dimensions of Katherine Dunham's dance pedagogy in "Katherine Dunham: Decolonizing Dance Education," highlighting the ways in which this innovative art form attempts to decolonize the Black body and Black identity. Exploring an often neglected area in the collective history of African American education, Cruz-Banks skillfully expands our understanding of how the evolution of this art form was consistent with other movements to foster a healthy Black self-identity in young people

Finally, in part 3, "Advancing the Race: African American Education and Social Progress," Black education is examined for its role in advancing African Americans through the social, political, and economic hierarchies of the United States. In chapter 7, "Live the Truth: Politics and Pedagogy in the African American Movement for Freedom and Liberation," Daniel Perlstein analyzes the work of the Black Panthers and the Student Nonviolent Coordinating Committee (SNCC) in setting up schools in the midst of civil rights struggles during the 1960s. Perlstein asserts that these organizations early in their creation utilized progressive educational philosophies and pedagogical approaches with young people. However, over time as state and police repression became more pronounced, as did internal organizational conflicts and power struggles, more didactic and rigid instructional approaches were soon adopted.

In chapter 8, "Black Schools, White Schools: Derrick Bell, Race, and the Failure of the Integration Ideal in *Brown*," Noel S. Anderson examines the life and writings of critical race theorist and legal scholar Derrick Bell to reassess the impact of the *Brown* decision over fifty years later. Anderson both historicizes and resituates Bell's ideas on *Brown* in the broader public discourse on resegregating public schools around the country. He asserts that *Brown* as a Supreme Court decision succeeded in striking down "separate but equal" but failed as an integration strategy.

Lastly, in chapter 9, A. A. Akom's "Research for Liberation: Du Bois, the Chicago School, and the Development of Black Emanicipatory Action Research" examines new, global-minded approaches to conducting research in Black education that acknowledges the diversity of cultures and histories within Black communities. Akom advances a Black Emancipatory Action Research framework (BEAR) that draws on critical race theory (CRT) as well as other progressive theories. BEAR not only questions notions of objectivity in research on Black education but underscores the ethical principles such as self-determination, social justice, equity, healing, and love as central to empirical work throughout the African Diaspora.

Education as Freedom not only presents an impressive range and diversity of thought and activism regarding Black education from scholars across the United States and abroad, but it concurrently reaffirms the legacy and invaluable contributions of African American educational ideas and activism to public education and to the direction and future of the United States.

Note

1. The terms "Black" and "African American" are used interchangeably throughout this book. When referring to historical time frames, terms such as Negro, colored, Black, and African American will be used by the contributors to this book.

Works Cited

Anderson, James. 1988. *The education of blacks in the south.* Chapel Hill: The University of North Carolina Press.

Foster, Michele.1997. *Black teachers on teaching.* New York: New Press.

Hall, Prince. 1792. *A charge delivered to the brethren of the African Lodge on the 25th of June, 1792.* Boston: Printed and sold by T. and J. Fleet at the Bible and Heart, Cornhill.

Kunjufu, Jawanza. 2002. *Black students—middle class teachers.* Chicago: African American Images.

Wright, Richard.1957. *White man, listen.* Westport, CT: Greenwood Press.

FROM BONDAGE TO FREEDOM: EARLY AFRICAN AMERICAN EDUCATIONAL THOUGHT AND ACTIVISM

I

Medical Doctor, Integrationist, and Black Nationalist
1

Black Nationalist
Dr. James McCune Smith and the Dilemma of an Antebellum Intellectual Black Activist

HAROON KHAREM

> *Through my veins flow, freely flow, dark Afric's proudest blood.*

—JAMES MCCUNE SMITH[1]

THE BIRTH OF THE UNITED STATES as an independent nation was plagued at its inception with racism, discriminatory practices, compromise, and expediency with regard to indigenous people, Africans, and those of African descent. This was especially true with slavery, which later split the nation into warring sections. In the North, racist sentiment was rooted deeply in white people's psyche against both an enslaved and a free Black population. Eighteenth- and nineteenth-century intelligentsia and religious leaders led the way in promoting Black inferiority.[2]

Slavery was an integral part of the colonial economy in both the North and South. Contrary to our collective memory (and school textbooks), New York and New England's economy depended upon the Atlantic Slave Trade, slave labor, and the products of slave labor from the 1600s to the 1850s. Especially in New York City, economic wealth was primarily dependent upon slave labor and the products produced through slavery until the Civil War.[3] By the 1800s, the South's dependence on slave labor was almost two centuries old, and its permanence appeared assured.

In response to the continual importation of enslaved Africans, the breeding of Blacks in the United States, and racial discrimination in the North,[4] the antebellum period witnessed the ascension of some of the most prominent and influential activists to come out of the Black community in the nineteenth century. Black activists set the tone for the abolitionist period, pushed the envelope against slavery, and openly confronted the racist ideology of Northern white abolitionists. Black activists were instrumental in changing the minds of many white abolitionists, such as William Lloyd Garrison, from the idea of "colonizing" of Blacks to the immediate end of slavery. Black activists differed in opinion concerning which action was best to abolish slavery: some advocated moral persuasion while others called for the use of physical force to end slavery as the better choice. They also debated whether Black people should integrate into Anglo-Protestant society or separate and emigrate to Africa. Nevertheless, they were of one mind, determined to put an end to slavery and racial discrimination.[5] They engaged in numerous rallies and conventions, and advocated and participated in aid societies to end slavery, to uplift the race, and to promote education and economic prosperity. Black activists in the antebellum period matured into a powerful rhetorical force and were the compelling force behind the abolitionist movement. Some of the most famous lecturers among the Black abolitionists were Charles B. Ray, Martin Delany, Frederick Douglass, Henry Highland Garnet, Charles Lenox Remond, and Samuel Ringgold Ward. However, men such as Lunsford Lane, Jermain Loguen, J. W. C. Pennington, and many others were also powerful orators. Talented yet untrained Black female orators such as Maria W. Stewart and Sojourner Truth were able to move multitudes and stood alongside the best male lecturers.

One Black activist whose name does not readily come to mind when one speaks of Black abolitionists is James McCune Smith, one of the most significant activists and intellectuals during the antebellum period. James McCune Smith was the first Black man in America to obtain a medical degree, the first Black man to practice his profession and own and operate a pharmacy in the United States. His patients were both Black and white, he published in prestigious journals of his day, became a member of the American Geographical Society, and served for twenty years on the medical staff of the Free Negro Orphan Asylum in New York City (Morgan 2003). McCune Smith was an integral part of the Negro Conventions; he petitioned for Black suffrage, was active with the Underground Railroad, contributed funds to the poor, and wrote articles for various publications like the *Emancipator*. Harriet A. Washington in her decisive book *Medical Apartheid: The Dark History of Medical Experimentation on Black Americans from Colonial Times to the Present* (2006) says that McCune Smith was a brilliant physician and statistical scientist and was superb in refuting scientific racism. Washington states that his lectures exposed "the scientific fallacy of phrenology . . . and offered scathing criticisms of . . . imputing character and intelligence from physiology" (Washington 2006, 94). John Stauffer in his scholarly work *The Black Hearts of Men: Radical Abolitionists and the Transformation of Race* (2001) says of James McCune Smith

> He was a brilliant scholar, writer and critic. . . . As a prose stylist and original thinker, McCune Smith ranks, at his best, alongside such canonical figures as Emerson and Thoreau. His essays are sophisticated and elegant, his interpretations of American culture are way ahead of his time, and his experimental style and use of dialect anticipate some of the Harlem Renaissance. (5–6)

The purpose of this essay is to examine the life of James McCune Smith and his contribution as a Black activist within the abolitionist movement, his activities to promote education and racial equality, and his dilemma as a Black intellectual. This will be achieved by investigating McCune Smith's life, his struggle against racism and colonization, and the emigration movements of free Blacks during the antebellum period. I also look at McCune Smith's dilemma as a middle-class Black intellectual in a white dominant society that found it hard to accept a Black man as an intellectual. McCune Smith held Black Nationalist opinions while at the same time he believed in integration. The objective is to provide the reader with sound knowledge of James McCune Smith, his dedication to the abolition of slavery, and his dedication to racial equality in the North. As a result, the reader will be able to derive an assessment of the life of James McCune Smith, his enduring legacy, and his dilemma as a Black intellectual. Hopefully the reader will understand the impact he made upon the struggle against slavery, colonization, and racism in the United States.

Historical Background

Emancipation laws in the North not only had an effect on Northern Blacks, but influenced the decisions of both enslaved and free Blacks who wanted to leave the South. While New York City along with other Northern cities became temporary and/or permanent havens for manumitted Blacks and those who liberated themselves from their enslaved status, many New England colonies passed laws that prohibited Blacks from entering their colonies and made them move into the wilderness, land still occupied by Native Americans. In the Dutch colony called New Netherlands (New York City), Africans and those of African descent had lived in the colony since the early 1600s. The first record of a Black entering what is now called New York Harbor was Esteban Gomez, a Portuguese pilot who sailed up the Hudson River in 1525. The first Black to set foot on the island of Manhattan was Jan Rodrigues in 1613, who was left there by a Dutch captain. Rodrigues would later be the interpreter between the Dutch and the indigenous people we call the Rockaway Indians (Hodges 1999, 6–7).

During the Dutch colonial period, Blacks became the first landowners of the area that is now Broadway and Chambers Street in lower Manhattan. Although enslaved Africans were sent to New Netherlands as cheap slave labor, they maintained their African culture, adopted Dutch culture, petitioned for wages and their freedom. A few Blacks were able to amass some sort of wealth while living in the Dutch colony. Anthony Jansen Van Vaes, a Black sea captain who sailed under the Dutch flag, lived in the Gravesend section of Brooklyn and was later given two hundred acres near Coney Island (Hodges 1999, 10–11)

In 1664, an English fleet invaded the Dutch colony forcing Peter Stuyvesant to surrender the colony. The colony was given to the Duke of York, the principal owner of the Royal African Company, a slave trading company, who began to use the colony and shifted the importation of large numbers of enslaved Africans from the Caribbean to New York (McManus 1966, 23). The Duke of York encouraged the importation of Africans and gave slave ships special privileges by removing property taxes and import tariffs on slaves, giving warehouse priorities, and supporting resolutions that promoted slave labor. Individual slave traders began to amass huge profits by selling enslaved Africans to slave owners in the city and to farmers, artisans, and the plantations throughout the colonies. The Royal African Company led the way to create laws to regulate slaves and restrict the movement of free Blacks at the same time the Virginia colony developed its laws to restrict Blacks, thus solidifying the foundation of white superiority and Black inferiority in its colonies.[6] In the early 1700s, men such as Gabriel Ludlow, Phillip Livingston, and Nicholas De Ronde, some of New York's most respected leaders, were the leading importers of enslaved Africans. They made slave trading New York's most profitable business. Pirates such as Captain Kidd, when he was not a paid mercenary for the English, engaged in the slave trade and transported them to New York. In addition, during the intercolonial wars with Spain for the control of the Caribbean, free Blacks serving in the Spanish navy captured by the English or Dutch were sold into slavery and sent to New York. The 1698 census counted 2,170 African slaves and by 1746 the slave population had risen to 9,000 (McManus 1973, 25–27).

In 1712, enslaved Blacks were accused of seeking freedom by becoming Christians and learning how to read. Elias Neau, a missionary, opened a school for Blacks and began to teach them how to read. Some of the students were implicated in an attempt to use force to gain their freedom. As a result, emancipation laws were passed prohibiting free Blacks from purchasing land within the city. Neau's school was closed for fear that education would motivate Blacks to seek freedom, which exacerbated the problem of importing Africans who were skilled artisans, fluent in Spanish, Dutch, French, and English as well as various African dialects. Slave owners were required to post a bond for any manumitted slaves as a guarantee that they could support themselves (Aptheker 1939, 19; Harris 2003, 35; Hodges 1999, 64–65). Northern colonies passed laws to restrict any upward mobility of Blacks in all parts of colonial society. Connecticut, Massachusetts, Rhode Island, and Maine refused to educate any nonresident Blacks and made interracial sex and marriage a crime. Pennsylvania and Rhode Island declared Blacks as noncitizens therefore unable to vote. Both New Jersey and Connecticut completely disfranchised free Blacks (McManus 1973). Alexis de Tocqueville witnessed white racism first hand as he traveled through the United States in 1831 and wrote *Democracy in America* (1835) commenting:

> Race prejudice seems stronger in those states that have abolished slavery than in those States where it still exists, and nowhere is it more intolerant than in those states where slavery was never known. . . . Negroes have been given electoral rights, but they would come forward to vote at the risks of their lives. When oppressed, they can bring action at law. But they will find only white men among their judges. It is true that the law makes them eligible as jurors, but prejudice wards them off. The Negro's son is excluded from the school the European's child goes . . . in the hospitals he lies apart. He is allowed to worship the same God as the white man but must not pray at the same altar. . . . The gates of heaven are not closed against him, but his inequality stops only short of the boundaries of the other world. When the Negro is no more, his bones are cast aside, and some difference in condition is found even in the equality of death. (343)

In 1815, Republicans gained control of New York from the Federalists and passed laws that required Blacks to obtain special passes to vote. Moreover, in 1821 Blacks were required to possess $250.00 to be able to vote, while this same requirement was abolished for white males.

In Brooklyn, there were 641 free Blacks by 1800 and by 1830 there were 1,253 free Blacks living in the Fourth Ward, Bedford, Gowanus, Red Hook, Fort Greene, and Williamsburg sections of Brooklyn. In 1817, Black congregates in Brooklyn's interracial Sands Street Methodist Church decided to leave and purchased property on High Street and formed the High Street Wesleyan Methodist Episcopal Church. In 1816, the Rev. Peter Croger, who later became pastor of the High Street Church, opened the first "African School" in his home. In Brooklyn, Black and white children attended the same public school in the early 1800s and were taught by a Black teacher named William M. Read. By the 1820s, Black students were completely driven from the school, but through the persistence by Black parents to educate their children, they built and maintained their own school (Connolly 1977).

Slavery had not yet been abolished in New York City when James McCune Smith's parents arrived; nevertheless, New York City was an ideal place for Blacks who sought freedom from their enslaved status. Although slave catchers and kidnappers were abundant in the city, enslaved Blacks took freedom into their own hands and took refuge in New York City; they were able to find support and assistance from the Black community and passage to other Northern regions and Canada. Those who chose to stay in New York found employment as bootblacks, housemaids, waiters, longshoremen, sailors, chimney cleaners, and in other jobs that required little skill. Free and enslaved Blacks were forced to live in the oldest and most deplorable sections of lower Manhattan and South Brooklyn. Without romanticizing Black unity, it is safe to say that racial discrimination, diseases, and the deplorable conditions forced most Blacks to become a closely knit community whereby they provided each other with relief and comfort. McCune Smith's mother, like most Blacks, lived a difficult life as a noncitizen that restricted her to dilapidated living quarters and probably domestic employment. Although McCune Smith's mother was free, as a child he was still a slave by law (in New York the children of free parents were still held as slaves) and like most Black children, he understood that he was chattel till 1827 when slavery was abolished in New York (Harris 2003).

By the early 1800s, there were close to 8,000 free Blacks living in New York City and most avoided living near the Eastern tip of Manhattan where many of the slave owning families resided. The majority of Blacks lived in segregated communities near present-day Houston Street and the Fresh Water Pond, the area presently near the African American Burial Ground memorial site (290 Broadway). Middle-class and wealthy whites avoided the Fresh Water Pond area because it was swampland that caused disease and was used as a dumping ground for the city's waste. Although the Pond was later filled in and dried up, its offensive smell kept many whites away and allowed Blacks a sense of independence (Harris 2003, 74). Somewhere around 1825 working-class Blacks began to obtain lots between what are now 83rd and 88th streets and 8th Ave in Central Park. Working-class Blacks settled in the area that became known as Seneca Village. By the 1840s, over 100 people were living there and by 1850 almost 300 Blacks and Irish people lived in Seneca Village. Finally, to make room for Central Park, Seneca Village was destroyed in 1858 through the Law of Eminent Domain, whereby the government can take private property for public use (Blackmar 1992, 64–73).

Although some Blacks were able to move into tenuous middle-class status, it did not change the racism or Black Codes they were bound to obey. White mobs could cause physical harm to body and/or property without any repercussions of the law. Middle-class Black men like Andrew Williams, a twenty-five-year-old bootblack, moved to escape the racist white mobs and the Black Codes; he purchased land that began Seneca Village. Thomas Downing, who owned the Oyster Bar on Broad Street and Cato's Tavern that catered to the white elite and politicians, voiced his protest to the Black Codes and white mobs that roamed the streets; both restaurants were well-known New York City establishments during the antebellum era. In 1820 William Brown lived in present-day Greenwich Village, opened the first pleasure garden for Blacks, (a recreation spot) known as the "African Grove" by whites. Williams ran a small theater in an apartment but was forced to close in 1823 because of complaints by whites. Brown's theater was the site of the first play written by a Black in the United States called "The Drama of King Shotaway" and was the training ground of the famous Black Shakespearian actor Ira Aldridge (Harris 2003, 79; Hubert and Mildred 1993). Instead of middle-class status giving Blacks economic stability, middle-class status was mostly a moral aspect than an economic point of view. While many middle-class Blacks lived a semi comfortable lifestyle, most held jobs or owned businesses that were considered working-class or low-income employment.

The African Free Schools

In 1787 John Jay, Alexander Hamilton, George Clinton, Lewis Morris, James Duane, and other elite New Yorkers founded the New York Manumission Society.[7] The Society allied itself to the struggle of Blacks and sought to convince whites that Blacks were worthy of freedom but not equality. They established themselves as the patron of free and enslaved Blacks in New York and provided legal assistance to free Blacks who were kidnapped and sold South. The Society also founded the African Free Schools to provide education to enslaved and free Black children (Rury 1983; 1985). The Society joined with the Federalists and saw themselves as guardians of New York's Black community and sought to monitor and influence the way Blacks lived and control their cultural norms. The Society believed in colonization whereby Blacks were to be sent to Africa. They believed America's greatest sin was the enslavement of Africans and to eradicate the stain of sin was to send them back to Africa. Also, the Society did not see Blacks as equal human beings alongside whites and sending them back to Africa would rid the United States of an inferior and immoral people (Bodo 1954; Harris 2003; Kharem 2006). At meetings, the Society maintained it had to "Keep a watchful eye over the conduct of such Negroes as have been liberated . . . [to] prevent them from running into immorality or sinking into idleness" (Rury 1985). The Society set out to control and stamp out the alleged inferior and savage culture of Black people. Although the Manumission Society accused Blacks of immoral behavior, they never specifically said what kind of immoral behavior Blacks exhibited.

The Manumission Society set out to accomplish their ideology through the African Free Schools by indoctrinating the children with Anglo-Protestant ideas and demeaning their African culture. They understood that it was easier to influence the minds of the children by imbuing them with the alleged superior tenets of Anglo-Protestant culture and history (Kharem 2000). The Society saw African culture as heathen and inculcating the children with the ideas of Anglo Protestant culture would rid the next generation of the allegedly deficient culture of Black parents. Although the Society believed that the African Free Schools would prove to whites that Blacks were as intelligent if given the opportunity, their main concern was instilling the children with moral values they perceived the parents lacked. Whites viewed dancing, loud music, and other cultural activities the Black community engaged in as demoralizing and sexually deviant. As a requirement for attending the African Free School, the families of the children were forbidden to associate with those who did not live by the Society's standards. In other words, the Society was preparing a Black elite/middle class that would shun their allegedly inferior Africanness and slave culture that had become a part of their lives (Harris 2003; Stuckey 1987; Kharem 2000; Rury 1985). The Society hired a white schoolteacher named Cornelius Davis as the principal to put their ideas into action.

However, the school kept experiencing low enrollments until they hired a Black named John Teasman (born a slave in New Jersey) as an assistant teacher in 1797.

While the Society used the African Free School as an ideological tool to imbue Black children with white values and cultural norms, the parents had other ideas and goals for their children. Blacks used the African Free Schools as the vehicle for upward economic mobility for their children. Teasman's presence added creditability to the school and with the assistance of Black community leadership, Teasman became the principal after two years. Teasman became a popular member in the Black community and was politically active in the Democratic Party (Swan 1992). The Manumission Society contended with an emerging Black middle class that held parades celebrating their freedom and their African past as they struggled for their civil rights. The Society had hoped Teasman would align himself with their views and tried to influence him from participating in the various parades Blacks organized in the city (Harris 2003, 68, 128). In 1809, frustrated Society members fired Teasman as the principal and hired Charles C. Andrews, a white abolitionist and a supporter the American Colonization Society (ACS), an organization that believed in the permanent inferiority of Black people and that they should be removed from the United States. His opinions and support of the ACS angered the Black community (Kharem 2000; Rury 1983; Staudenraus 1961). Blacks protested against Andrews' views on colonization and responded by removing their children from the school. Teasman and his wife started a school under the sponsorship of the New York African Society for Mutual Relief (Hodges 1999, 187; Swan 1992). In 1830, the conflict between the Manumission Society and the Black community led to Andrews' termination and the hiring of a few Black teachers.

Another problem that concerned the white elite in New York City was the fear of mob rule coupled with fears of an expanding free Black population. This fear led to the creation of crime pamphlets that depicted various racial and ethnic groups, especially Blacks, as prone to crime and a threat to society. Black cultural lifestyle was consistently linked as a danger to the white elite and middle class. This criminalization of Blacks renewed itself when whites feared that their cultural norms were threatened. Moreover, whites feared labor competition, upward economic mobility of Blacks, and miscegenation (Bodo 1954; Harris 2003; Kharem 2006; McIntyre 1984). In 1834, white mobs attacked abolitionist meetings and any new immigrant groups but the worst violence was turned against the Black community on Center Street at St. Philip's African Episcopal Church.

Rumors had spread that the renowned Black Rev. Peter Williams had officiated over an interracial wedding in the church. White mobs destroyed the inside of the church and the fighting spilled into the streets of Five Points. The mob destroyed the homes or dwelling of Blacks and encouraged white families to distinguish their homes from Blacks by burning candles in their windows. Some blamed the riot on the abolitionist meetings or economic competition from free Blacks, but the greatest fear was miscegenation. After the riot, continual fears of interracial sexual unions led to new laws against any interracial socialization as journalists and social reformers depicted interracial sex as a problem among the city's poor (Harris 2003, 194–98; Hewitt 1980; Kerber 1967). James McCune Smith was born in a city and nation that had no intention of solving its racism or acheiving any acceptance of its free Black population. McCune Smith was among thousands of Blacks who struggled to define themselves as not just Americans but as African Americans.

James McCune Smith's Early Years

James McCune Smith was born a slave in 1813 in New York City, the son of Samuel Smith. Samuel was believed to be a slave-owning merchant from Charleston, South Carolina, who relocated to New York City. James's mother was an enslaved Black woman, also from Charleston, named Lavinia (most likely Samuel Smith's slave), who in later years acquired her freedom. According to Stauffer (2006), McCune Smith wrote a letter to Frederick Douglass, dated February 12, 1852, melancholically stating that like Douglass he never knew his father.

One can only imagine the mental and emotional stress of McCune Smith and hundreds of other young Black males seeking to define themselves as young Black men. Enslaved young Black males had to learn to navigate the streets of New York City and avoid slave catchers and kidnappers, dodge white mobs, survive dilapidated living conditions, and somehow obtain an education or skill for employment. Despite all the dangers and racial obstacles, McCune Smith lived in a time when Blacks were beginning to form a sense of community. McCune Smith's mother met the requirements of the Manumission Society for her son to attend the African Free School #2 located on Mulberry Street along with some of the most efficacious Black activists of the Antebellum Period (Harris 2003, 65–66). Alumni were like Alexander Crummell, a future African Episcopalian minister and Pan Africanist influential in establishing the Negro Academy in Washington, D.C., and the idea of the Talented Tenth (Moses 1989). Henry Highland Garnet, who later also became a minister and suffrage activist and abolitionist who supported emigration to Africa, was an educator and would become the first Black to give a sermon in Congress commemorating Lincoln's birthday (Pasternak 1995; Swift 1989). Some of his other schoolmates included George Thomas Downing; Samuel Ringgold Ward, future minister and one of the greatest antislavery orators; Patrick Reason, an engraver; and his brother Charles L. Reason, who later became a teacher at the African Free School and a professor of literature and language at Central College in McGrawville, New York (Harris 2003, 235; Ripley 1991). The African Free Schools graduated some of the most outspoken Black activists, which included Edward V. Clark, a prominent businessman in New York City; others were Rev. Theorore Wright, Peter Williams Jr., and John Peterson; Ira Aldridge, the famous Shakespearian actor, and numerous others attended the African Free School in New York City. Charles Andrews instructed these young males until he was terminated when he was repudiated by Blacks for voicing his support for the ACS.

In 1824, the #2 school was visited by the Marquis de Lafayette, Greenville Sharpe, and Thomas Clarkson who were elected as honorary members of the institution. The following address by McCune Smith, then eleven years old, shows the quality of education and scholarship the students received at the African Free Schools. McCune Smith stepped forward and addressed the Marquis de Lafayette in the following manner:

> In behalf of myself and my fellow school mates, may I be permitted to express our sincere and respectful gratitude to you for the condescension you have manifested this day, in visiting this Institution, which is one of the noblest specimens of New York philanthropy. Here, Sir, you behold hundreds of the poor children of Africa, sharing with those of a higher hue, in the blessing of education; and, while it will be our pleasure to remember the great deeds you have done in America, it will be our delight also to cherish the memory of General la Fayette as a friend to African Emancipation, and as a member of this Institution. (Andrews 1969, 52–61)

McCune Smith and his schoolmates Isaiah G. Degrass, Thomas Sidney, Elwer Reason, George R. Allen, and others mentioned earlier established themselves as scholars early and were very conscious of their duty and commitment to the race. Their antislavery essays and the development of their oratory skills at the African Free School prepared them as future crusaders against slavery and racism. Their education prepared them to refute the proslavers and the scientific and romantic racists by listening to speeches and reading various antislavery newspapers and pamphlets. They planned schemes to free their enslaved brethren and promised to start slave revolts when they had finished their education (Andrews 1969, 61, 65–68, 130–41). McCune Smith had no idea that he would later in life support John Brown and his scheme of arming enslaved and free Blacks to cleanse the nation of slavery.

McCune Smith and his schoolmate's ideological opinions were also being shaped and influenced by the Black leadership that was emerging in New York City and throughout the North. Established Black men such as the Reverend Theodore Wright, Reverend Samuel Cornish, James Forten, Richard Allen, Lewis Woodson from Pittsburgh, John B. Russwurm, James Varick, and others were already involved in the struggle against racism. McCune Smith and his schoolmates read their editorials, letters, and other advertisements in Cornish's *Freedom's Journal* and other antislavery newspapers. They saw and experienced racism and were able to understand the heart-stirring speeches on topics of racial justice by Black ministers such as Cornish, Wright, and others that laid the groundwork for what became known as Black Nationalism (Miller 1975). McCune Smith and his schoolmates probably read David Walker's *Appeal* (1829), heard their parents and friends conversing about Africa and their everyday experience with racial discrimination. They saw their parents assist in the Underground Railroad as the city was always full of roaming slave catchers and kidnappers. Every Fourth of July, McCune Smith's boyhood friend, Henry Highland Garnet, would sway the other students to agonize over slavery and resolved not to celebrate Independence Day as long as slavery existed (Pasternak 1995, 8).

When McCune Smith and his colleagues graduated from the African Free School, racial discrimination made it hard for them to find any employment worthy of their skills. Garnet and others took to the sea as stewards, cooks, or dockhands. Others remained in the city to work as waiters, coachmen, barbers, and house servants. Leonard P. Curry in his work *The Free Black in Urban America, 1800–1850* (1981) states that racism kept most "ambitious young men, still living with their parents unable to successfully practice the skills they had learned in school" (22–23). McCune Smith was one of the few fortunate enough to leave the United States and fulfill his dream of furthering his education (Harris 2003, 120, 238, 231; Hodges 1999, 218).

Nevertheless, other graduates refused to allow racism keep them from fulfilling their destiny. As stated earlier, Charles L. Reason became a professor of literature. George T. Downing followed his father's footsteps and became a successful businessman and Black activist. Garnet returned from the sea and joined Alexander Crummell and Thomas Sidney to attend William Scale's Noyes Academy in Canaan, New Hampshire. Crummell would leave the America for Liberia and teach there for twenty years before returning to the United States. Garnet moved on to become a minister, political activist, and president of Avery College in Pittsburgh, and in 1881 he was appointed as the foreign minister to Liberia.

After McCune Smith graduated with honors from the African Free School in 1828 he worked as a blacksmith's apprentice and studied languages under the tutelage of the Rev. Peter Williams Jr. McCune Smith became fluent in Latin and Greek and applied to Columbia College and Geneva medical schools, but was denied because he was Black. In 1832, McCune Smith applied and was accepted at the University of Glasgow in Scotland to study medicine. The Rev. Peter Williams and other Black leaders in New York City raised the funds for his education and living expenses. He studied for five years and earned his B.A. in 1835, his M.A. in 1836, and his M.D. in 1837. During his studies at Glasgow, McCune Smith was respected among his peers as a devoted scholar and fervent abolitionist, passed his orals with honors, and graduated near the top of his class in all three degrees (Blight 1985; Morgan 2003; Stauffer 2006).

McCune Smith was one of the first to give a scholarly rebuttal that disproved the scientific theories of racial inferiority. In 1837, after returning to the United States with three degrees from the University of Glasgow, McCune Smith quickly became involved the abolitionist movement and scholarly activities giving speeches in New York and Philadelphia on the fallacy of phrenology promoted by racist scientists such as Josiah Clark Nott, Samuel George Morton, Louis Agassiz, and George Robins Giddon. These men believed that Blacks were physically and mentally inferior and that the development of a Black person's brain was limited to that of a child, based on their pseudo scientific data (Tucker 1994; Washington 2006, 94). McCune Smith attended the American Anti-Slavery Society in 1838, where he was the keynote speaker refuting white abolitionist perceptions of Black revolutionaries of the Haitian Revolution. He published an article, "Abolition of Slavery and the Slave Trade in the French and British Colonies," that appeared in the *Colored American*, and in 1839 became its editor for six months. In 1841, McCune Smith published a pamphlet titled *A Lecture on the Haytien Revolutions: With a Sketch of the Character of Toussaint L'Ouverture*. His pamphlet examined slavery globally and praised the Haitian revolutionary Toussaint as a messiah seeking justice for his people. The *New York Tribune* and the *Liberator* published McCune Smith's article "Freedom and Slavery for Africans" in 1844; and in 1859 the Anglo-African Magazine published his article "Civilization: Its Dependence on Physical Circumstances." McCune Smith published numerous other articles for the *Anglo-African Magazine* and *Hunt's Merchants' Magazine*. His scholarship and knowledge of the sciences, history, literature, and languages caused many to consider McCune Smith the most scholarly Black of his day (Stauffer 2001; 2006).

McCune Smith's Later Years

In a time when whites debated and refused to accept Blacks as skilled practitioners, intellectuals, or even as the same species as whites, McCune Smith was one of the most highly educated men in the United States. He was fluent in Latin, Greek, French, and Hebrew, and acquainted with German, Italian, and Spanish. McCune Smith read Aristotle, Virgil, Shakespeare, and Mills, as well as, Melville's *Moby Dick*, and was familiar with the writings of Walt Whitman. He was acknowledged by white physicians and was asked to join and help draft the constitution for the Statistic Institute where he remained a leading component (Fredrickson 1971; Stauffer 2001, 66; 2006). Although McCune Smith was a well-respected doctor and surgeon in New York City, throughout the North, and parts of Europe, more important than any of the accomplishments in life, McCune Smith's legacy rests largely on his activities for racial equality.

McCune Smith's lectures and essays challenged the racial conceptions white people held toward Black people. He wrote and published essays in many of the Black and predominately white newspapers and joined numerous anti-slavery and Black aid societies that supported Black communities. In 1843, McCune Smith gave a series of lectures to an assembly of prominent New Yorkers, "Comparative Anatomy and Physiology of the Races." He particularly assailed the pseudoscientific racists who argued about the alleged small size and weight of the brains of Black people, the inferior intelligence of Africans and those of African descent, and received an ovation from the audience.

In 1846, *Hunt's Merchants' Magazine* published McCune Smith's essay titled "The Influence of Climate Upon Longevity," in which he used his vast scientific knowledge and his literary skills to refute Senator John C. Calhoun of South Carolina and other proslavery arguments. Calhoun, a slave owner and slave trader, used the 1840 census to make erroneous claims that free Blacks had a high rate of lunacy, vice, and pauperism. Proslavers argued that slavery was more suited to Black people and freedom drove them mad. McCune Smith's scholarship was hailed as a masterpiece of statistical and scientific analysis that silenced Calhoun and his supporters. McCune Smith proved the data to be false and misleading to the U.S. Senate. His research provided evidence that there were more whites in asylums, involved in vice, and in pauperism than Blacks; and in the northern towns Calhoun claimed mentally ill Blacks lived, McCune Smith proved no Black residents existed at all (Washington 2006, 148–50).

In 1859, McCune Smith article "Civilization: Its Dependence on Physical Circumstances" appeared in the January edition of the *Anglo-American Magazine*. While making no mention of Johann Fredrich Blumembach, he refuted Blumembach's doctoral dissertation *On the Natural Varity of Mankind* (1775), where he coined the three races through some skulls that were bought to him. At the same time McCune Smith's essay invalidated the racist philosophies of Voltaire's *Of the Different Races of Men* (1765), and Immanuel Kant's *Of the Different Human Races* (1777).[8]

As a companion article to his January essay in 1859, McCune Smith published "On the Fourteenth Query of Thomas Jefferson's *Notes on Virginia*" in the August issue of the *Anglo-African Magazine*, where he cogently disproved Jefferson's fourteenth query with the same scholarly skill that present-day scholars proved Herrnstein and Murray's argument on Black inferiority in the Bell Curve as false. Jefferson, who was considered a genius and is praised as the "founding father" of the United States, is also one of the founding fathers of white supremacist ideology on Black inferiority in the United States (Joshi 1999). In his work *Notes on the State of Virginia* (1787), Jefferson asserted Blacks were mentally inferior, were ashamed of their color and wanted to be white, and that Black women preferred orangutans as sexual partners (Jefferson 1787; Smith 1859; Washington 2006, 78, 98). American literature was overflowing with claims of Black inferiority, that Blacks were fit for enslavement, needed to be cared for as little children, and would never be full citizens.[9]

In his essay, McCune Smith confronted Jefferson's racist opinions and argued that there are more differences within a race than between races and showed Jefferson's own racial conflict of trying to defend Black inferiority while at the same time engaging in sexual intercourse with Black women, especially a fifteen-year-old Black girl named Sally Hemming, who produced his children. While McCune Smith's Christian tenets sought after a redeemed nation free from the sin of slavery and racism and that Blacks and whites can live together in harmony, he also held Black Nationalist opinions concerning culture and education (Rogers 1967; Sloan 1992). In 1841, he gave a lecture that was published in 1843 titled *The Destiny of the People of Color: A Lecture Delivered before the Philomathean Society and*

Hamilton Lyceum. McCune Smith's rhetorical Black Nationalist sentiments reminded the reader that the same God who raised up leaders to deliver the Hebrew people from bondage will do the same for Blacks in America. McCune Smith argued in an essay published in the August 8th edition of *Frederick Douglass' Paper* (1856) urging Blacks to take their freedom and stop waiting for white assistance. McCune Smith used the names of Denmark Vesey and Nat Turner, and the incident in Christina, Pennsylvania, where Blacks defended themselves against white slave catchers, to stir the hearts of enslaved people and inspire them into action. He said that one day Blacks would be victorious from white oppression through the power of literature and music, break down social barriers, and redefine American cultural expressions.[10] Although McCune Smith believed in integration, he advocated and supported separate Black schools, a curriculum that reflected a Black perspective, and the idea that Black teachers had more success with Black kids than did white teachers. He also believed that white abolitionists were not suited to fight the Black man's battles nor able to grasp the things that concerned Black people (Kharem and Hayes 2005, 76).

McCune Smith's intellectual abilities were far ahead of his time; his proclamation that Black literature and music would change the cultural expressions of American society came to pass during the Harlem Renaissance and the civil rights movement, and still influences American society today. He identified himself as a teacher and intellectual who preferred to work out of the public eye. McCune Smith desired and hoped that someday his work and efforts would be recognized by his people and appreciated by American society as a whole.

McCune Smith's educational success and light complexion led some of his peers to accuse him of being too successful, that he lived in too much luxury and spent too much time in idle reading (Pease and Pease 1974, 292–93; Stauffer 2006, 69). Jane H. Pease and William H. Pease (1974) say McCune Smith lived a comfortable middle-class lifestyle in a large mansion on Leonard Street near Sixth Ave built by white labor, wore tailored clothing, and frequented white barbers. He married Malvina Barnet, the daughter of a respected Black family who also held scholarship in high esteem (Morgan 2003; Pease and Pease 1974, 293). Yet, McCune Smith understood that being a confident educated Black man in America who had a grasp of race, power, and privilege made him unacceptable and dangerous to the dominant white male culture in America. McCune Smith was also out of place amongst his own people and faced many of the same struggles many Black intellectuals deal with today who live in both a Black and white world. He was always reminded that he was an embellishment for white liberal abolitionists, an advocate for his people, and that racism implicitly defined both roles (Blight 1985).

As McCune Smith grew older he lost faith in his white allies to end racism and began to express Black Nationalist views of self-reliance and Black education. He believed that it was the duty of Black leaders to create opportunities for Blacks to learn the ideals of traditional values of thrift, hard work, punctuality, and moral discipline. McCune Smith saw education as the cornerstone to eradicate idleness and unemployment; he hoped that Black men would instill within themselves an esprit de corps. He was acutely aware that he was part of the privileged elite while most of his people were wallowing in abject poverty. McCune Smith understood that while he advocated self-improvement, he could not ignore the issue of "class" among his own people who were subject to "caste" within the larger dominant society. At the Negro Conventions and in New York suffrage campaigns, McCune Smith pushed his belief that the elevation of the race rested in the education of Black youth and sought to establish schools. Frederick Douglass and McCune Smith called for the establishment of an Industrial College and Manual Labor College at the 1853 Negro Convention in Rochester. McCune Smith empathized with what it meant to be rejected by educational institutions and called it an atrocity that will disfigure Black youth. McCune Smith shared some of the educational ideals of both Booker T. Washington's emphasis on manual labor skills and W. E. B. Du Bois's need for intellectual pursuits (Blight 1985). The elevation of the race, which included race consciousness and self-help, was more important to McCune Smith and other Black leaders than was a focus on moral values espoused by whites (Cooper 1972).

At some point, McCune Smith moved into the Williamsburg section of Brooklyn and lived there until his death in 1865 from an enlarged heart. According to Thomas M. Morgan (2003), his family continued to live in Williamsburg on 3rd Street and later on Marcy Ave. John Stauffer (2006) says McCune Smith's obscurity lies in the fact that his writings are not easily accessible to the public. Stauffer also argues that McCune Smith's descendants wanted him erased from the historical records as a Black man (Stauffer 2006; Smith 1843, xvi). The decisions to run away from racial discrimination and the label of racial inferiority could have influenced McCune Smith's descendants' choice to reject their progenitor's "Afric's proudest blood" and pass as white (Stauffer 2006; DeCuir-Gunby 2006). His children quickly buried their Blackness. The 1870 census listed his descendants as white and the majority of them continue to do so to this day (Stauffer 2006, xvii–xviii). McCune Smith was buried in Cypress Hills

Cemetery. How ironic that this Black man who advocated for the uplifting of the race lies in a cemetery that today borders a segregated low-income Black and Latino community of East New York in Brooklyn.

Conclusion

McCune Smith's scientific scholarship is important because it reveals and acknowledges the fact that Blacks were not sitting around allowing whites to fight their battles but were major players in the struggle for equality from the beginning. Blacks refuted scientific racism and proslavery arguments throughout the antebellum period. The almost complete erasure of McCune Smith's life and scholarship also show us that the exclusion of historical events and historical periods can leave many thinking that Blacks played no key role in the quest for freedom and equality. This erasure also leaves many to assume that Blacks were not capable of disproving proslavery scholarship in a scholarly manner. McCune Smith's scholarly work itself invalidated proslavery arguments and any scientific racist scholarship that claims Blacks were incapable of thinking in the abstract or generating scientific knowledge. History textbooks have been and are continually written in such a way that gives the impression that Blacks hardly had anything to do with their own struggle for freedom and equality.

Our collective memory has been trained to believe that slavery and racism was scarce in the North. Carl L. Becker in his work *Everyman His Own Historian: Essays on History and Politics* (1935) argues that history has become a convenient blend of reality and fantasy to "preserve and perpetuate the social traditions; to harmonize, as well as ignorance and prejudice" (247). Although the National Council for the Social Studies states that teachers should teach about race and racism, very little if any is actually taught, discussed, nor is an integral part of classroom curriculum (Branch 2003). In addition, the New York State Council for Social Studies has published a curriculum where teachers can access resources for teaching about slavery and resistance in New York written by Professor Alan Singer of Hofstra University titled "New York and Slavery: Complicity and Resistance." Noam Chomsky (2000) and Singer (2005) argue that schools are representatives of the dominant state apparatus that systematically deprives students of their autonomous collective memory and instills in them a nationalist memory that is basically totalitarian. The official curriculum continues to serve to reinforce the notion that Blacks, Latinos, and other subjugated people are relatively insignificant and disparaged. Even white students are given a curriculum that resembles a totalitarian system yet at the same time validates their collective histori-cal heritage. School curricula inculcate students to accept and live with the contradictions yet do not tolerate students to question the inaccurate pictures of reality (Loewen 1995; Zinn 2005). William L. Griffin (1979) says, "the dominant class by virtue of their control of ideological institu-tions such as schools, that shape perception . . . [exclude] crucial facts and viewpoints limits profoundly the ways in which students come to view historical facts" (163).

Paulo Freire (1985) states that we are "naïve" if we expect the domi-nant class to legislate education reform that will permit the oppressed (or for that matter any student) to critically examine social injustice (102). The mental violence and abuse schools perpetuate upon children involves not only illiteracy but an illiterate violence that incapacitates the mind to read the world critically. School curricula deposit information that elevates Anglo-American history and culture while at the same time devalues the history and cultures of subjugated students. Thus the collective memory of students' historical and cultural artifacts is erased to promote a "poison-ous pedagogy" of obedience (Macedo 1994, 67). Some teachers assert a colorblind ideology that does not see race or ethnicity and therefore do not discuss racism and the consequences it has left upon our society. This ideological stance of colorblind pedagogy by some teachers infuriates stu-dents of color and results in not only a lack of respect towards teachers and schools but also a resistance to learn (Branch 2003). Thus many events and historical figures are never mentioned or are erased from our collec-tive memory and are forgotten until someone or something shakes off the dirt and dust of time to expose what was reflexively or deliberately erased and forgotten.

Whether James McCune Smith was forgotten by mistake or on pur-pose, he is remembered and acknowledged among various history scholars. For some reason, however, he has never been included in the "canon" of Black leaders as have Frederick Douglass and other influential Black activ-ists. McCune Smith's picture does not decorate any classroom walls as a model of Black genius or as a model of academic and scholarly achieve-ment.

Notes

1. James McCune Smith in Stauffer (2001).
2. See, for example, Adams (2003), Fredrickson (1971), Jordan (1968), Kharem (2006), Litwack (1961), Tice (1987), and Wood (1999).

3. See Alderman (1972), Gronowicz (1998), Harris (2003), Hodges (1999), and McManus (1973).

4. See Bancroft (1959), Johnson (1999), Katyal (1993), Spears (1970), and Sutch (1972).

5. See Dick (1974), Harding (1981), Harris (2003), Kharem and Hayes (2005), and Miller (1975).

6. See Higginbotham (1978), Jordan (1968), 91–98, McManus (1973), 24, Morgan (1975), and Zinn (1980)

7. Hereafter cited in text as the Society.

8. On the ideas and writings of Johann Fredrich Blumembach, Voltaire, and Immanuel Kant on race, see Bernasconi and Lott (2000).

9. See Fredrickson (1971), Jordan (1968), Joshi (1999), Tice (1987), and Tucker (1994).

10. See Kharem and Hayes (2005), Moses (1989), Pease and Pease (1974), Smith (1843), and Stauffer (2006).

Works Cited

Adams, Francis D. 2003. *Alienable rights: The exclusion of African Americans in a white man's land, 1619–2000.* New York: Harper Collins Publishers.

Alderman, Lindsey C. 1972. *Rum, slaves and molasses: The story of New England's triangular trade.* Great Britain: Baily Brothers & Swinfen Ltd.

Andrews, Charles C. 1969. *The history of the New York African free-schools: From their establishment in 1787, to the present time; embracing a period of more than forty years: Also a brief account of the successful labors of the New York manumission society, with an appendix.* New York: Negro University Press, 52–61. (Orig. pub. 1830.)

Aptheker, Herbert. 1939. *Negro slave revolts in the United States 1526–1860.* New York: International Publishers Co.

Bancroft, Frederic. 1959. *Slave trading in the old South.* New York: Frederick Ungar.

Becker, Carl. 1935. *Every man his own historian: Essays on history and politics.* Chicago: Quadrangle Books.

Bernasconi, Robert, and Tommy L. Lott, eds. 2000. *The idea of race.* Indianapolis: Hackett Publishing Company, Inc.

Blackmar, Elizabeth, and Roy Rosenzweig. 1992. *The people and the park: A history of Central Park.* Ithaca, NY: Cornell University Press, 64–63.

Blight, David W. 1985. "In search of learning, liberty, and self definition: James McCune Smith and the ordeal of the antebellum black intellectual." *Afro-Americans in New York Life and History* 9:7–25.

Bodo, John R. 1954. *The Protestant clergy and public issues, 1812–1848.* Princeton, NJ: Princeton University Press.

Branch, Andre J. 2003. "A look at race in the national standards for the social studies." In *Critical race theory: Perspectives on social studies,* ed. Gloria Ladsen-Billing, 99–120. Greenwich, CT: Information Age Publishing

Chomsky, Noam. 2000. *Chomsky on miseducation*. Lanham, MD: Roman & Littlefield Publishers.

Connolly, Harold X. 1977. *A ghetto grows in Brooklyn*. New York: New York University Press.

Cooper, Frederick. 1972. "Elevating the race: The social thoughts of black leaders, 1827–1850." *American Quarterly* 24:601–25.

Curry, Leonard P. 1981. *The free black in urban America, 1800–1850*. Chicago: University of Chicago Press, 22–23.

DeCuir-Gunby, Jessica T. 2006. "'Proving your skin is white, you can have everything:' race, racial identity, and property rights in whiteness in the supreme court case of Josphine DeCuir." In *Critical race theory in education: All God's children got a song*, ed. Adrienne D. Dixon and Celia K. Rousseau. New York: Routledge.

Dick, Robert C. 1974. *Black protest: Issues and tactics*. Westport, CT: Greenwood Press.

Fredrickson, George M. 1971. *The black image in the white mind: The debate on Afro-American character and destiny, 1817–1914*. Hanover, CT: Wesleyan University Press.

Freire, Paulo. 1985. *The politics of education: Culture power and liberation*. South Hadley, MA: Bergin & Garvey Publishers.

Griffin, William L. 1979. *Teaching the Vietnam War: A critical examination of school texts and an interpretive comparative history utilizing the Pentagon Papers and other documents*. Montclair, NJ: Allenheld, Osmun & Co.

Gronowicz, Anthony. 1998. *Race and class politics in New York before the Civil War*. Boston: Northeastern University Press.

Harding, Vincent. 1981. *There is a river: The black struggle for freedom in America*. San Diego: Harcourt Brace Jovanovich.

Harris, Leslie M. 2003. *In the shadow of slavery: African Americans in New York City, 1626–1863*. Chicago: University of Chicago Press.

Hewitt, John H. 1980. "The sacking of St. Philip's Church, New York." *Historical Magazine of the Protestant Episcopal Church* 99:7–20.

Higginbotham, Leon A., Jr. 1978. *In the matter of color: Race and the American legal process: The colonial period*. New York: Oxford University Press, 36–46, 115.

Hodges, Russell G. 1999. *Root and branch: African Americans in New York & East Jersey*. Chapel Hill: University of North Carolina Press.

Hubert, Marshall, and Mildred Stock. 1993. *Ira Aldridge: The negro tragedian*. Washington, DC: Howard University Press & Stock.

Jefferson, Thomas. 1787. *Notes on the state of Virginia*. Ed. William Peden. Chapel Hill: University of North Carolina Press. (1992 Reprint.)

Johnson, Walter. 1999. *Soul by soul: Life inside the antebellum slave market*. Cambridge, MA: Harvard University Press.

Jordan, Winthrop D. 1968. *White over black: American attitudes toward the negro 1550–1812*. New York: W. W. Norton & Company.

Joshi, S. T., ed. 1999. *Documents of American prejudice: An anthology of writings on race from Thomas Jefferson to David Duke.* New York: Basic Books.

Katyal Neal K. 1993. "Men who owned women: A Thirteenth Amendment critique of forced prostitution." *Yale Law Journal* 103: 791–826.

Kerber, Linda K. 1967. "Abolitionists and amalgamators: The New York City race riots of 1834." *New York History* 48:28–39.

Kharem, Haroon. 2000. "The African free schools: A black community's struggle against cultural hegemony in New York City, 1820–1850." *Taboo: The Journal of Culture and Education* 4:27–36.

———. 2006. *A curriculum of repression: A pedagogy of racial history in the United States.* New York: Peter Lang.

Kharem, Haroon, and Eileen M. Hayes. 2005. "Separation or integration: Early black nationalism and the education critique." In *Black protest and education,* ed. William H. Watkins. New York: Peter Lang.

Litwack, Leon F. 1961. *North of slavery: The negro in the free states, 1790–1860.* Chicago: University of Chicago Press.

Loewen, James W. 1995. *Lies my teacher told me: Everything your American history textbook got wrong.* New York: Simon & Schuster.

Macedo, Donaldo. 1994. *Literacies of power: What Americans are not allowed to know.* Boulder, CO: Westview Press.

McIntyre, Charshee C. 1984. *Criminalizing a race: Free blacks during slavery.* New York: Kayoed Publications, Ltd.

McManus, Edgar J. 1966. *A history of Negro slavery in New York.* Syracuse, NY: Syracuse University Press.

———. 1973. *Black bondage in the north.* Syracuse, NY: Syracuse University Press.

Miller, Floyd. 1975. *The search for a black nationality: Black emigration and colonization, 1787–1863.* Urbana: University of Illinois Press.

Morgan, Edmund S. 1975. *American slavery American freedom: The ordeal of colonial Virginia.* New York: W. W. Norton & Company

Morgan, Thomas. 2003. "The education and medical practice of Dr. James McCune Smith (1813–1865), first black American to hold a medical practice." *Journal of the National Medical Association* 95:2–13.

Moses, Wilson J. 1989. *Alexander Crummell: A study of civilization and discontent.* Amherst: University of Massachusetts Press.

Pasternak, Martin B. 1995. *Rise now and fly to arms: The life of Henry Highland Garnet.* New York: Garland Publishing, Inc.

Pease, Jane H., and William H. Pease. 1974. *They who would be free: Blacks search for freedom, 1830–1861.* New York: Atheneum.

Ripley, Peter, ed. 1991. *Black abolitionist papers vol. III: The United States, 1847–1858.* Chapel Hill: University of North Carolina.

Rogers, J. A. 1967. *Sex and race: A history of white, Negro, and Indian miscegenation in the two Americas: The new world.* New York: Helga M. Rogers.

Rury, John. 1983. "The New York African free school, 1827–1836: Conflict over community control of black education." *Phylon* 44:187–197.

———. 1985. "Philanthropy, self help, and social control: The New York Manumission Society and free blacks, 1785–1810." *Phylon* 46:231–41.

Singer, Alan, ed. 2005. "New York and slavery: Complicity and resistance: A document-based curriculum guide prepared for the gateway to the city teaching American history project grant project." *New York State Council for the Social Studies*. Available at www.nyscss.org/resources/publications/NYandSlavery/Chapter%20A/Introduction.pdf.

Sloan, Samuel. 1992. *The slave children of Thomas Jefferson*. Berkeley, CA: Orsden Press.

Smith, James McCune. 1843. *The destiny of the people of color: A lecture delivered before the Philomathean Society and Hamilton Lyceum*. New York: Cornell University Library

———. 1859. "On the fourteenth query of Thomas Jefferson's notes on Virginia." *Anglo-African Magazine* 1:225–38.

Spears, John R. 1970. *The American slave trade*. Manchester, UK: Cornerhouse Publications.

Staudenraus, P. J. 1961. *The African colonization movement, 1816–1865*. New York: Columbia University Press.

Stauffer, John. 2001. *The black hearts of men: Radical abolitionists and the transformation of race*. Cambridge, MA: Harvard University Press, 5–6.

———, ed. 2006. *The works of James McCune Smith: Black intellectual and abolitionist*. Oxford: Oxford University Press, xxi.

Stuckey, Sterling. 1987. *Slave culture: Nationalist theory and the foundations of black America*. New York: Oxford University Press.

Sutch, Richard. 1972. *The breeding of slaves for sale and the western expansion of slavery, 1850–1860*. Institute of Business and Economic Research. Berkley: University of California Press.

Swan, Robert. 1992. "John Teasman: African-American educator and the emergence of community in early New York City, 1787–1815." *Journal of the Early Republic* 12:331–56.

Swift, David E. 1989. *Black prophets of justice: Activist clergy before the Civil War*. Baton Rouge: Louisiana State University Press.

Tice, Larry E. 1987. *Proslavery: A history of the defense of slavery in America, 1701–1840*. Athens: The University of Georgia Press.

Tocqueville, Alexis de. 1969. *Democracy in America*. Ed. J. P. Mayer. New York: Harper Perennial, 343.

Tucker, William H. 1994. *The science and politics of racial research*. Urbana: University of Illinois Press.

Washington, Harriet A. 2006. *Medical apartheid: The dark history of medical experimentation on black Americans from colonial times to the present*. New York: Doubleday, 94.

Wood, Forrest G. 1999. *The arrogance of faith: Christianity and race in America from the colonial era to the twentieth century*. New York: Alfred A. Knopf.

Zinn, Howard. 1980. *A people's history of the United States 1492–Present*. New York: Harper Perennial.

———. 2005. *On democratic education*. Boulder, CO: Paradigm Publishers.

John Mercer Langston and the Shaping of African American Education in the Nineteenth Century   2

JUDITH E. KING-CALNEK

THERE HAVE BEEN MYRIAD MOVEMENTS, schools of thought, pedagogies, and people who have shaped the American educational discourse over time. When surveying the voices that defined the early years of American educational thought, we would be remiss not to include the life and work of John Mercer Langston. Unfortunately, too often his contributions have been overlooked, often overshadowed by others. Although not usually considered an educator in the same vein as educational philosophers such as Horace Mann, John Dewey, or Maxine Greene, or the Brazilian pedagogue Paulo Freire, Langston's influence on nineteenth-century American education was of great importance. In addition to his better known achievements as orator, abolitionist, attorney, elected official, and diplomat, he was a schoolteacher, educational organizer, and university administrator; and as a member of Congress he actively promoted education. This chapter is an attempt at reinserting John Mercer Langston into his proper place in the annals of the history of American education.[1]

African American Education in Antebellum Virginia

The nineteenth century was a time of great change in American society. The country was still relatively young, in the process of defining itself, and there was much debate about how to simultaneously live the ideals of liberty and freedom that had been put forth during the War for Independence, and maintain a social order. Moreover, there was the question of how far to extend these new ideals. That is to say, should all members of society, women as well as men, Americans of African descent[2] and Natives as well as whites, and poor as well as landed people, enjoy the same level of rights and privileges? If not, to what degree? What would be the social codification? How does a nation that champions individual liberty justify enslaving some of its members? Within the context of this ongoing debate, many saw the function of education as key in shaping a new social order—whatever it might be. Questions that fueled the educational discourse were: For what purpose are we Americans educating our children? Who is included as "American" and "our children"? Do we educate all to the same degree and in the same manner? How do we link education to the larger society and social organization? The answers to these questions were not uniform, rather they varied over time and depended on who addressed them.

For Americans of African descent, who were struggling for individual and collective freedom and an end to slavery, education was seen as a path from their subaltern status to full citizenship, but according to many whites, if permitted at all, education for Blacks was to maintain a racially stratified society (Anderson 1988, 1). Therefore, for Blacks, the fight for education was twofold: to obtain it and to ensure that it was quality education, designed to prepare them for full rather than partial or second-class citizenship.

It is important to understand, however, that while there was great opposition to both freedom and education for Americans of African descent, the nineteenth (and even the eighteenth) century was not a static period and this antagonism was not exerted by a monolithic, constant force. Antislavery sentiment surged about the time of the War for Independence as both abolitionism and independence were viewed as part and parcel of the "principles of natural equality and individual liberty" (Russell [1913] 1969, 10, 55). Hence, the number of slave owners who manumitted their slaves increased significantly.

Toward the end of the eighteenth century, when the country experienced an increase in the antislavery movement, and its subsequent backlash, violent opposition to the education of people of African descent emerged. The fear was that too much freedom, especially for Americans of African descent, would disrupt the social order. The concepts of "the inseparable relationships between popular education and a free society" (Anderson 1988, 1), and that a free nation could not be ignorant, were espoused by Thomas Jefferson before he became president. However, the educational legislature he proposed for the Commonwealth of Virginia was for a public educational system[3] that would exclude children of color (free or enslaved), who made up more than 40 percent of the state's youth. Anderson asserts that this is illustrative of governmental leaders' view that ensuring the nascent republic's future depended on simultaneously suppressing Black literacy while educating whites (1988, 1). Hence, while the few Blacks who managed to be lettered received primarily private and church-sponsored education, white education took a different form.

In the first decades of the nineteenth century, public schools were sprouting up for whites, in the North and, although at a slower pace, the South, but the idea of procuring formal schooling became more and more elusive for the country's darker population. For Blacks, so forceful was the notion of gaining education that a group of ninety-one free Americans of African descent in Richmond petitioned the government of the commonwealth for the right to open a school:

> the number of free persons of colour and slaves has become very considerable and although few of them can boast any knowledge of letters, yet that they are always desirous of receiving such instruction from public and divine worship as may be given by sensible and prudent Teachers of religion . . . Your Petitioners for these reasons humbly pray that your honourable body will pass a law authorizing them to cause to be erected within this city a house of public worship which may be called the Baptist African church. (Henrico County 1823, A 9335; Russell [1913] 1969, 142)

However, between 1800 and 1835 most Southern states criminalized teaching enslaved children how to read or write (Anderson 1988, 2). Furthermore, in Virginia, a law extended the prohibition to include free Blacks, whose numbers went from just under 37,000 in 1820 to near 50,000 by 1840 (Russell [1913] 1969, 13). This law, enacted on April 7, 1831, which was extremely restrictive as it addressed not only education, but made other assemblies of groups of people of African descent vulnerable, ruled illegal:

> all meetings of free negroes or mulattoes at any school-house or other place for teaching them reading or writing, either in the day or night, under whatever pretext. (Acts of the General Assembly of Virginia 1830–1831, 107; Russell [1913] 1969, 143–44)

While the law was not uniformly enforced, it was quite harsh nonetheless, and many instructors of Virginia's Blacks, most of whom were women, were jailed for breaking the law (Russell [1913] 1969, 141, 143; Jackson [1942] 1969, 20). For African Americans, punishment for violating the law was thirty-nine lashes; whites were subject to a fine of fifty dollars, which was substantial for the day, as well as imprisonment (Acts of the General Assembly of Virginia 1830–1831, 107; Russell [1913] 1969, 143–44).

The ban on formal education of Blacks forced most schools to close; however, it did not halt learning. One group of sixteen free Blacks in Fredericksburg, Virginia, petitioned the state government to allow them to open a school[4] rather than send their children north to study (Legislative Petitions of Virginia, Spottsylvania, Mar. 16, 1838; Acts of the General Assembly of Virginia 1838, 76; Jackson [1942] 1969, 20; Russell [1913] 1969, 144–45). Their petition was denied and untold numbers preferred to study in secret rather than remain illiterate and uneducated.

The fear was that Blacks would read anti-slavery literature (Jackson [1942] 1969, 19), which was prevalent and clearly threatened a racist, slavery-based society.

The state's attempt at prohibiting the education of free Blacks continued and in 1842 the laws became even more restrictive so that:

> every assemblage of negroes for the purpose of religious worship, when such worship is conducted by a negro, and every assemblage of negroes for the purpose of instruction in reading and writing, or in the night time for any purpose, shall be deemed an unlawful assembly. (Acts of the General Assembly of Virginia 1840–1842, 21; 1847–1848, 120; Russell [1913] 1969, 144)

Prior to this law, free Blacks in Virginia had managed to establish formal schooling in virtually all towns of the Commonwealth (Jackson [1942] 1969, 20). In short, while Blacks were struggling to acquire education, for pro-slavery whites, educating Blacks was a dangerous proposition as it was necessary to keep them ignorant and enslaved. For Blacks, there were only a few roads to freedom, and education was one.

Langston's Early Years in Antebellum Virginia and "Free" Ohio

Knowledge and physical mobility of Americans of African descent were of concern to slavers. The growing number of free Blacks in Virginia (and other states) had already caused the state government to restrict their movement. As early as 1793 Virginia had instituted a law requiring Blacks to register every one to three years, depending on the size of their town, with the county clerk (Abercrombie 1994, v–vi; Jackson [1942] 1969, 4–5; Russell [1913] 1969). While the imposition these obstacles placed on the lives of many is grievous, these documents make for a rich supply of data to help contemporary researchers piece together information about the lives of these early Americans. It was into this atmosphere that John Mercer Langston was born in 1829 in Louisa, Virginia. Possibly the earliest record on Langston is found in a Louisa County court register of "Free Negroes and Mulattoes" where he is described,

> John Langston son of Lucy Langston dec'd., said John was born free bright mulatto boy age 7 years, about 3'8" high, scar near center of forehead, hair inclined to be straight. Reg. 4 Oct. 1834. (Louisa County Court Office Records, 163; Abercrombie 1994, 47)[5]

Langston, who was born free, was the youngest child of Lucy Jane Langston, a Native American/African American who had been enslaved, but was manumitted in 1806 (Louisa County Deed Book K, 226; Abercrombie 1994, 164), immediately before the law that forced emancipated slaves to leave the state or risk being re-enslaved was enacted (see Jackson [1942] 1969 and Russell [1913] 1969 for an extensive discussion of the severity of these laws). His father was Captain Ralph Quarles, a wealthy white man, and the former owner of Lucy Jane Langston. While it was not uncommon for an enslaved woman to bear a child by a white slaveowner, what made the Langston-Quarles family unique was that Ralph Quarles never took a white wife, only had children (daughter Maria and sons Gideon, Charles, and John)[6] with Lucy Jane Langston, and lived as a family on one of his plantations (Langston [1894] 2002; Cheek and Cheek 1996; and Hunter n.d.). Due to anti-miscegenation laws, the two were not married and the children all carry the Langston surname. While Quarles was alive he saw to it that his children were well educated, but John, who was only four years old when both his parents died, did not benefit directly from the instruction Quarles provided (Cheek and Cheek 1996).[7] Langston's parents died within months of each other, and when Quarles died in 1834, he willed virtually all of his vast wealth to his three sons to ensure their financial and educational future (Langston [1894] 2002; Louisa County Will Book 9, 110; Abercrombie 1994, 154–56; Cheek and Cheek 1996).[8] Although a child when he lost his parents, John Mercer Langston spoke of them both with great affection and of his father, he explained,

> Captain Quarles insisted that it was his desire, as it was his purpose, to have them so advanced and improved by study and learning, as to make them useful, influential members of society. (Langston [1894] 2002, 40–41)

Soon thereafter, the Langston boys—John, with his older brothers Charles and Gideon—left Virginia for Ohio, as it was a free state and was, therefore, a safer place for them,[9] and offered more educational opportunities for Americans of African descent. In Ohio John lived with the family of Colonel William Gooch, his father's friend and one of the executors of his father's will (Langston [1894] 2002, 23–50; Cheek and Cheek 1996, 18–22; Louisa County Will Book 9, 110; Abercrombie 1994, 154–55). It had been the practice for numerous free Blacks in Virginia to send their children north to be educated, but by 1838 the Virginia legislature passed an act stating that such people would not be allowed to return to the state (Legislative Petitions of Virginia, Spottsylvania, Mar. 16, 1838; Acts of General Assembly of Virginia 1838, 76; Jackson [1942] 1969, 20; Russell [1913] 1969, 144–45). This was a hard blow for African Americans in Virginia as it cut off one of their main sources to supply the population with newly educated people.

During Langston's initial years in Ohio he experienced an assortment of living arrangements, as his guardianship changed a number of times, yet he managed to acquire a sound educational foundation, studying ancient history, math, grammar, and basic science (Langston [1894] 2002, 60). In his autobiography he recalls these early years:

> At this time, in the State of Ohio, there were no public school opportunities furnished colored youth. The educational advantages offered them could only be found in private schools, and these were very limited in number, and often difficult to reach and attend. The best and most accessible school of this character in the State for all such youth as lived in its southern section, was the one located in the city named, kept by . . . two scholarly white men, well disposed to the colored race, and willing to labor for its education. To this school, occupying the basement story of the Baker Street Baptist Church of Cincinnati, John was sent. (Langston [1894] 2002, 59)

Without chronicling all of the details of Langston's personal educational history, suffice it to say he and his brothers eventually made their way to Oberlin preparatory school where, in about 1844, he began studying Greek, Latin, advanced math, bible studies, and rhetoric (Langston [1894] 2002, 77, 81). He later received his bachelor's degree, a master's, and a degree in theology from the college.

Even in the free states Blacks were not always welcomed in white schools (Tyack 1974, 109–25; Douglass 1881, 194–95) and, with the exception of the some of the progressively integrated public schools in Oberlin (Cheek and Cheek 1996, 130), there were still few options for schooling, especially public schooling, for African Americans. Langston, recollecting his own experience as a rural schoolteacher in a small town near Chillicothe, Ohio, while still in his teens (Langston [1894] 2002, 82–83, 85), reinforced this fact:

> It is to be remembered that at this time there were no public-schools provided in Ohio for colored persons, and no public money given for the support of any schools which they might establish among themselves for the education of their children. So far as such education was concerned, it depended wholly upon their own efforts and their own special outlays. It will be understood then, that the organization of the committee named, and the establishment of this school with the employment of the teacher, depended entirely upon the enterprise and purpose of the colored people, composing, mainly, the population of the Settlement. (84)

Like Virginia, the laws in Ohio were adversarial to Blacks and constantly made it difficult to establish and maintain schools. One 1848 law declared that taxes should go toward the education of African American children; however, that law was complicated the following year when the manner in which taxes were to be collected and allocated was reconfigured, thus confounded the educational efforts of Ohio's Black residents (Cheek and Cheek 1996, 80). In Cincinnati, local officials went so far as to refuse funding for Black school heads on the grounds that they declared it in violation of the state constitution. Other government authorities thwarted educational endeavors by establishing a minimum of thirty Black students in order to open a school, making it virtually impossible to do because of the size of the African American population in many small towns. Still other towns repealed Blacks' rights to elect their own school officials—one of the few voting rights held by Americans of African descent at the time. John Mercer Langston was among those at the forefront of this struggle and strongly argued that the law was "notoriously perverted; to the great injury of the cause of education" (Langston 1852; Cheek and Cheek 1996, 180–81).

In their richly detailed biography of John Mercer Langston's life and work through the Civil War, Cheek and Cheek (1996) point out that while the state of education for African Americans in Ohio was lacking, it was not too far below the quality of white education, especially in rural areas (184). A fundamental difference, however, was in the way education was legislated and enforced for African Americans, compared to whites. It is clear from the number of hostile laws that were enacted, interpreted, and misinterpreted that, for the most part, the state was adversarial to the idea and reality of Americans of African descent having access to and receiving a quality education.

In an attempt to address this need, John Mercer Langston was selected by the Black community of Oberlin to assume the newly created position of school agent in September of 1851. Langston's mandate was to work with various communities of white abolitionists and African Americans throughout the state of Ohio, including the Young Women's Anti-Slavery Society, "arousing, directing, and utilizing public feeling among the colored people for their educational welfare," with special emphasis on supplying teachers, both white and Black, from Oberlin College (Cheek and Cheek 1996, 181–82; Langston 1852). For Langston, and the numerous others involved, education was an integral part of the pursuit of full freedom, closely linked to the abolition movement in its "aid in promoting the abolition of American slavery, and in devising some judicious plan for the elevation of the half-free of the Northern states" (Langston 1852).

Following his assignment as school agent, in January 1852 Langston chaired the state's Black convention committee[10] on education and recommended the election (by Blacks) of a state superintendent of colored schools (Cheek and Cheek 1996, 182). Confronted by combative laws, undereducated teachers, and clergy, Langston persevered and these difficulties only reinforced his conviction of the importance of public schooling as he saw the existing private and church schools insufficient. To this end he professed, "the free schools in the State be supported and encouraged in preference to all others, for upon them depend the education of the colored youth of Ohio" (Langston 1852).

It should be noted that his was not a proposal for separate Black schools, but in the spirit of the democratic education he received in Oberlin, schools were to be public and open to all. Cheek and Cheek (1996) lament the spotty data available from the state of Ohio on the specificities of African American schooling in these years; however, there are sufficient records to claim that immediately preceding the Civil War 159 African American schools boasted an enrollment of almost 7,000, which was approximately ten times greater than in the preceding eight years (184). John Mercer Langston was not acting alone, so we cannot attribute this success solely to his undertakings, but that his was a role of leadership in this movement cannot be ignored.

Reconstruction: Dismantling Slavery and Constructing Educational Paths to Freedom

After the Civil War, with the emancipation of millions of African Americans, Blacks were hopeful that they would be afforded the status of full American citizenship that they were promised. Countless scholars have analyzed the intricacies of the Reconstruction era and the deception African Americans experienced as their hopes for full inclusion in society were continuously dashed. The intention of this chapter is not to revisit those essays. What is of concern here is how the philosophy and practice of education for the newly freed people fit into the overall scheme of rebuilding the nation especially the South, which was home to the majority of African Americans. More specifically, despite a multitude of efforts to strip African Americans of education opportunities by either denying access altogether, or compromising its quality, how did Blacks continue to fight for and gain education? Further, within this struggle the work of John Mercer Langston was instrumental in educational gains. While Langston had been a strong advocate for the African American community prior to the Civil War, after Emancipation, his work continued as the task at hand augmented with the newly freed Americans' desire for education. According to Anderson (1988), for Blacks there were both short-range and long-range aims; the former was to make available basic literacy and "citizenship training for participation in a democratic society," and the latter was aimed at developing a class of Black leaders who would "lead them to freedom and equality" (31). It was apparent that although African Americans had been emancipated, they were still not "free and equal" and somehow education was to be a means of reaching this goal.

With Reconstruction underway, Langston was appointed inspector general of the Bureau of Refugees, Freedmen, and Abandoned Lands, known as the Freedmen's Bureau, in 1867 (Langston [1894] 2002, 249–74). One of the abounding tasks of the Freedmen's Bureau, along with other benevolent societies, was to establish schools throughout the South (Anderson 1988, 6–32; Langston [1894] 2002, 249–74). Newly empowered free Blacks used the planters' need for their labor as leverage to demand that their work contracts include an educational clause, guaranteeing that in exchange for retaining their labor, planters must provide educational opportunities on site. Needless to say, although the mandate to furnish schools for Blacks came from the federal government, African Americans faced great antipathy from growing numbers of whites. Some racist planters who believed that only whites were capable of teaching prohibited white instructors from teaching Blacks on their lands; however, as noted in a report from one Louisiana educational superintendent, "In this they are mistaken, as many of the most prosperous schools in the State are taught by competent colored teachers" (Frank R. Chase, July 1867, cited in Anderson 1988, 21–22). So determined were freed African Americans to get an education, that there were numerous instances in which they took matters into their own hands and established their own colored schools, rather than wait for the government or Northern missionaries, of whom they were increasingly skeptical.

In 1867, the year Langston assumed command as inspector general, the *Freedmen's Record* affirmed that increasingly, Black Southerners opted for their own private schools, despite the fact that the cost was more than the "northern white-dominated" public schools (Anderson 1988, 6, 12). Often leery of Northerners, in an effort to be on par with their educational standards, many Southern Black educators began to adopt teaching models that emulated a classical liberal curriculum as found in Northern schools (Anderson 1988, 28). Even before the Civil War, the public schools of Massachusetts, under the direction of Horace Mann, were seen as a model of enlightened education. According to Mann's Massachusetts Board of Education Annual Reports, the challenge was to somehow orchestrate educational and social unity in the form of the common school, and the ultimate task of the common school was to educate a citizenry for social democracy (Mann 1847/1848, 59). This message was especially strong in his Ninth Annual Report in 1845 in which he declared that people must understand the "laws of reason and duty" in a democratic society in order to obey them, and that training or "apprenticeship" for this sort of "self-government" must begin in childhood (57–58, 63, 77). The notions of self-government and "voluntary compliance" were perhaps at the heart of this issue, which he considered the "highest point of excellence attainable by a human being" (57). In fact, Mann saw education as not just a privilege, but a right of the members of society and it was the duty of the government to shape people through education (63). Additionally, he averred that schools were to provide an opportunity "for all the children within [the school's] territory" (36) to encourage them to rise above the "common level" (31).[11] This philosophy resounded with the newly freed Americans as it spoke directly to the dynamic between liberty and citizenship, and considered education as the glue that cemented the relationship between the two.

Similar to Horace Mann, John Mercer Langston was a strong believer in the common school and long since registered his views on the matter.

In a speech commemorating the anniversary of the fifteenth amendment, Langston (1874) put forth,

> A common school should be one to which all citizens may send their children, not by favor, but by right. It is established and supported by the Government . . . [and it] belongs as much to one as to another citizen; and no principle of law can . . . justify any arbitrary classification which excludes the child of any citizen or class of citizens from equal enjoyment.

Further, Langston saw the common school as an equalizing force in society, having two main objectives: "bring every child, especially the poor . . . a reasonable degree of elementary education" and provide equal education to all, so that students "enter upon business or professional walks with an equal start in life" (Langston 1874).

Thus, the newly freed Blacks began to "grab education" in whatever form it was now available to them. Exercising their new rights, Black politicians participated in constitutional conventions and fought to establish universal public education in the same states that had so adamantly opposed to extending it to Blacks, and less than a decade after Emancipation, Southern states included provisions for state funded public education (Anderson 1988, 19). As Anderson attests, "fundamentally, the ex-slaves' struggle for education was an expression of freedom" (18), and their efforts paid off as the Black literacy rate increased dramatically, so that in the fifty years after 1860 it climbed from 5 percent to 70 percent (31). The endeavors of the Freedmen's Bureau toward improving the lives of the newly freed Americans spanned a number of years and their successes were the result of countless inspectors, agents and activists. However, again, one must note that John Mercer Langston's position of leadership, especially in the early years of the Bureau, played a significant role, which we must not overlook.

This era also witnessed the establishment of the nation's first historically Black colleges and universities, and it is in this context that we next see Langston making his mark on American education as administrator at two institutions of higher learning, Howard University and Virginia Normal and Collegiate Institute, the present-day Virginia State University. [12] After his assignment with the Freedmen's Bureau, he was called to organize Howard's law department, and later served as acting president. What made it a unique venture was that it was "the first law school known in the world for the special education of colored youth, male and female," and was open to all students, regardless of race or gender (Langston [1894] 2002, 297). Quite proud of the democratic ideals and equal opportunity the school offered, Langston boasted that under his supervision in June of 1872, the first graduating class of ten students "for the first time in the history of the world a young lady was found in the class, sustaining full membership, who graduated with her associates" (Langston [1894] 2002, 298, 303). Having been denied entrance into law school himself, even though he was well qualified, Langston fully appreciated the notion of "sustaining full membership" in a school of law and was happy to be able to extend this status to women, who also occupied a subaltern status in American society.

Indeed, during the initial part of his tenure at Howard, the university seemed to enjoy not only government sanction for the establishment of the law department, but genuine sympathy from federal leaders, of which Langston was keenly aware, "General [Ulysses] Grant was especially interested in the education of colored youth, and in more than a hundred ways showed his deep concern for the success of Howard University and the work of its law department" (300).

Similarly, as president of Virginia Normal and Collegiate Institute, from 1885–1887, Langston focused his attention on cultivating a new group of leaders by increasing enrollment and raising educational standards. He reported that he not only received support from the Republican party, of which he was a loyal member, but the Black population of Petersburg, Virginia, welcomed his appointment, as they wanted to avoid white management of a Black institution (411) for fear their best interests would not be taken into consideration. His concern went well beyond ensuring sound instruction at the school, for his interest was

> always . . . in a high intellectual, moral and Christian training for colored youth as the only means by which they might be brought to a wise, comprehensive understanding of their situation and duty as American citizens, and thus enabled to free themselves from prejudices which exist against them as brought, educated, cultured and refined, to take their places in general society. (437)

According to Langston, their "places in society" were as full and equal citizens. And it is upon this point that much of the controversy rested as there were still many whites who were contrary to the emerging social order.

Political and social opposition from whites became "constant," "bitter," got to the point where it was "outspoken and demonstrative," and eventually seeped into the board of trustees at which point it began to undermine Langston's authority as president of the school. He vividly remembered the antagonisms as "narrow-minded and illiberal, full of prejudice against the colored classes, with strong feelings against their extended and various education" (423–25). This back and forth between support and hostility from white officials that Langston experienced at both Howard University and Virginia Normal and Collegiate Institute is reflective of the ongoing polemic and treatment of African American education. It was part of what Anderson (1988) describes as "a social ideology designed to adjust Black southerners to racially qualified forms of political and economic subordination" (3). Despite the abuses, and keeping in mind that the long-term goal for African Americans was to train future leaders, these two institutions were pivotal in educating a cadre of one of the earliest generations of the nation's Black leaders. In the years Langston functioned as president of Virginia Normal and Collegiate Institute, the numbers of teachers trained more than doubled, and upon his resignation from the institution, he received high praises and accolades from his faculty and students (Langston [1894] 2002, 422, 429–30).[13]

In her study of Callie House's visionary campaign to petition the federal government for reparations, Mary Frances Berry recounts how the few Blacks in the legislative branch during Reconstruction fought to gain assistance for "education as compensation for slavery" in addition to protecting voting rights. Langston, in his capacity as representative from Virginia, along with Henry P. Cheatam of North Carolina and Thomas Miller of South Carolina, were instrumental in this struggle (Berry 2006, 39–42). Langston won a contested election and took his seat in Congress in December of 1890, but left in 1891. Cheek and Cheek (1988) assert that although he was a "lame duck congressman," Langston managed to "put into the national record" the need for "popular suffrage and higher education for Blacks" (123). During his brief term in Congress he professed, "what we want is the means of obtaining knowledge and useful information, which will fit the rising generation for honorable and useful employment" (Berry 2006, 42, 70; Langston [1894] 2002, 508–9; Veterans Administration 1892–1916).

A staunch advocate for literacy, as a member of the Fifty-first Congress, John Mercer Langston introduced a resolution that was a Constitutional amendment on voting rights, and included the clause that "no elector shall be allowed to vote at any such election who cannot read and write the English language" (Langston [1894] 2002, 510–11). Ironically the strategy of tying voting rights to literacy was later viewed as detrimental to African Americans and others who did not have the benefit of quality education; however, at the time Langston and many others saw this as a way of ensuring that Blacks would receive and maintain both voting rights and universal schooling. As a member of the Committee on Education, commissioned by the Speaker of the House, he was a vocal member and, of the bills he proposed, declared "the most important was one to provide for the establishment of a national industrial university for the education of colored persons residents of the United States" (511). So strong were his beliefs in the need for this university, Langston documents the entire bill, word for word, in the body of his autobiography. The university was to be coeducational, located on ten thousand acres of public lands, and

> the purpose and aim in this university to educate and to train young men and women in all the branches of the highest scholarship and in all the callings of general industry, art, and trade, fitting all students graduating . . . for the best . . . labor in life. (511–13)

Emphatic about the project, Langston furthered,

> the importance and necessity of such legislative national action cannot be exaggerated when the educational and industrial wants of the colored youth of the country, and the general benefits of their improvement in such directions are duly estimated and considered. (513)

The bill did not pass the House, which Langston attributed to lack of time. Although his time in Congress was curtailed, John Mercer Langston's was a voice that was heard as he made known the concerns and needs, educational and other, of the nation's newly freed population.

Closing Remarks: The Timelessness of Langston's Educational Philosophy

It has been the intention of this chapter to consider the often overlooked life and labors of John Mercer Langston as a significant force in defining African American education in the nineteenth century. While we must consider Langston within the context of the times in which he lived and worked, both antebellum and after the Civil War, there is a tendency to assume that we would discover a major shift in his work that echoed corresponding changes in American society. This, however, is not the case. His educational endeavors both prior to and after the Civil War were of the same focus. What distinguished his work after Emancipation was that he was able to attain positions from which his accomplishments reached a broader audience. Thus, it was the scope, rather than the nature of his efforts, that were impacted by the new social and political conditions that African Americans began to experience. The truth of the matter is that although, according to law, Americans of African descent now had more educational (and other) rights, the reality was that the practice of their new freedom was continually under siege as the situation of African American education was precarious. That they were subjected to the whims of unjust state officials whose "interpretation of cloudily worded statutes . . . and the vagaries of . . . politics" (Cheek and Cheek 1986, 81) proved challenging.

We are reminded of historian Kim Butler's depiction of the struggle for "full free" for people of African descent in the Diaspora. Butler's (1998) study of post abolition Brazil, in many ways, parallels that of African Americans in the United State in the sense that although, with the abolition of slavery, people were no longer legally enslaved, they did not command all of the rights and privileges of full citizens as their white compatriots. Similarly, in his study of free Blacks in antebellum Virginia, Russell ([1913] 1969) also poses the question "whether the free negro in Virginia was a citizen either of the Commonwealth or of the United States" (120). He theorizes that the answer is based on how we choose to define "citizen." Surely the promise made to and belief held by Americans of African descent was not that with emancipation they would inch from slavery to second-class citizenry (120–22). Theirs was supposed to be one of equal status or "full free." As personal liberty was to be realized through the exercise of citizenship, the type of education Blacks received was key; it was to prepare them for their new role in American society. However, the educational options for the nation's white and non-white inhabitants reflected "two contradictory traditions of American education" (Anderson 1988, 1),[14] which surfaced during the antebellum era and solidified after Reconstruction. In short, the answers to the initial questions *For what purpose are we Americans educating our children? Who is included as "American" and "our children"?* and *Do we educate all to the same degree and in the same manner?* varied, based on whether one subscribed to the belief of "full free" or second class "citizen" for Americans of African descent.

Revisiting the language Langston ([1894] 2002) uses to describe his philosophy of education as imperative for Blacks to "understand . . . their situation and duty as American citizens, and thus enabled to free themselves from prejudices which exist against them" (437), it is clear that as for the millions of other African Americans, whether born free or newly emancipated, "universal schooling was a matter of personal liberation and a necessary function of a free society" (Anderson 1988, 17–18). In this sense, Langston's voice redoubles Ralph Waldo Emerson's. This is not surprising as Langston was an admirer of Emerson, and in his autobiography he mentions Emerson's visit to Howard Law School at the time when it was under Langston's supervision (Langston [1894] 2002, 301). The same volume begins by invoking the concept of self-reliance, perhaps a nod to Emerson. However, Langston's take on self-reliance seems to diverge from Emerson's when it comes to the role of education. While Emerson suggested that a "universal system of education foster(ed) restlessness" (Emerson n.d., 35) and somehow stifled one's voice, Langston was a dedicated agent of such—a difference, possibly due to Emerson's privileged vantage point in society. Here Langston is more in agreement with another of his contemporaries (and sometimes rival)[15] Frederick Douglass. Douglass, unlike Langston, was a former slave, but both men believed that learning to read was the "direct pathway from slavery to freedom" (Douglass 1881, 97) and emphasized the role of education in a democracy.

The belief in the "equalizing power of schooling" (Tyack 1974, 110, 122), put forth by nineteenth century thinkers such as Langston and his contemporaries, became a widely held notion in America. In the first part of the twentieth-century classic *Democracy and Education*, John Dewey wrestles with some of the inherent challenges of providing quality education in a democratic society. Dewey ([1916] 1944) is critical of an educational system that "draw[s] a line between menial and liberal" by dividing it into "base/mechanical" and "liberal/intellectual" (252–53, 308–9). In that view, slave or peasant class would receive a base or mechanical education whereas an upper class or full citizens receive an intellectual or liberal education. Dewey posits that "the problem of education in a democratic society is to do away with the dualism and to construct a course of studies which makes thought a guide of free practice for all" (261). This recurring theme has framed much of the discourse that has continued in schools of education until today.

Recently, critical pedagogues have cautioned that schooling has become increasingly corporatist in a way that fosters learning environments to stifle critical reflection and questioning, and encourages students to be consumers rather than critical thinkers, doers and active citizens in a democracy (Brulé 2004; Feigenbaum 2007, 337; Giroux 1993; Greene 1988, 1996; King-Calnek 2004, 458–59; Weiler 1988). This is perhaps not new, but an old theme reconfigured in postmodern trappings. We can learn by taking a page from Langston in the hopes of understanding and addressing this criticism. His concerns with linking education to abolition and instructing newly emancipated Americans so they could "free themselves from prejudices which exist against them" (Langston [1894] 2002, 437) is strikingly similar to contemporary critical pedagogues' concern with getting learners to better understand the workings of power in society.

When surveying American educational thought, sadly it is rare that we come across the name of John Mercer Langston, despite the fact he was an active and vocal force in affecting educational policy and instruction in nineteenth-century America. In light of his accomplishments and contributions to the discourse, we would be remiss not to include him as a prominent figure. Nor should his role in education be the only thing for which the orator, abolitionist, educator, diplomat, and congressman be remembered.

Notes

1. The author would like to thank Ann Avery Hunter and Davida L. Zike for generously sharing genealogical and historical data, feedback, and encouragement. Newfound kin, Zike, like the author, is a descendent of Maria Langston and Joseph Powell, and Hunter is a Quarles cousin. Many thanks are also given to Aimee Lee Cheek and William Cheek for reviewing a draft of this chapter.

2. Just as the nation struggled to define its relations on a global level, individuals and groups/members of society were also in the process of forming new identities. There were many ways the population of African descent was categorized, including "Negro," "mulatto," "colored," and later "Black." A single person's designation may have changed during his or her lifetime. For the purpose of this chapter, the terms "Black," "Negro," "African American," "people of African descent," or "people of color" are used interchangeably. It should be noted, however, that many of this population also claimed Native American heritage; however, that identity was often subsumed by the "colored" designation, which later transformed into "African American," an issue of contention among Native Americans as many of their descendants have experienced a disconnect to that side of their past.

3. The educational system proposed by Jefferson offered three years of schooling to every white child of the state, with the most academically advanced boys going on to grammar school and college (Anderson 1988, 1).

4. Similarly, Anderson points to a later group of ex-slaves in Louisiana who petitioned governments to make universal education available and even expressed willingness to be taxed additionally to cover the expense (Anderson 1988, 9–10).

5. It is the author's belief that Langston's age is a misread/misprint of the original document, as he would have been four, a few months from his fifth birthday, not seven in October of 1834. As the "4" and "7" keys are near each other on numerical keyboards, it is most likely a typographical error.

6. The author is a direct descendant of John Mercer Langston's oldest sister, Maria Langston Powell. For a discussion of the life of her descendants, see Jackson (1947) and King-Calnek (2007). Charles Henry Langston became an abolitionist, involved in the Underground Railroad and the Oberlin-Wellington Rescue. He

was also the grandfather of the great American poet Langston Hughes. It should be noted that Lucy Langston had three other children, Mary, William, and Harriet Langston, who were not Quarles's.

7. In their biography of Langston, the instruction Gideon and Charles received from their father is described as rigorous. They reported to their father at five in the morning where he used his extensive library to tutor them in English studies and geography, among other things (Cheek and Cheek 1996, 17).

8. Ralph Quarles had already provided for his daughter Maria by making available to her a substantial amount of land; see Langston ([1894] 2002, 20), Cheek and Cheek (1996, 7–22), and King-Calnek (2007). Lucy Langston had three other children, William, Harriet, and Mary, who were not by Quarles. In her will she provided for those surviving children, who did not receive land or money from Quarles (Louisa County Will Book 9, 1833–1837, Reel 23, Library of Virginia).

9. Maria Langston was the only one of that generation to remain in Virginia, where she married Joseph Powell, who was a slave. For a discussion on the lives of both free and enslaved African Americans who stayed in Virginia after the law of 1806, which stated that all manumitted slaves had to leave the state within a year or become re-enslaved, see Russell ([1913] 1969) and Jackson ([1942] 1969).

10. Charles Henry Langston, John Mercer Langston's brother and an active abolitionist, also served on the committee.

11. Although Mann was a strong advocate of universal public school, he did not see its function as primarily an equalizer, but rather an important instrument in shaping the social order. The tone and emphasis in Mann's (1847/1848) Massachusetts Board of Education Annual Reports varies. At times his voice is that of an administrator concerned with socializing students and teaching the rudiments, while in other reports his stance is more philosophical, even ministerial as he ponders the fundamental issues of universal rights versus privileges and the "natural" order of government, education, and people in society. At other times he prescribes specific pedagogical techniques.

12. Some years later Charles James Daniel, the grandson of Langston's sister Maria Langston Powell, would also serve the same institution as secretary. Daniel Hall, now Daniel Gymnasium, is named for him. Continuing in the family's tradition, from the next generation, niece Addie Poindexter taught at Virginia Normal and Collegiate Institute before her marriage in 1900, and others attended the school as students (Jackson 1947, 54–57).

13. In his address to the class, in 1887 Virginia's governor Fitzhugh Lee cited that participation in the teachers' summer institute went up from 129 to 131 and that the Normal School increased from 8 to 18 from the previous year, cited in Langston ([1894] 2002, 422).

14. Anderson characterizes it as a "struggle between two social systems— slavery and peasantry on one hand, and capitalism and free labor on the other" (Anderson 1988, 1–2).

15. See Cheek and Cheek (1988, 123–25) for a comparison of Langston and Douglass. Historian Benjamin Quarles in Langston ([1894] 2002) alludes to a rivalry between Langston and Douglass in the introduction of Langston's autobiography, but he does not elaborate on the background of their relationship and reasons for the rivalry. On another note, interestingly, a genealogist's search reveals that Quarles was most likely the descendant of one of the slaves owned by Langston's father Ralph Quarles (Hunter, personal communication, 2007). Whether this was known to Quarles at the time of his writing is unknown to this author.

Works Cited

Abercrombie, Janice L., transcrib. 1994. *Free Blacks of Louisa County Virginia: Bonds, wills & other records.* Athens, GA: Iberian Publishing Company.

Acts of the General Assembly of Virginia, 1807–1865.

Anderson, James D. 1988. *The education of blacks in the south, 1860–1935.* Chapel Hill: University of North Carolina Press.

Berry, Mary Frances. 2006. *My face is black is true: Callie House and the struggle for ex-slave reparations.* New York: Alfred A. Knopf.

Brulé, Elizabeth. 2004. "Going to the market: Neoliberalism and the social construction of the university student as an autonomous consumer." *In corporate u: women in the academy speak out,* ed. Marilee Reimer. Toronto: Sumach Press, 104, 255.

Butler, Kim D. 1998. *Freedoms given, freedoms won: Afro-Brazilians in the post-abolition São Paulo and Salvador.* New Brunswick, NJ: Rutgers University Press.

Cheek, William, and Aimee Lee Cheek. 1988. "John Mercer Langston: Principle and politics. Black leaders of the nineteenth century," ed. Leon Litwack and August Meier, 103–26. Urbana: University of Illinois Press.

———. 1996. *John Mercer Langston and the fight for black freedom, 1829–1865.* Urbana: University of Illinois Press.

Dewey, John. [1916] 1944. *Democracy and education.* New York: The Free Press.

Douglass, Frederick. 1881. *Life and times of Frederick Douglass.* Hartford, CT: Park Publishing Co.

Emerson, Ralph Waldo. n.d. *Selected essays.* Mount Vernon, NY: Peter Pauper Press.

Feigenbaum, Anna. 2007. "The teachable moment: Feminist pedagogy and the neoliberal classroom." *The Review of Education Pedagogy & Cultural Studies* 29 (4): 337–49.

Giroux, Henry A. 1993. *Border crossings, cultural workers and the politics of education.* New York: Routledge.

Greene, Maxine. 1996. "In search of a critical pedagogy." *Breaking free, the transformative power of critical pedagogy,* ed. Pepi Leistyna, Arlie Woodrum, and Stephen A. Sherblom, 13–30. Cambridge, MA: Harvard Educational Review.

————. 1988. *The dialectic of freedom*. New York: Teachers College Press.

Henrico County Court Records. 1776–1860. Richmond, VA.

Hunter, Ann Avery. n.d. The Clopton Chronicles. Clopton Family Genealogical Society. Available at homepages.rootsweb.com/~clopton/anncmill.htm#_ftnl.

Jackson, Luther Porter. [1942] 1969. *Free negro labor and property holding in Virginia, 1830–1860*. New York: Atheneum.

————. 1947. "The Daniel family of Virginia." *Negro History Bulletin* 11 (3): 51–58.

King-Calnek, Judith. 2004. "Review of *Black American students in an affluent suburb* by John Ogbu." *Intercultural Education* 15 (4): 457–60.

————. 2007. The Langston-Quarles family: a study of free people of color in antebellum Virginia. Paper presented at Norfolk State University Conference, Norfolk, Virginia.

Langston, John Mercer. 1852. *Proceedings of the state convention of the colored citizens of Ohio . . . Cincinnati . . . January, 1852*. Cincinnati, OH.

————. 1874. *Equality before the law: The treatment of the American man of color before and since the adoption of the Thirteenth Amendment*. Electronic Oberlin Group. Available at www.oberlin.edu/external/EOG/LangstonSpeeches/equality.htm. Accessed, June 2008.

————. [1894] 2002. *From the Virginia plantation to the national capitol*. North Stratford, NH: Ayer Company Publishers, Inc.

Legislative Petitions of Virginia, 1776–1860.

Louisa County Court Office Records. *List of free Negroes and mulattoes in Louisa County, 1816–1865*. Louisa County Deed Book K, Louisa County Will Book 9. Louisa, VA.

Mann, Horace. 1847/1848. The First Annual Report (1837). Eleventh/Twelfth Annual Report (1847/1848).

Russell, John H. [1913] 1969. *The free negro in Virginia, 1619–1865*. New York: Negro Universities Press.

Tyack, David B. 1974. *The one best system: A history of American urban education*. Cambridge, MA: Harvard University Press.

Veterans Administration. 1892–1916. *Correspondence and reports pertaining to ex-slave pension movement, 1892–1916*. Record Group 15, National Archives.

Weiler, Kathleen. 1988. *Women teaching for change: Gender, class and power*. New York: Bergin and Garvey Publishers.

On Classical versus Vocational Training 3
The Educational Ideas of Anna Julia Cooper
and Nannie Helen Burroughs

KAREN A. JOHNSON

> *There is no social activity that more vitally concerns the life of a people than the problem of education. The Colored people of the United States . . . want for themselves and their descendants . . . all the advantages and opportunities of education as the term is interpreted and understood in the most favored groups in our American civilization.*

> —ANNA JULIA COOPER[1]

> *Education and justice are democracy's only life insurance. There is no substitute for learning . . . it is the investment of our hopes and dreams for the generations that are to come.*

> —NANNIE HELEN BURROUGHS[2]

ANNA JULIA HAYWOOD COOPER (1859–1964) and Nannie Helen Burroughs (1879–1961) were among the most influential African American educators of the late nineteenth and early twentieth centuries. As educators and social activists, Cooper and Burroughs dedicated their entire lives to the education and empowerment of African American youth and adults. The above two quotes by these women are reflective of their commitment to and passionate belief in the power of education as a vehicle to social, economic, and political freedom for disfranchised African Americans, during the era of legalized segregation.

During the nineteenth century, the time period in which Cooper and Burroughs began their careers as educators, white Americans' apprehension and distress about the fate and integration of people of color into American society was evinced by ardent discourses around race. In America as well as Europe, the "idea of white supremacy was constituted as an object of modern discourse," argues philosopher Cornel West, via the emergence of pseudoscientific racial theories, which claimed the inherent "inferiority" of people of color and the superiority of whites (Graves 2004; West 1999, 70–71; Winant 2001, 19). As explained by sociologist Joe Feagin, it was an era in which "thousands of articles and books ha[d] been written, as well as speeches given, as part of an ideological machine that constantly defend[ed] white supremacy and [anti-black] racial oppression" (Feagin 2000, 82). As a result, these racist, white supremacist ideologies justified the political and social subordination of nonwhites to whites in America and abroad. It was also a period when women were oppressed politically and economically due to their gender status in society. "To be a Black woman in nineteenth and early twentieth century America," argues historian Dorothy Sterling, "was to live in double jeopardy of belonging to the 'inferior' sex of an 'inferior' race" (Sterling 1984, ix).

In their efforts to chip away at the interlocking matrix of domination, Cooper and Burroughs initiated and implemented pioneering educational reforms that reflected their distinctive vision of education for African Americans, females, and working-class people. These educators' vision of education challenged the dominant racist and sexist notions concerning how African Americans and females should be educated by offering alternative ways of educating these disfranchised groups.

Similar to many African American female educators of their time, Cooper and Burroughs integrated their roles as educators with social and political activism. Cooper and Burroughs believed educators and administrators played a key role in the struggle for a better world for their students and for Black civil society. They clearly understood that the progress and success of their own lives as well as the lives of their students and the overall Black community were all interrelated (Franklin 1990, 39–64). Therefore, their social and civic advocacies included the founding of various institutions, social service programs, clubs, and other organizations that were centered on ameliorating the social plight of African American communities; programs such as literary clubs for adults and youth, settlement houses, kindergartens, orphanages, medical clinics, and homes for the elderly, and so forth. They were also involved in anti-lynching struggles, and women's rights; and most importantly, they were involved in establishing educational institutions that offered vocational and liberal arts curricula (Johnson 2000; Shaw 1995).

Indeed, Cooper and Burroughs's philosophies on education in addition to their social and civic advocacies were framed by their social location as African American middle-class women in an era when few Blacks and few women were educated, and when most were rendered to subordinated statuses in a repressive social order. Cooper, who lived to be 105 years old, witnessed several critical periods in United States history—from the antebellum era to the Civil Rights Movement of the 1960s. Driven by a deep commitment to helping her race and gender through education, Cooper rose to head one of the most prestigious African American high schools in the nation's capital—the Washington Colored High School (later nicknamed "M Street" and still later renamed Paul Laurence Dunbar High School), by 1902. Later on, in 1930, Cooper served as second president of Frelinghuysen University, an independent university for working-class African Americans. After working many years as an educator, Cooper eventually earned a Ph.D. in 1925 from the Université de Paris, Sorbonne, at the age of sixty-seven.

Burroughs, who was an advocate for an education that would build the fiber of a sturdy, moral, industrious, and intellectual female, grew up during the Post-Reconstruction era and died at the height of the Civil Rights period. With the collaborative efforts of the Women's Convention, an auxiliary of the National Baptist Convention, Burroughs founded The National Training School for Women and Girls (later renamed The National Trade and Professional School for Women and Girls, NTPS) in 1909, a Christian school for African American females. This school, which continues to operate to day as an early childhood and elementary school, attracted a national and international student body, from the Black Diaspora.

The intent of this chapter is to examine Anna Julia Cooper's and Nannie Helen Burroughs's educational perspectives, particularly as they relate to their distinctive vision of education for the racial advancement and empowerment of African Americans. The examination of Cooper's and Burroughs's beliefs is situated within the framework of the social, cultural, and historical era of the Reconstruction, Post-Reconstruction and "Jim Crow." Their educational ideas are also situated within the context of the industrial versus classical educational debate and Victorian beliefs about the education of females. The questions this chapter addresses are: What were Anna Julia Cooper and Nannie Helen Burroughs' beliefs about education as it related to the advancement of Black civil society and to the classical versus industrial education debate? How did their educational perspectives contribute to a distinctive teaching praxis or idea that was geared toward transforming inequitable educational experiences for African American students? And how did Victorian beliefs impact Cooper and Burroughs's beliefs about educating African American females?

Teaching for Self-Help and Racial Uplift

Those of us fortunate enough to have an education must share it.
. . . We must go into our communities and improve it.

—MARY CHURCH TERRELL[3]

Education has always been greatly cherished in the Black community. It has been one of the "consistent themes in the life, thought, struggle, and protests of African Americans" (Collier-Thompson 1982, 173). The African American's passionate thirst and quest for an education is very revealing in the following observation made by educator and school founder Booker T. Washington after the Civil War:

> This experience of a whole race beginning to go to school for the first time [after the Civil War] presents one of the most interesting studies that has ever occurred in connection with the development of any race. Few people who were not right in the midst of the scenes can form any exact idea of the intense desire which the people of my race showed for an education. . . . It was a whole race trying to go to school. Few were too young, and none too old, to make the attempt to learn. As fast as any kind of teachers could be secured, not only were day schools filled, but night schools as well. Day schools, night schools, Sunday schools were always crowded and often many had to be turned away for want of room. (Washington 1901, 44–45)

Cooper writes the following of this time frame also,

> Our girls as well as our boys flocked in and battled for an education. Not even then was that patient, untrumpeted [*sic*] heroine, the slave-mother, released from self-sacrifice, and many an unbuttered crust was eaten in silent content that she might eke out enough from her poverty to send her young folks off to school. She "never had the chance," she would tell you, with tears on her withered cheek, so she wanted them to get all they could. (Loewenberg and Bogin 1976, 330)

Clearly, as indicated in Washington's and Cooper's observations, the battle for an education on the part of the newly freed was enlightened by the sanguinity of the Reconstruction era. Hope for freedom—social, political, and economic—seemed to have been the theme throughout the Reconstruction period within the African American community. Educational institutions were constructed, offering the newly emancipated persons an opportunity to gain literacy skills—one of the keys to their liberation. In fact, no facet of the African American freedom struggle in this nation has been as "charged with revolutionary fervor as the effort to gain access to education at all levels" (hooks 1989, 98). "For the freed," argues educational historian James Anderson, "schooling was a matter of personal liberation and a necessary function of a free society" (Anderson 1988, 18). For many of the newly freed, a formal education was a "lamp unto their feet and a light unto the path of freedom" (Davis 1981, 105). African Americans linked literacy and schooling to the freedom and acquisition of race, gender, and class equality for the overall Black community (Anderson 1988; Franklin 1984). An education would remove the vestiges of slavery, illiteracy, joblessness, and caste-like segregated economic and political powerlessness.

The idea of self-help and racial uplift and its linkage to education as a vehicle for group freedom and social reform became a rallying call embraced by Black educators and other Black intelligentsia from the Reconstruction to the "Jim Crow" era (Gaines 1996). In response to lynching, mob violence, literary attacks on Black women's morality, legalized segregation, and in particular the abysmal living conditions of African Americans, Black leaders and educators articulated a universal call for self-help and "racial uplift." As explained by historian Kevin Gaines, racial uplift "describes a group struggle for freedom and social advancement" (among other things), wherein education was viewed as the major tool toward political, social, and economic empowerment (1). From the antebellum era through the *de jure* segregation period, some Black educators, such as Cooper and Burroughs, possessed a discerning perspective about the interconnection between formal schooling and self-help, racial advancement, and liberation. They "understood that formal education played a key role in either encouraging true democracy or sanctioning a system of continued oppression" (Beauboeuf-Lafontant 1999, 4). Hence, some of these educators partook in "abetting or subverting a social system of [race, class, and gender] domination" (4).

With regards to their own educational experiences, Cooper and Burroughs, like other Black educators of the Reconstruction and Post-Reconstruction generation, received an education that instilled in them an "ethic of social responsible individualism," and self-help—a belief that their education is not just for their own development *but* for the purpose of Black community development and empowerment (Collins 2000; Shaw 1995). As explained by sociologist Patricia Hill Collins,

> The commitment to the value of an education by prominent black women such as Anna Julia Cooper . . . [and] Nannie Burroughs . . . goes far beyond the themes of gaining the technical skills essential to African American employability, or mastering the social skills required for white acceptance . . . education [was] a cornerstone of black community development. (Collins 2000, 210)

Cooper and Burroughs as well as several other Black educators of their period believed that they had a special responsibility to their students and to their respective community, which they alone could fulfill (Harley 1982). As nineteenth-century educator and activist Mary Church Terrell explains, "Those of us fortunate enough to have an education must share it . . . We must go into our communities and improve them" (Mary Church Terrell).[4] School founder and former student of W. E. B. Du Bois, Lucy Craft Laney, argued that the, "educated Negro woman . . . is needed in the schoolroom, not only in the kindergarten, [or] . . . the primary and secondary schools, but [also] . . . in [the] high schools . . . and the colleges" (Loewenberg and Bogin 1976, 300). Educating the African American community was of utmost importance that Black educators, such as Cooper, Burroughs, Laney, Terrell, and race leaders took on during the Reconstruction period to the "Jim Crow" era.

When Cooper and Burroughs embarked on their journey as educators they came ready for a life dedicated to service to women, girls, the race, and the poor. In Cooper's reflections on her duty and commitment to teaching her people she writes, "There is nothing in life really worth striving for but . . . a sincere effort to serve the best of one's powers in the advancement of one's generation" (Cooper n.d.). As an educator concerned about the quality of education of her people, Cooper passionately felt that, "The black race has need . . . of wise teachers and far-seeing leaders to help them up the thorny road of life. When . . . planning a program of Negro education we . . . need the clearest thought, the wisest counsels, [and] the broadest charity" (Cooper 1988, 251).

Burroughs shared a similar viewpoint as Cooper. As a faithful Christian, educator, and activist, Burroughs felt a moral obligation to guide the so-called less fortunate of the race to social, political, and educational progress. She was convinced that in order to uplift the masses as well as dismantle white supremacist behaviors and legal dictums, which resulted in the educational, economic, and civil disfranchisement of African Americans in

U.S. society, Black teachers, preachers, and other Black professionals had to unite in their efforts to engage in a battle toward the progress of the race. In her article "Must Uplift the Masses," Burroughs contends,

> The vital problems and basic needs of the Negro masses are: (1) improvement and transformation of character and conduct; (2) proper training for . . . work; [and] (3) improvement in home and community life. To these three basic needs, all preachers, missionaries, teachers, professional men and women and welfare workers should unite . . . and work intensively and continuously until the masses . . . are affected and influence to move upward and forward on the highway of life. (Burroughs 1982, 27)

Although the racial uplift/advancement educational ideals Cooper and Burroughs embraced were used to subvert the repressive social order and empower the women and the race, it was at times contradictory and paradoxical in that "they were implicitly endorsing educational perspectives whose values were antithetical to their own experience" (McCluskey 1991, 12). According to historian Kevin Gaines, the racial uplift concept contained "vestiges of paternalistic, conservative neo-Calvinist morality grounded in cultural assumptions of human depravity" (Gaines 1996, 25). Cooper and Burroughs, as well as many of their contemporaries, "never questioned the suppose superiority of the middle-class way of life or . . . notions of the inherent nobility of the . . . uneducated masses" (Giddings 1983, 95).

Cooper and Burroughs's critiques of oppression at times spoke to their social location as middle-class women, in that they failed to intersect class oppression with race, gender, and institutional structures of industrial capitalism. Too often the masses were blamed for their own victimization. But then on the other hand, the ideology of racial uplift that Cooper and Burroughs embraced was not necessarily imposed on the "masses" as some scholars suggests but was indeed a concept that reflected a shared widespread consensus within the African American community. Without a doubt, Cooper and Burroughs were committed to social advocacies and educational reforms that would ameliorate the social ills that plagued the Black community. They clearly understood that their fate as middle-class women was bound with that of the poor. Their experiences with the interlocking forms of oppression linked them more intimately to the "masses" (Johnson 2000, 160). Oppression and exploitation in Cooper and Burroughs' lives as well as the lives of the overall Black community were real. In the 1896 *Plessy v. Ferguson* case, the U.S. government sanctioned *de jure* segregation that in turn denied African Americans basic rights and access to class privileges, restricted their movements, and limited their career opportunities (*Plessy v. Ferguson* 1896). Refusing to be victims, these educators pulled their resources together with other community activists and became advocates for social change. The organizations Black women educators created undertook educational, philanthropic, and welfare activities to address the problems experienced by the Black community. As a result of their educational and social advocacies, Cooper and Burroughs and their contemporaries built a host of educational institutions as well as a number of social welfare reform establishments, which laid a foundation for Black community development.

The next section of this chapter examines Anna Julia Cooper and Nannie Helen Burroughs's educational philosophies within the context of the industrial versus classical education of the late nineteenth and early twentieth centuries. The Booker T. Washington and W. E. B. Du Bois debate over industrial versus classical education has framed much thinking and writing about the history of Black education to the point of rendering to the margins the educational perspectives of Black women educators such as Cooper and Burroughs. Specifically, this section speaks to how Cooper and Burroughs endeavored to implement a curriculum that sought to nurture the intellect of their students and empower them.

Industrial versus Classical Education: Cooper and Burroughs's Ideals

The contours of Anna Julia Cooper and Nannie Helen Burroughs's educational beliefs were shaped by the controversial issue regarding the industrial versus the classical educational debate that raged during the late nineteenth and early twentieth centuries; as well as by the rousing of an emergent group of prominent Black women educators who, during this time frame, put forth their own educational viewpoints regarding the education of Black females and the overall Black community (McCluskey 1991; Johnson 2000). During the nineteenth century, educational endeavors for the schooling of African Americans were the results of a mixture of missionary Christian fervor, the industrial and agricultural educational movement, and uplift and self-help ideals. Due to the prevailing social attitudes around race, white Northern reformers and philanthropists of this period maintained that the best type of education for African Americans was industrial education, which allowed for practical instruction for domestic work and manual labor, as opposed to preparation for higher education. Like many

African American educators of their era, Cooper and Burroughs maintained that the best educational programs included both classical liberal arts and industrial vocational education. However, the type of industrial educational programs Cooper and Burroughs were proposing were ones that prepared students for practical trades and business skills such as carpentry, tailoring, millinery, and so on. They espoused the belief that a combination of industrial and classical education provided practical usefulness in the trades and business field as well as cultivated the intellect. In an article titled "On Education" Cooper argued,

> The only sane education . . . is that which conserves the very lowest stratum, the best and most economical . . . [because it] . . . gives to each individual according to his capacity that training of head, hand and heart, or more literally, of mind, body and spirit which converts him into a beneficent force in the service of the world. (Cooper 1998, 250)

In making her case before the Women's Convention committee [WC] for the type of curriculum that should be implemented at the National Trade and Professional School, Burroughs stated,

> I believe that an industrial and classical education can be simultaneously attained and it is our duty to get both. . . . We [the members of the WC] are anxious for our girls to learn to think but it is indispensable that they learn how to work. (Tennessee National Baptist Convention Publishing Board 1902, 8)

Burroughs maintained that at her trade and professional school, "the trade courses are correlated with the academic and neither is stressed at the expense of the other" (Burroughs 1930, n.p.). She explains that, "we can't teach a trade without giving an academic [liberal arts course of study, thus] . . . we offer the literary subjects . . . in order to round out the necessary qualifications for useful citizenship" (Burroughs 1942, n.p.). Similar to Washington, Cooper and Burroughs understood and appreciated the necessity to provide industrial training, especially because they believed that it played a crucial function in female education. They recognized the fact that late-nineteenth- and early-twentieth-century Black females were in need of training that offered scientific methods in the basics of sanitation, family health care, infant child care, and food preparation, so that they would better care for their families as well as be in a position to ameliorate the enormous array of health problems that plagued the Black community at that time. These educators also had pragmatic views about industrial vocational education. They believe it gave their students an alternative choice to classical education, especially being that not many of their students would attend college. For example, at the Second Hampton [Institute] Negro Conference in 1893, Cooper declared,

> I believe in industrial education with all my heart. We can't all be professional people. We must have a backbone to the race. . . . There is a crisis ahead in the labor question. The foreign elements is [sic] unstable and restive, ready for strikes, and as a rule impatient of control. The people of this country will inevitably look around for a stable working class. When the time comes for the need to be appreciated and satisfied, the Negro must be ready to satisfy it; there will be no prejudice against the colored man as a worker . . . if our young men are to have trades they must get them in industrial schools. (Cooper in Hutchinson 1981, 61)

Similar to Cooper, Burroughs gives the following reasons for a vocational education:

> The race is overstocked with teachers of academic subjects, but is in dire need of skilled artisans and qualified teachers of handicrafts. . . . [In addition] three million Negroes live outside the South. Not many of the Colored graduates from normal schools or colleges are accepted in the public school system, as teachers, in the North. . . . [Thus,] a trade school will open new avenues of employment to girls who are shut out of teaching in public schools because they live in sections where Colored teachers are not generally employed. (*School Brochure* 1928–1929, 6)

Cooper and Burroughs also stressed the importance that vocational education courses provide for their students practical usefulness that went beyond just preparing them to becoming skilled hands. They strongly believed that industrial educational courses would professionalize certain vocational fields. As explained by Cooper, "the trained domestic, like the trained nurse, will demand pay . . . and treatment that are accorded intelligent and efficient services rendered professionally in what ever calling of life" (Cooper 1998, 225). Burroughs believed that "every girl should learn a useful trade out of which she can make a living" (Burroughs n.d).

Although Burroughs's school combined elements of industrial vocational arts and classical liberal arts courses, she was much more pragmatic in her educational views and was a strong supporter of certain ideals of Booker T. Washington's philosophies on industrial education. Like Washington, Burroughs's school emphasized cleanliness, morality, racial pride, solidarity, and habits of industry. The vocational aspect of her school was created to prepare her female students to work as domestic laborers, missionaries, and individuals working in the business industry, among other things. The goal of her school was to train Black women to perform vocational education type of jobs as professionally as possible rather than fight directly against the gender and racial discrimination that limited employment opportunities for African American women during the early twentieth century. By the 1900s, Black women constituted the vast majority of domestic servants, washerwomen, cooks, and cleaning ladies of government office buildings in the District of Columbia (Harley 1988, 165). Hence, in view of that fact Burroughs felt a calling to prepare Black women for their future outlook. As she explains,

> the majority of our women make their living at service and the demand is for trained servants. Unless we prepare ourselves we will find within the next few years that our women will be pushed out of their places, filled by white foreigners who . . . taking advantages of the instruction . . . in schools of domestic science. . . . Since we must serve, let us serve well. (Executive Committee of the Women's Convention 1901, 6)

She also desired that the graduates of her school would garner respect for vocational educational type fields from the greater community, due to the negative images of African American women that society had inscribed on them. As historian Evelyn Brooks Higginbotham explains, "for Burroughs, mastery of the most ordinary trade taught students accuracy, thoroughness, self-reliance, and an appreciation of [her students'] own achievement and usefulness. . . . In her opinion, an ideal education provided academic background and . . . a trade so that students could enter a specific vocation upon graduation" (Higginbotham 2006, 213–14).

Unlike Washington, Burroughs never believed that an industrial curriculum would end race, class, and gender exploitation. She believed that the "measure of black progress rested not upon [Du Bois's] 'talent tenth,' but upon the economic and moral status of the great mass of laboring people, especially the women" (Burroughs 1905, 213). As explained by Burroughs, "we believe that upon the highest development of womanhood, her spiritual development, her moral development, and her intellectual development, depends on the salvation of . . . the race" (1905).

The concept of the "talent tenth" coined and espoused by W. E. B. Du Bois was embraced somewhat by Cooper and Burroughs, however more so the ideals on liberal arts curriculum than the talent tenth ideals. Cooper was a passionate advocate of liberal arts education; perhaps this was due to her own educational experiences as well as to her stance that the purpose of an education was to prepare African Americans for service to their race. Hence, a classical education from Cooper's perspective would be better suited to prepare her students for the tasks of community, development, empowerment, and advancement. Cooper was also a stronger supporter of Du Bois and a hesitant supporter of Washington. She, however, never partook in the anti–Booker T. Washington discourses. In fact, Cooper's position on classical versus industrial education predates Booker T. Washington's rise to national prominence and prior to the historical philosophical debates between Washington and Du Bois (Hutchinson 1981, 60). Burroughs's school was very distinctive from other Black schools that were founded during the late nineteenth and early twentieth century in that her school did not depend upon funding from white philanthropists—philanthropists who often dictated or controlled the curriculum at Black schools (Anderson 1988; Watkins 2001). Her funding came mainly from the Black community and the Black Baptist churches. Thus, Burroughs had the liberty to provide liberal arts courses along with the vocational courses. While Burroughs was able to develop and control the type of curriculum she implemented in her school, Cooper's efforts to do the same at "M Street" Public High School was unavoidably and negatively impacted by the Tuskegee Institute model and its industrial educational ideology. This issue will be discussed in the next section.

Education as a Fulcrum for Advancement

Anna Julia Cooper and Nannie Helen Burroughs firmly believed that education was the fulcrum for advancement and social change and the role of the educator was one of social and moral change agent. Educating Black youth, females, and adults to be productive citizens and social activists not only defined Cooper and Burroughs's philosophies, but it also became their ultimate mission for educational equity.

As educators for social change, Cooper and Burroughs utilized pedagogical practices and ideals that were focused on transforming the social and educational experiences that circumscribed the lives of Black students. Their pedagogy was political in that it was rooted in an antiracist and antisexist struggle. Fighting for equitable educational opportunities for Black youth became intertwined with the fight for women's rights and the rights of the poor. Hence, teacher as social agent became a theme in each educator's writings, lectures, and pedagogy. As teacher activists for social change, Cooper and Burroughs developed pedagogies that were intended to subvert the rules that circumscribed the lives of their students' academic experiences. For example, in the 1905–1906 academic year, Cooper was

fired from her position as principal at "M Street" because she staunchly refused to allow the Board of Education to dismantle the college-preparatory
classical curriculum at the school and replace it with the type of industrial
educational curriculum that was found at Tuskegee. Cooper felt that the
type of industrial arts curriculum that prepared Black students on a minimal
academic level rendered the Black community in a perpetual segregated,
subservient status. She argued:

> no people can progress, without the vivifying touch of ideas and ideals.
> The very policy of segregation renders all the more the necessary leader-
> ship that has been on the Mount. If any group or class cannot be allowed
> living contact through seeing, hearing, feeling the best of life in their day
> and generation, there is no compensation morally or socially except to let
> them find their thrills through the inspiration of the broadest education
> and generously equipped schools. (Cooper in Hutchinson 1981, 83)

For Cooper, the classical arts, particularly at a school like "M Street,"
"gives direction of thought-power, power of appreciation, power of willing the right," she posits, "and to the divine possibilities in all human
development" (Cooper 1998, 252). She believed that "teachers from Aristotle to the present have sifted and analysed [sic] the various branches of
learning to get at [the classical arts] worth as educative factors. . . . They
are universally accepted by teachers and thinkers as a reasonable and proper
basis for the education of [humankind]" (252).

Cooper had a successful track record with her students at "M Street."
She utilized a variety of teaching methods that aided in her students passing
required standardized exams. Also, Cooper and her teaching staff decided
collectively not to use the school board–adopted textbooks on English
history. They chose to secure another textbook, which they felt was more
appropriate for their students' abilities. The alternative pedagogical practices she implemented gave rise to successful school achievement of many
of her students. Her successes also demonstrate a need for teachers to have
an understanding and knowledge and concern about the school community in which they worked. It also illustrated the need for teachers to be
empowered to have a voice in the education of their students. During her
time as principal at the school, "M Street" graduated multitudes of African
American students who went on to attend major research universities in
the U.S." (Robinson 1980; Terrell 1917, 255–57).[5]

Cooper worked with her students to ensure that they would fulfill their
intellectual destiny. In spite of her battle to keep the classical curriculum
as well as her success record of getting a significant number of her students

enrolled in major universities, Cooper was removed from her position of leadership because she represented a substantial force against the racist and classist dominant view of the type of education should be appropriate for African Americans. Cooper's pedagogy was political and was rooted in anti-racist strategies. Cooper's fight for equitable educational opportunities for her students indeed became a fight for the dignity and self-determination of the overall community.

As for Burroughs, she was a champion for the poor and unlettered of her race, and particularly, African American women were her main focus of consideration, given that their special educational preparation was essential to challenge their racial oppression as well as to lead the race. As explained by Burroughs, "There is such a great need for young women of . . . leadership ability . . . that we [her faculty] have highly resolved to find and train leaders" (Burroughs 1947). While there were a limited number of schools established specifically for girls, very few were set up to cater to the special vocational training of Black females. Thus, when Burroughs set out to establish her school, she envisioned an institution that would uplift and ameliorate the "greatest unmet need in the Negro race," she posits, " the need of a vocational training school for girls" (Burroughs 1932). Burroughs was passionately committed to her students and their academic success. Desiring to inspire, impact, and improve the lives of her students and the African American community, Burroughs worked effortlessly to "offer a quality . . . education that will make our women dynamic and socially distinctive so that their lives will have power to revitalize the spirit of a distressed race" (Burroughs 1938, 5). In her struggle to uplift the women and the race, Burroughs wanted her teachers and students to "keep in close touch with the masses," she argued, "study their condition and needs, [in an effort to] shape [the] curriculum to meet the actual needs of the race" (National Training Center for Women and Girls 1925–1926, 15).

Cooper and Burroughs engaged in deep reflections about what education should be about and how they could invest in the lives of their students, in an effort to assist their students build productive lives and realize their full potentials. As explained by Cooper, "the elemental principal [*sic*] and foundation of all education everywhere, [is] the fullest development of the individual in and by and for the best possible environing society" (Cooper n.d). "Education," explains Cooper, "should be aim[ed] at the making of men rather than constructing machines" (Cooper 1998, 249). Burroughs articulated that, "all education is continued growth . . . in everything, in our thinking, our methods of teaching, in our choice of books . . . and also in our professional attitudes" and that the "greatest service that a school can render to help young people discover their talents and glorify it through training and devoted service" (*Teachers Conference* 1941).

Burroughs consciously and tirelessly worked to create a caring milieu that was student-centered. As an the visionary leader of her school in the early 1900s, Burroughs required her teachers to implement teaching methods that included: (a) "ongoing conferences with students; (b) the accepting and utilizing of the students' voice, opinions or experiences; (c) student evaluation of their own and other students' work; (d) students creating their own exams" (*Good Teaching Procedures* n.d).

Victorian Views Embedded in Cooper and Burroughs's Educational Beliefs

It is important to understand that Cooper's and Burroughs's educational ideals were at times contradictory and paradoxical. Their perspectives contained late Victorian bourgeois systems of beliefs that redefined the "ideal" Black woman (for the purpose of informing the role of the educated Black woman), intersected with the two prevailing philosophies of education for Black people, that is, industrial education and classical education; and formed the bases for Cooper's and Burroughs's educational theories (Perkins 1987, 17). According to Carol Perkin, the concept of the "ideal" Black woman differed from the majority culture's ideal woman because her social "responsibilities seem to end at her own front door. [However,] black women felt that they could not afford the luxury of being concerned only about their own households when the race as well as society in general suffered from a vast array of problems" (17).

Their Victorian viewpoints were reflective in both their educational perspectives regarding the education of African American females. Both argued passionately and eloquently for the education of African American women. They perceived that it was *only* the Black female who was capable of being pivotal players in the advancement of the race. Cooper argued,

> I ask the men and women who are teachers and coworkers for the highest interests of the race that they give the girls a chance! . . . Teach them that there is a race with special needs which they and only they can help. . . . The earnest well trained Christian young woman, as a teacher, as a homemaker, as a wife, mother, or silent influence . . . is as potent a missionary agency among our people as the theologian. (Cooper 1988, 78–79)

Like Cooper, Burroughs declared similar Victorian views, when she stated, "Teachers, preachers and leaders cannot solve the problems of the race alone. The race needs an army of skilled workers and the properly educated Negro woman is the most essential factor" (Higginbotham 2006, 213). In spite of the fact that Cooper and Burroughs internalized Victorian bourgeois assumptions about women's role in a patriarchal society, they passionately argued for equal educational opportunities for female students on every level. Cooper undertook a stronger stance for higher education, because she believed higher education would prepare a special cadre of women for a role as race leaders and for a role in establishing new values that would redefine the very basis of Western culture. In contrast, Burroughs positioned herself on the side of vocational training as the appropriate form of education for the masses of African American women whom she hoped would be very much a part of the world in action and thought as skilled workers, capable leaders in their chosen fields and "biblical Dorcas," and activists in the community.

Conclusion

Anna Julia Cooper and Nannie Helen Burroughs were educators and visionary educational leaders in the African American communities during the late nineteenth and early twentieth centuries. Cooper and Burroughs were consummate educators who tirelessly advocated for equitable educational opportunities for African American youth and adult students. These women benevolently worked to produce accomplished students who would not only seek out intellectual pursuits and human fulfillment but who would be committed to working for the economic, political, and social advancement of the Black community. The school Burroughs founded and the schools Cooper headed were not only milieus where the learning of academic skills was imparted, they were also centers where these two educators attempted to transform the lives of their students in meaningful and impacting ways. Their most significant achievement has been their rearticulation of the late-nineteenth- and early-twentieth-century curriculum for Black people that would indeed contribute to the liberation of this community.

Anna Julia Cooper's and Nannie Helen Burroughs's effectiveness as educators provides a valuable resource and significant addition to contemporary literature on minority education and social justice education. The themes of racial, gender, and social justice are found throughout their work as educators. These themes are significant, particularly in light of the fact that for many low-income, urban youth, the promise of educational equitable experiences continues to be a fleeting reality in contemporary society, fifty-three years after the passage of the Supreme Court *Brown v. Board of Education* decision, a decision that declared that the "separate but equal" dictum had no place in public education (*Brown v. Board of Education of Topeka* 1954). Yet, there continues to be a nagging and unrelenting persistence in de facto school segregation or re-segregation of public schools nationwide (Kozol 2005; Orfield and Lee 2006). The ongoing pervasive disparities in the academic achievement among racial/ethnic student groups, and students from low-income and affluent socioeconomic backgrounds, are a well-documented dilemma in this nation's public schools. This major problem has indeed drawn national attention to the urgent need to improve the academic achievement for all children via initiatives that would close the achievement gaps between various student groups. If we as a nation are committed to the equitable educational experiences of urban minority youth, we need to explore a different, more proactive approach to educating them. Research has revealed that for the most part Black educators from the past and the present have produced valuable cultural paradigms that could inform educational research on how to effectively educate African American students. In today's society we need educators such as Cooper and Burroughs, who sincerely believed that "all [students] are capable and desirous of living a life of meaning and that all can be educated to be free and responsible" (Purpel 1989, 10). We need educators who are committed to teaching in the urban school setting, implementing a curriculum that is inclusive and reflective of culturally, linguistically, racially diverse urban school populations. Finally we need educators such Cooper and Burroughs who will not only "provide the conditions under which all people can express their full human potential," but who will, like Cooper and Burroughs, would tear down the walls of race, class, and gender oppression and in its place build institution that support educational equities and justice for minority students (Purpel 1989, 10). Hence, the legacy Cooper and Burroughs leave for those of us in the present is a vision for a more just experience for all students, particularly for those on the fringes of the U.S. dominant social hierarchy.

Notes

1. See Cooper (n.d.).
2. See Burroughs (1982, 55).
3. Mary Church Terrell, quoted in Baker (2006, 3).

4. Mary Church Terrell quoted in Baker (2006, 3).

5. This paper was lent to this author, courtesy of Dr. Paul Philips Cooke's private collection.

Works Cited

Anderson, James. 1988. *The education of blacks in the south, 1860–1935.* Chapel Hill: University of North Carolina Press.

Baker, R. Scott. 2006. *Paradoxes of desegregation: African American struggles for educational equity in Charleston, South Carolina, 1926–1972.* Columbia: University of South Carolina Press.

Beauboeuf-Lafontant, Tamara. 1999. "A movement against and beyond boundaries: Politically relevant teaching among African American teachers." *Teachers College Record Online* 100.

Brown v. Board of Education of Topeka, 347 U.S. 483. 1954.

Burroughs, Helen N. n.d. *Education: Build on character, culture, christianity.* Nannie Helen Burroughs Papers, courtesy of the Library of Congress Manuscript Division. Hereafter, NHB Papers, courtesy of LC.

———. 1905. *Women's part.* NHB Papers, courtesy of LC.

———. 1930. *Philosophy.* NHB Papers, courtesy of LC.

———. 1932. *Letter to Colonel Wade Cooper.* NHB Papers, courtesy of LC.

———. 1938. *The Worker.* NHB Papers, courtesy of LC.

———. 1942. *Washington DC.* NHB Papers, courtesy of LC.

———. 1947. *Letter to Butler.* 1947. NHB Papers, courtesy of LC.

———. 1982. "Education and Justice." In *Think on these things.* Washington, DC: Nannie Helen Burroughs Publications.

———. 1982. "Must uplift the masses." In *Think on these things.* Washington, DC: Nannie Helen Burroughs Publications.

Collier-Thompson, Bettye. 1982. "The impact of black women in education: An historical overview." *Journal of Negro Education* 51.

Collins, Patricia H. 2000. *Black feminist thought.* New York: Routledge.

Cooper, Anna J. n.d. *Educational aims.* Anna Julia Cooper's papers, courtesy of Moorland-Spingarn Research Center, Washington, DC. Hereafter AJC papers, courtesy of MSRC.

———. 1988. "The Higher Education of Women." In A *voice from the South,* 78–79. New York: Oxford University Press.

———. 1998. "On Education." In *The voice of Anna Julia Cooper: Including a voice from the South and other important essays, papers, and letters,* ed. Charles Lemert and Esme Bhan. New York: Rowman & Littlefield Publishers.

Davis, Angela. 1981. *Women, race, and class.* New York: Random House.

Executive Committee of the Woman's Convention. 1901. *First annual report of the executive committee of the woman's convention, auxiliary of the national Baptist convention.* NHB Papers courtesy of LC.

Feagin, Joe. 2000. *Racist America*. New York: Routledge.

Franklin, V. P. 1984. *Black self-determination: A cultural history of the faith of the fathers*. Westport, CT: Lawrence Hill & Company.

——. 1990. "They rose and fell together: African American educators and community leadership, 1795–1954." *Journal of Education* 172:39–64.

Gaines, Kevin. 1996. *Uplifting the race: Black leadership, politics, and culture in the twentieth century*. Chapel Hill: University of North Carolina Press.

Giddings, Paula. 1983. *When and where I enter: The impact of black women on race and sex in America*. New York: William Morrow.

Good Teaching Procedures. n.d. NHB, courtesy of LC.

Graves, Joseph. 2004. *The race myth: Why we pretend race exists in America*. New York: Dutton Press.

Harley, Sharon. 1982. "Beyond the classroom: The organizational lives of black female educators in the District Columbia, 1890–1930." *Journal of Negro Education* 51:254–65.

——. 1988. "For the good of the family and race: Gender, work and domestic roles in the black community, 1880–1930." In *Black women in America: Social science perspectives*, ed. M. Malson. Chicago: University of Chicago Press.

Higginbotham, Evelyn. 2006. *Righteous discontent: The women's movement in the black Baptist church, 1880–1920*. Cambridge, MA: Harvard University Press.

hooks, bell. 1989. *Feminist theory: From margin to center*. Boston: South End Press.

Hutchinson, Louise. 1981. *Anna J. Cooper: A voice from the South*. Washington, DC: Smithsonian Institution Press, 61.

Johnson, Karen A. 2000. *Uplifting the women and the race: The educational philosophies and the social activism of Anna Julia Cooper and Nannie Helen Burroughs*. New York: Garland.

Kozol, Jonathan. 2005. *The shame of the nation: The restoration of apartheid in schooling in America*. New York: Three Rivers Press.

Loewenberg, Bert, and Ruth Bogin. 1976. "Anna Julia Cooper." In *Black Women in Nineteenth Century American Life*, 317–31. University Park: Pennsylvania State University Press.

——. 1976. "Lucy Craft Laney." In *Black Women in Nineteenth Century American Life*, 296–301. University Park: Pennsylvania State University Press.

McCluskey, Audrey. 1991. "Mary McLeod Bethune and the education of black girls in the south, 1904–1923." Doctoral diss., Indiana University.

National Training School for Women and Girls. 1925–1926. *Circular of information for the seventeenth annual session of the national training school for women and girls*. NHB Papers, courtesy of LC.

Orfield, Gary, and Carol Lee. 2006. *Radical transformation and the changing nature of segregation*. Cambridge, MA: Harvard University Civil Rights Project.

Perkins, Carol. 1987. "'Pragmatic idealism': Industrial training, liberal education, and women's special needs. Conflict and continuity in the experience of Mary McLeod Bethune and other Black women educators, 1900–1930."

Doctoral dissertation, Claremont Graduate School and San Diego State University.

Plessy v. Ferguson, 163 U.S. 537, 1896.

Purpel, David E. 1989. *The moral and spiritual crisis in education*. Granby, MA: Bergin & Garvey.

Robinson, Henry. 1980. "The M Street High School, 1891–1916." Unpublished paper.

School Brochure. 1928–1929. p. 6. NHB Papers, courtesy of LC.

Shaw, Stephanie. 1995. "Black club women and the creation of the national association of colored women." In *We specialize in the wholly impossible: A reader in black women's history*, ed. Darline Hine Clark and Wilma King, 433–48. Brooklyn, NY: Carlson Publishing.

Sterling, Dorothy. 1984. *We are your sisters: Black women in the 19th century*. New York: W. W. Norton.

"Teachers Conference." 1941. NHB papers, courtesy of LC.

Tennessee National Baptist Convention Publishing Board. 1902. *Second Annual Report of the Executive Board Woman's Convention*. Birmingham, AL. NHB Papers, courtesy of LC.

Terrell, Mary Church. 1917. "History of the high school for negroes in Washington." *Journal of Negro History* 2:255–57.

Washington, Booker T. 1901. *Up from slavery: An autobiography*. New York: A. L. Burt Company, 44–45.

Watkins, William. 2001. *The white architects of black education: Ideology and power in America, 1865–1954*. New York: Teachers College Press.

West, Cornel. 1999. "Race and modernity." In *The Cornel West Reader*, 70-71. New York: Basic Civitas Books.

Winant, Howard. 2001. *The world is a ghetto: Race and democracy since World War II*. New York: Farrar, Straus & Giroux Press.

THIS SKIN I'M IN: AFRICAN AMERICAN IDENTITY AND EDUCATION

II

Womanist Conceptualizations of African-Centered Critical Multiculturalism
Creating New Possibilities of Thinking about Social Justice

SABRINA N. ROSS

ISTORICALLY, BLACKS IN THE UNITED STATES have understood the significance of education for social justice (Bush 2004; Murtadha and Watts 2005; Williams 2005). U.S. Black scholars of the past and present (Du Bois 1935; Hilliard 1995, 2001, 2004; Rashid 2005; Shujaa 1994; Woodson 1933/1990) have articulated the importance of educating Black learners in ways that counter white hegemony and foster educational and social empowerment. Yet proposed strategies for achieving Black liberation have been diverse. To thwart racial oppression, many Black scholars and activists have at one time or another eschewed direct Anglo-European influence in their affairs (though they may have utilized European frameworks to inform their philosophies) and espoused beliefs in Black independence and self-reliance (e.g., Marcus Garvey, Elijah Muhammad, Malcolm X), while others have advocated developing alliances with whites as well as other marginalized groups at various stages in their careers (e.g., W. E. B. Du Bois, Martin Luther King Jr., Cornel West) to increase access to power and the likelihood of goal attainment. While much of earlier Black liberation efforts were subsumed within a modernist discourse (hooks 1993), increasing numbers of contemporary Black scholars have called for attention to the postmodern condition relevant to strategies of liberation (Anderson 1995; hooks 1993; West 1993). The persistence of Black oppression despite a long and dedicated history of Black resistance efforts in education and other social areas necessitates a closer examination of these various strategies for Black liberation.

This chapter utilizes a womanist perspective to explore new possibilities for Black educational liberation. Originally coined by author and activist

Alice Walker (1984) and later refined by ethical and theological scholars to denote a standpoint that draws on Black women's experiences of and resistance to oppression, womanism emphasizes dialogue to build coalitions for social justice (Cannon 1995; Collins 1996; Williams 1993). Significant for this chapter is the "hermeneutical posture of suspicion" (Williams 1993, 188) used by womanist scholars in their social justice work; this interpretive framework assumes that taken for granted ways of reading the world often serve to maintain oppression. Thus womanist scholars express hope for fruitful coalition building while remaining critically aware of ways in which those coalitions could also facilitate oppression. Relevant to this chapter, the usage of a womanist perspective indicates an emphasis on conceptual dialogue and collaboration between African-centered thought and critical multiculturalism for Black liberation. Moreover, a womanist hermeneutic of suspicion will be used to outline the benefits as well as the potential dangers of the proposed dialogical encounter.

Specifically, African-centered pedagogy (exemplifying self-reliance and modern discourse) and critical multiculturalism (exemplifying coalition building and postmodern discourse) will be explored to determine their potential for facilitating Black educational and social progress. Though seemingly incompatible—African-centered pedagogy gives primacy to African cultural unity and issues of racial oppression while critical multiculturalism disavows notions of fixed identity, views race, class, and gender oppression as having equal significance, and emphasizes coalition building among diverse groups—it will be argued that African-centered pedagogy and critical multiculturalism can be understood as complimentary disciplines that can enhance each other in ways that contribute to Black educational progress.

Independent of one another, African-centered pedagogy and critical multiculturalism both hold liberatory potential. African-centered educators have made progress in successfully educating Black youth (Giddings 2001; Gill 1991; Kifano 1996; Institute for Independent Education 1991; Njuguna 1997; Richardson 2000; Shujaa and Ratteray 1988), whom public educational systems have largely been unsuccessful in educating (Hilliard 1995; King and Wilson 1994; Lomotey 1992; Madhubuti 1994). Yet African-centered educators lack the financial and human resources to educate the nation's Black youth in large numbers (Njuguna 1997). Similarly, critical multiculturalists have worked to establish transformative agendas within which Blacks and other marginalized groups can receive emancipatory education and social justice (Kincheloe and Steinberg 1997). Yet, theories of critical multiculturalism have been critiqued for their difficulty of application in real world settings (Ladson-Billings 2003). Thus, despite the potential these discipline holds, it seems unlikely that either one is capable of fully realizing Black educational liberation alone.

Womanist scholars emphasize the important role that honest and respectful dialogue contributes to the realization of social justice (Cannon 1995; Thomas 1998). Through critical dialogue, individuals can share ideas and resolve conflicts in mutually beneficial ways. The premise of this chapter is that through dialogical encounter, African-centered scholars can provide critical multicultural scholars a greater appreciation of the necessity of African-centered pedagogy for the mental and psychological well-being of Black youth and, in doing so, gain the support necessary to expand the provision African-centered pedagogy to Black students in public schools. Similarly, African-centered scholars can strengthen the theoretical precision of understandings of Black identity in ways that honor the multiple and competing forms of Blackness that are manifested in the Black community. Informed by a critical multicultural understanding of identity (i.e., as fluid and contested), African-centered scholars can develop a more inclusive and liberatory African-centered pedagogy for all members of the Black community.

The organization of this chapter is as follows. Key concepts of African-centered pedagogy and critical multiculturalism will be discussed. Next, points of commonality, tensions, and challenges among the two disciplines will be addressed, organized around the themes of: (1) modern versus postmodern understandings of Black identity; (2) politics of self-reliance versus politics of coalition building for Black liberation; and (3) the uses of Eurocentric epistemology for Black liberation. For ease of discussion, key concepts relevant to African-centered pedagogy and critical multiculturalism will be presented within the context of the broader multicultural education movement in the United States.

Emergence of a Multicultural Education Movement

The emergence of multicultural education and the resultant U.S. multiculturalism movement in the late 1960s and early 1970s can be attributed to Black and other race/ethnic minority groups' efforts to influence educational institutions in ways that would realize social justice (Banks 1989, 2001; Newfield and Gordon 1996; Sleeter 1996). During the Civil Rights movement, Blacks and other race/ethnic groups targeted educational and other public institutions as sites within which to challenge discriminatory practices because these sites blatantly and hostilely countered democratic ideals of racial equality (Banks 1989, 1995; Gorski 1999). Thus, multicultural education developed through the insistence of social activists, community leaders, and parents for decision-making in the education and socialization of their children (Gorski 1999; Sleeter 1996). These groups challenged the hegemony of white power in public education by demanding the implementation of diverse curricula, textbook revision, increases in minority teachers and administrators, and increased community control of schools serving Black and other race/ethnic minority students (Banks 2001; Sleeter 1996).

Initial demands for multicultural education yielded seemingly auspicious results. Educational institutions at the K–12 and postsecondary level responded to these demands by introducing programs, practices, and policies intended to diversify, to varying degrees, educational curricula and practices (Gorski 1999). Yet these initial responses lacked the careful thought and planning necessary to achieve multicultural education's goals of creating school environments where the cultures of diverse groups within society are respected, valued, and have an equal opportunity to learn (Banks 1997, 2001). As might be expected given the numerous stakeholders involved in the concepts of multiculturalism and multicultural education, a high degree of variety was found in understandings and implementations of multicultural education. The two forms of multicultural education to be discussed in this chapter are African-centered pedagogy and critical multiculturalism.

African-Centered Pedagogy

African-centered thought (also referred to as Afrocentric thought) is a worldview that uses critical knowledge of African and Western culture and history for the personal transformation and liberation of those belonging to the African Diaspora (Carruthers 1994; Hilliard 1995; Shujaa 1994). African-centered scholars share a belief in the connectedness of Blacks in the United States with others in the African Diaspora (Hilliard 2001; Madhubuti 1994; Shujaa 1994), a recognition of and commitment to fight against white supremacy and the hegemonic means through which the dominant culture oppresses, alienates, and culturally denigrates Black people through schooling and other social systems (Hilliard 1995, 2001; King and Wilson 1994; Shujaa 1994), a belief in self-determination for Africans as well as other cultural groups (Asante 1996; Richardson 2000), and a belief that critical education (as opposed to schooling) grounded in African ways of knowing, culture, history, and value systems can promote well-being (Ani 1994; Shujaa 1994), educational equity (Hilliard 2001), intellectual freedom (Carruthers 1994), and a transformation of existing power relationships (Carruthers 1994; King and Wilson 1994; Shujaa 1994).

African-centered pedagogy is one element of African-centered thought; it focuses on the thoughts and actions of educators who are committed to the holistic development of members of the African Diaspora. African-centered educators strive to nurture the intellectual and psychological development of Black youth (Asante 1996; Shujaa 1994) and to instill in these youth the importance of preserving the unity of the African cultural community (Hilliard 2001; King and Wilson 1994; Shujaa 1994). Additionally, proponents of African-centered pedagogy acknowledge the persistent negative effects of historical and present day racial oppression of Africans and their descendants both in the United States and abroad (Lee and Lomotey 1990) and contend that a reclaiming of African history and culture is needed to repair the damages of cultural domination to Black people (Hilliard 1995, 2001; Lee and Lomotey 1990; Teasley and Tyson 2007). Consequently, African-centered thought conceptualizes Black people as active agents in history, rather than as subjects (Asante 1996) and articulates ways in which the educational system, along with other social systems in the United States, collude in the perpetuation of white hegemonic domination of Black life (Gordon 1994; Hilliard 1995, 2001; Shujaa 1994).

While numerous educators who embrace the above-mentioned worldview specifically refer to their pedagogical processes as "African-centered pedagogy" (e.g., Akoto 1994; Murell 2002; Shujaa 1994), others do not invoke this term, yet still address the unique sociohistorical and cultural needs of Black youth and work for Black liberation (e.g., Delpit 2006; Foster 1997; Ladson-Billings 1994; Woodson 1933/1990). For the purposes of this chapter, all educators implementing culturally relevant pedagogy for Black liberation will be subsumed within the context of African-centered pedagogy. Thus, it is argued here that the ethos of African-centered pedagogy predates the multicultural education movement of the 1960s and 1970s (though it experienced large growth during this time) and continues to be articulated in the present.

Such an ethos was characterized by former slaves in the late 1800s who staffed and financed African schools to educate themselves for freedom (Bush 2004; Potts 2003), by Edward W. Blyden (1832–1912) and Carter G.

Woodson (1875–1950), both of whom understood and prescribed amelioration for the ways in which mental slavery served as a road block to Black liberation, by the SNCC Freedom Schools formed during the early 1960s, the Liberation Schools of the Black Panther Party formed in 1969, and the schools affiliated with the Council of Independent Black Institutions, founded in 1972 (Potts 2003). Moreover, an African-centered pedagogy continues to be articulated in the culturally relevant pedagogy of educators such as Gloria Ladson-Billings (1994), Lisa Delpit (2006), and Michele Foster (1997).

As the diversity of educators who embrace African-centered pedagogy might suggest, there is no "right way" to implement African-centered pedagogy (Murrell 2002). What African-centered educators share is a curriculum that centers on Black culture, Black history, and Black accomplishments in which Black role models are presented for Black youth to identify with (Asante 1996). Such a focus is designed to provide Blacks with a sense of pride, enhanced self-esteem, and an accurate knowledge of their cultural history (Lee and Lomotey 1990; Shujaa 1994b). When applied to course curricula, an African-centered pedagogy could be demonstrated through discussions of literature by Black authors, math instruction that teaches children to count in an African language or that identifies aspects of geometry in African hair-braiding techniques, history classes that reinterpret African and U.S. history from the point of view of those Blacks and Africans who helped to shape history, and so on. What defines African-centered pedagogy is the centrality of African history and culture, the care for and nurturance of the whole student, and the necessity of a positive relationship between the student and teacher (Foster 1997; Shujaa 1994a; Murrell 2002).

While it is important to note that African-centered thought as a theoretical construct (i.e., Afrocentrism) was developed by Molefi Asante at Temple University and spread thereafter to other Black studies and African studies programs (Marable 2000), this chapter limits its discussion to the application of African-centered thought in elementary and secondary school curricula. While some African-centered scholars have explored possibilities of introducing African-centered pedagogy into public schools as part of a multicultural curriculum (see for example Delpit 2006; Gordon 1994; Hilliard 1995, 2001), difficulties associated with these efforts have prompted many other African-centered scholars to endorse independent educational systems capable of shielding Black youth from the direct impact of the cultural domination that manifests itself through public schooling and other social institutions (Akoto 1994; Ani 1994;

Carruthers 1994). In independent schools (and a few noteworthy public school systems) African-centered pedagogy has been established as a viable system of education for Black youth (Giddings 2001; Gill 1991; Institute for Independent Education 1991; Kifano 1996; Richardson 2000; Shujaa and Ratteray 1988).

Critical Multiculturalism

Emerging in the 1990s in response to perceived limitations in the multicultural education movement (Kincheloe and Steinberg 1997; Ladson-Billings 2003; May 1999), critical multiculturalism embraces the reality of diverse populations living in the Western world and directs efforts toward resisting forms of hegemonic domination and realizing the full democratic participation of all members of society (McLaren 1995). Two perspectives utilized to pursue the efforts of critical multiculturalism include critical race theory and critical pedagogy.

Critical Race Theory (CRT) is an intellectual movement developed by legal scholars in the 1970s to counter Black racial oppression (Ladson-Billings 2003). Recently, CRT has been appropriated by a number of educational scholars (i.e., Jay 2003; Ladson-Billings 2003; Ladson-Billings and Tate 1995; Solorzano 1997, 1998; Solorzano and Yosso, 2000; Tate 1997) to call attention to the continued primacy of race (and other issues of marginalization) in the treatment of individuals in public systems and to identify and alter the ways in which the educational system perpetuates the oppression of marginalized groups. For example, in the following passage Ladson-Billings (2003) uses a CRT perspective to analyze aspects of public school curricula, instruction, and assessment that reinforce each other and result in the legitimization of perceived deficiencies of poor students and students of color. She writes:

> In the classroom, a poor-quality curriculum, coupled with poor-quality instruction, a poorly prepared teacher, and limited resources add up to poor performance on the so-called objective tests. CRT theorists point out that the assessment game is merely a validation of the dominant culture's superiority. (60)

CRT as applied to the field of education is a relatively new venture (Jay 2003; Ladson-Billings 2003) that is likely to gain more exposure in time. In contrast, the work of critical multiculturalists such as Peter McLaren, Joe Kincheloe, and Shirley Steinberg, who utilize a critical pedagogy perspective has, for a number of reasons, achieved greater prominence in the field of education than has CRT. Therefore, it is the "critical pedagogy of multiculturalism" (Kincheloe and Steinberg 1997, 22) utilized by Peter McLaren, Joe Kincheloe, and Shirley Steinberg that will be used in this chapter's conceptual encounter with African-centered pedagogy.

Critical multiculturalists examine ways in which power shapes individual consciousness. More specifically, they attend to the ways in which intersecting "markers of difference" such as race, class, gender, and sexuality are socially constructed through relations of domination (Kincheloe and Steinberg 1997). By embracing these fluid understandings of identity formation, critical multiculturalism positions itself as a postmodern critique of stable and essentialized notions of identity.

Teacher education programs are major avenues for the application of critical multicultural thought (Kincheloe and Steinberg 1997; Ukpokodu 2003). Given the cultural mismatch between a largely white teaching population and a largely racial/ethnic minority student population in public schools (Kincheloe and Steinberg 1997; Murrell 2002; National Center for Education Statistics 2003, 2006) it should not be surprising that critical multicultural theorists pay special attention to the identity of whiteness and ways in which whiteness is a social construction that, at the same time, operates as a very real means of domination for both whites and other racial/ethnic groups. Thus, critical multiculturalism attempts to separate whiteness as hegemony from individual white identities that, like all other identities (as understood from a critical multicultural standpoint), change based on one's sociohistorical and cultural context.

As noted earlier in this chapter, the implementation of multicultural education projects has taken varied forms. While a detailed account of these various manifestations is beyond the scope of this chapter, it is necessary to briefly delineate these other implemented modes of multiculturalism to clarify concepts germane to critical multiculturalism. Critical multiculturalists identify for critique (to varying degrees) four expressions of multiculturalism: conservative, liberal, pluralist, and left-essentialist. Conservative multiculturalists attempt to assimilate differences into a common U.S. culture and in this way uphold the superiority of Western culture (Kincheloe and Steinberg 1997; McLaren 1994, 1995). While conservative multiculturalism includes culturally diverse groups in school curricula, representations of these groups are not integrated throughout the curricula but are instead presented in ways that perpetuate social marginalization (Ladson-Billings 2003). Liberal multiculturalism downplays difference and espouses an innate equality among racial/ethnic and gender groups

(Kincheloe and Steinberg 1997; McLaren 1994), but tends not to question existing power structures that perpetuate inequality (Ladson-Billings 2003) or ways in which a discourse of diversity is actually used to reference Eurocentric norms (Kincheloe and Steinberg 1997). Pluralist multiculturalism espouses the importance of bicultural literacy (i.e., knowledge of and exposure to both mainstream and marginalized cultural contexts) and economic and educational equality, but generally fails to give attention to the social, economic, and political realities that exist between whites and other racial/ethnic groups; in the absence of such attention, critical multiculturalists caution that superficial celebrations of difference do more to perpetuate the status quo than to promote social justice (Kincheloe and Steinberg 1997). Finally, left-essentialist multiculturalism (also referred to as left-liberal multiculturalism) highlights cultural difference and posits such difference as crucial to individual identity (Kincheloe and Steinberg 1997; McLaren 1994, 1995). It should be noted here that Kincheloe and Steinberg (1997) identify Afrocentricity as one expression of left-essentialist multiculturalism.

The main critique critical multiculturalists level against each of these forms of multiculturalism is that they lack a transformative agenda capable of altering the existing social order. Critical multiculturalists therefore attend carefully to the politics of how various expressions of multiculturalism maintain existing power relations and perpetuate domination (Ladson-Billings 2003; May 1999) through hegemonic control (Kincheloe and Steinberg 1997) and class exploitation (McLaren 1994, 1995). As a goal, critical multiculturalists work to transform multicultural education into both a critique of domination and a plan for developing culturally diverse coalitions to ameliorate race, class, and gender oppression (Kincheloe and Steinberg 1997). Because of the broad range of issues tackled by critical multiculturalists (e.g., critical multiculturalists McLaren, Kincheloe, and Steinberg have written books on intelligence, whiteness, multiculturalism, curriculum reform, literacy, educational policy, educational psychology, etc.), application of their ideas to the school environment has taken diverse forms.

In teacher education programs, educators embracing a critical multicultural perspective invite pre-service teachers to interrogate their social positions and "consciously engage in the construction of knowledge, critique the various forms of inequities and injustices embedded in the educational system, and strive to gain the empowerment needed to engage in culturally responsive and responsible practice" (Ukpokodu 2003, 19).

In terms of curricular reform, critical multiculturalists analyze how presentations of knowledge serve to perpetuate the status quo and argue for replacing the uncritical, predominantly Western interpretation of history commonly presented in public schools with "rigorous historical scholarship that explores not only excluded race, class and gender histories but also the construction of the public memory about both subjugated and dominant cultural groups" (Kincheloe and Steinberg 1997, 231).

Armed with a critical knowledge of history, teachers can then engage in critical multicultural praxis that forges alliances with marginalized community members to highlight and be further enlightened by their subjugated knowledge (Kincheloe and Steinberg 1997). Through the retelling of individual stories, critical exploration of history, and willingness to learn from and engage in solidarity with marginalized groups, critical multiculturalists hope to unearth previously suppressed ways of knowing that open new spaces for theorizing about and acting on democracy and freedom (Fischman 1999; Kincheloe and Steinberg 1997).

Having detailed key concepts and points of application for African-centered pedagogy and critical multiculturalism, this chapter proceeds to its main purpose—a dialogical conceptual encounter between the ideas that support African-centered pedagogy and critical multiculturalism. Though markedly different, both African-centered pedagogy and critical multiculturalism recognize white hegemony and the ways hegemony interacts with culture to provide degrees of privilege and penalty for all members of society. Additionally, both share a commitment to the improved life-outcomes, psychological well-being, and liberation of Black people from social and economic oppression. While this goal is for critical multiculturalists, part of an inclusive goal of liberation for all marginalized groups (Kincheloe and Steinberg 1997), it nevertheless represents the foundational point of commonality from which this chapter's argument for a mutually beneficial coalition between scholars of African-centered pedagogy and critical multiculturalism is based.

Despite the possibilities for liberation a dialogical encounter between these two perspectives holds, such an encounter also is potentially dangerous for both African-centered scholars and African-centered pedagogy. The tensions existing within and among African-centered pedagogy and critical multiculturalism must be articulated before the benefits of a dialogical encounter can be ascertained. These tensions include: (1) modern versus postmodern understandings of Black identity, (2) a politic of self-reliance versus a politic of coalition building for Black liberation, and (3) uses of Eurocentric epistemology for Black liberation.

Modern versus Postmodern
Understandings of Black Identity

Although African-centered scholars such as Asa Hilliard (2001) disavow biological/racialized understandings of connections among the "African family," the argument for experiential and cultural connectivity (Hilliard 1992, 2001; Shujaa 1994) with others of the African Diaspora nevertheless suggests a stability of Blackness and a modern understanding of Black identity. Hilliard (2001) and Shujaa (1994) demonstrate the stability of the collective African identity by arguing that African identity transcends both temporal and geographical location.

Of course, the adherence to a stable, collective African cultural identity serves as a means of fostering resistance to oppression and domination and also serves as a source of philosophical, mental, and spiritual guidance for future direction (Hilliard 2001; Shujaa 1994). Such stable understandings of cultural identity facilitate Black survival of U.S. racial and economic oppression by connecting Blacks to a rich cultural history and providing assurance that present-day situations of oppression are not the sole determinants of Black existence (Hilliard 1998).

The insistence of African-centered scholars on the primacy of a collective Black identity for liberation finds its origins within the context of the same "modernist sensibility" that ushered in ideologies of Black power and other static understandings of Blackness expressed through racial discourse (Anderson 1995; hooks 1993). To be sure, the reliance on Black identity politics is understandable given the history of racial oppression against Blacks in the United States. Identifying racial oppression as the "nexus" of domination for Blacks (Gordon 1995) of all socioeconomic statuses and religious orientations was a practical and effective means of historically mobilizing diverse groups of Blacks to push for change in the educational, employment, and legal systems of the United States (Collins 2000; Shelby 2005).

Yet, the endorsement of stable understandings of identity for Black people has been more than a mere political strategy. One of the many detrimental aspects of U.S. slavery and racial segregation was the erasure of Black subjectivity. The common Southern plantation practice of referring to Black adult slaves as "boy," "gal," "auntie," or "uncle" served to legitimate the Black/white racial hierarchy by denying Black subjectivity. Today African-centered scholars work to recover ways in which members of the African Diaspora have exercised active agency in history precisely because Black subjectivity has traditionally been denied through Western practices and historical accounts (Collins 2000). Understood from this context, the assertion of a collective Black identity can also be viewed as a means of asserting Black subjectivity.

Yet despite the appeal of modern identity politics for establishing Black political progress and subjectivity, numerous Black scholars have noted the problematics associated with stable understandings of Black identity. For example, Cornel West (1993a, 1993b), bell hooks (1993), Victor Anderson (1995), and Patricia Hill Collins (2000) have all attended to ways in which social and economic changes in the United States and abroad have altered the saliency of Black identity politics. Similarly, other Black scholars have made problematic the usage of Black racial identity as an organizing principle for social progress (Anderson 1995; Shelby 2005).

Clearly, no one form, image, or norm of Blackness exists (Collins 2000; Hill 1999; Kincheloe and Steinberg 1997). Therefore, when a modern discourse of racial identity is implemented (as through African-centered pedagogy), Blacks experiencing forms of oppression other than race/ ethnicity are denied creative spaces from which to strive for their own liberation and are required instead to subordinate aspects of their own identity for racial solidarity (Ladson-Billings 2003). As a liberatory project, African-centered pedagogy can ill afford to mimic oppressive practices. The difficulty here is that conceptualizations of identity must be theorized that encourage Black solidarity while also honoring multiple and competing expressions of Blackness (e.g., Shelby 2005). The first point being made through this discussion is that the issue of identity is an important and complicated one for African-centered scholars. The second point is that ideas found in critical multiculturalism could be used to strengthen the theoretical precision of African-centered scholars' conceptualizations of identity.

While African-centered pedagogy is representative of the modern identity project, critical multiculturalism embraces postmodern understandings of identity. Critical multiculturalists understand identity as contested and constantly in a state of flux (Kincheloe and Steinberg 1997). Because critical multiculturalists view identity as unstable, they resist politics of identity founded solely on the authority of shared history. Such politics are, for Kincheloe and Steinberg (1997), of dubitable liberatory potential because they fail to acknowledge ways in which identity formations change over time and afford possibilities for new political alliances. From a critical multicultural standpoint, the insistence on a stable collective African identity means that the effectiveness of libratory projects based on that identity are limited to those who accept it. Potential group members who do not identify with the established criteria for African identity are lost. Indeed Hilliard (2001) summarizes the place for Blacks who do not identify with an African identity in the following passage. He states:

> The fundamental question, as I have stated elsewhere, for people of African ancestry is, "To be or not to be African?" For some of us, ethnicity does not matter at all. In fact, some run from it as fast as is humanly possible. *I have no message for them*, nor will I argue for or against their position. Their struggle, if any, is of a different order. (24; emphasis mine)

In practical terms, the conceptualizations and pedagogy of African-centered scholars needs to reach a broader audience to further the cause of Black educational liberation. If rigid understandings of African identity result in the rejection of Blacks who could further liberatory efforts, such understandings need to be revisited.

While critical multiculturalism can inform African-centered scholars' conceptualizations of identity, such work would indicate an alliance or coalition, at least temporarily, between African-centered and critical multicultural scholars. The potential and challenges inherent in such a coalition will be discussed in the next section of this chapter.

A Politic of Self-Reliance versus a Politic of Coalition Building for Black Liberation

Patricia Hill Collins (2000) discusses the benefits of coalition building (referred to by Collins as transversal politics) in her book *Black Feminist Thought*. For Collins (2000), coalition building is necessary for social justice because "each group possesses a partial perspective on its own experiences and on those of other groups" (247). No group is capable of achieving social justice alone because their partial perspective fails to reveal the full complexities of relationships of domination. Collins's understanding of coalition building suggests that the liberatory potential of both African-centered pedagogy and critical multiculturalism are both limited to partial perspectives on oppression and social justice. By engaging in conceptual dialogue, scholars from these two disciplines may gain a fuller understanding of mechanisms necessary for social justice and thereby work to realize Black liberation and ultimately, the liberation of all marginalized groups in the United States.

African-centered educators have experienced success in independently educating Black youth (Bush 2004; Lomotey 1992; Njuguna 1997), but have not reached, in large numbers, Black youth in public schools. Should doubt exist as to the need for alternatives to traditional methods of school-ing experienced by Black youth in public schools, consider the following statistics:

Seventy percent of all Black students in the United States currently at-tend schools where the enrollment is more than 50 percent minority and 36 percent of Black students in the United States attend schools where the minority enrollment is 90 percent or greater (Kozol 2006; Orfield 2001). Research indicates that students in majority Black schools are consistently under-resourced in favor of richer and whiter schools (Liu 2006; Weiner and Pristoop 2006). Moreover, as a result of the disproportionate negative effects of accountability mandates such as No Child Left Behind (NCLB), Black youth in public schools also suffer from increased levels of teacher turnover and increased dropout rates, especially for low-income Black youth (Kohn 2006), as well as increases in placement in special educa-tion, behaviorally disruptive, and low-ability classes (Kohn 2000; Lee and Orfield 2006).

Given these findings it should not be surprising that as their time in public schools increases, Black students, especially Black male students, experience decreasing levels of excitement for learning and school achieve-ment (Comer and Poussaint 1992; Kunjufu 1996). Clearly, the educational treatment of Black youth in public schools has been decidedly negative (Delpit 1995, 1998; Hilliard 1998, 2001), and suggestive of "cultural geno-cide" (Hilliard 1998). Given the success of African-centered pedagogy in independent Black schools, its provision to Black students in public schools seems a preferable alternative to the above outcomes.

A coalition with critical multiculturalists who avow interest in ending Black oppression holds promise for allowing African-centered pedagogy to reach Black youth whom the public school systems have largely failed (Hilliard 1995; Shujaa 1994). Such a coalition could also serve the impor-tant purpose of creating a wider audience for the dissemination of African-centered thought. The persistent silencing of Black scholars (Gordon 1995; hooks 1993) is a reality in U.S. culture. In a perfect world the thoughts of African-centered and other Black scholars would be judged on their merit rather than the race/ethnicity of their authors. Yet scholars such as bell hooks (1993), Lisa Delpit (1988), and Patricia Hill Collins (2000) have spoken eloquently about the use of white power to silence Black voices. Relevant to African-centered scholarship, the result of this silencing is that the very ideas espoused by African-centered scholars fail to reach the ma-jority of Americans, Black or otherwise.

In addition to silencing Black voices, whiteness can also be used to distort the intellectual contributions of Black people. The power of the dominant society to publicize overly simplistic and often erroneous portrayals of African-centered thought was demonstrated by academics such as Diane Ravitch (1990) and Arthur Schlesinger (1991). Such distortions continue to color the views of the larger society about African-centered pedagogy. The resulting silencing and/or distorting of African-centered thought, then, reduces opportunities for Black educational liberation. As Gloria Ladson-Billings and William Tate (1995) recognize, whiteness "is valuable and is property" (59). Whiteness in the United States affords reputation and status (Ladson-Billings and Tate 1995). The unpleasant reality is that in the United States, white critical multiculturalists such as Peter McLaren, Joe Kincheloe, and Shirley Steinberg, by virtue of their whiteness, enjoy greater access to and greater authority in the public sphere than do most African-centered scholars. What is being argued here is that this commodity of whiteness could intentionally be used in the service of Black educational progress to insert into the public dialogue an endorsement of African-centered pedagogy.

For their own part, critical multiculturalists champion the cause of solidarity (McLaren 1995) and work toward the coalition of marginalized groups "in the mutual struggle for democracy and empowerment" (Kincheloe and Steinberg 1997, 33). However, while a coalition between African-centered scholars and critical multicultural scholars could create a broader audience for African-centered scholarship and ultimately result in the provision of African-centered pedagogy to more Black students, African-centered scholars such as Madhubuti (1994) have expressed concerns about such ventures. Although critical multicultural scholars have committed themselves to the cause of solidarity with Blacks and other marginalized groups (Fischman 1999; Kincheloe and Steinberg 1997), the persistent historical and present-day oppression of Black people in the United States (Collins 2000; Hilliard 2001) gives African-centered scholars little evidence that alliances with those sharing membership in the dominant society will not be used to further oppress Black people.

The skepticism over the success of coalitions between Blacks and members of the dominant society is evident in the work of Black scholars previously cited in this chapter who have attempted to participate in the largely Eurocentric postmodern project. Cornel West (1993a), for example, expresses suspicion of "postmodernism" because the ideology of its "modern" precursor was instrumental in the devaluation and exploitation of oppressed people. Additionally, West (1982, 1993a) observes that while Blacks in America existentially experience the postmodern condition of the Other, they will unlikely find in postmodernism tools of liberation because postmodern exploration of concepts such as difference and otherness remain disengaged from the plight of the oppressed in Black America. Similarly, while bell hooks (1993) is hopeful of the liberatory potential of postmodern discourse for oppressed Black Americans, she, like West, also is critical of exclusionary academic debates on postmodernity that appropriate the concepts of difference and otherness but fail to "incorporate the voices of displaced, marginalized exploited, and oppressed black people" (hooks 1993, 512). Finally, Patricia Hill Collins (2000) calls attention to the exclusive language of postmodernism that acts as a barrier of access to many marginalized people. More importantly perhaps, Collins (2000) and hooks (1993) both question the benefits to the dominant society of a set of theories that interrogate notions of subjectivity and authority and thereby undermine Black people's group authority at the exact time when Blacks and other marginalized individuals are gaining voice around these attributes. The above critiques are significant for this project as critical multiculturalism embraces the same notions of the postmodern that are being questioned by Collins, hooks, and West.

While there is much to be gained from a conceptual coalition between African-centered scholars and critical multicultural scholars, clearly, much is also at stake. For Black scholars, a coalition with members who possess white privilege (McIntosh 2003) would clearly be one of unequal power. Thus, African-centered scholars engaging in a coalition of this sort would be vulnerable to white hegemony.

To summarize, the power of white hegemony is evidenced in a system of public school accountability, ostensibly put in place to promote Black student achievement, but persistently produces negative educational outcomes for Black youth. The risks are further evidenced through the experiences of Black scholars with the postmodern project; a project which purportedly breaks away from the universal to create spaces for those fragmented and marginalized by systems of totality, yet finds ways to appropriate notions of otherness and alienation in ways that still leave Black people silenced and displaced (hooks 1993). Finally, these risks are made evident through the disparaging treatment of African-centered thought in the public sphere (Asante and Ravitch 1991) exemplified through the work of Diane Ravitch (1990) and Arthur Schlesinger (1991)—work indicative of the power of cultural hegemony to distort and silence Black thought. While it is argued in this chapter that the potential for Black educational liberation is worth chancing the fore-mentioned risks, the risks neverthe-less highlight a troubling aspect of critical multicultural thought relevant to the proposed project—the reliance of critical multicultural scholars on Eurocentric theories of power to produce the liberation of Blacks and other marginalized groups. For many African-centered scholars, reliance on Eurocentric theories points to a broader acceptance of the values and interpretations of European or Anglo-American culture that have been historically used to oppress African and Black people.

Uses of Eurocentric Epistemology for Black Liberation

As highlighted above, a final challenge relevant to a dialogical encounter between African-centered pedagogy and critical multiculturalism is the Eurocentric ways of knowing espoused in critical multiculturalism. The term "Eurocentric ways of knowing" refers to understandings of the world that are representative of European and Anglo-American culture, values, and interests. Activist and poet Audre Lorde (1984) writes that "the master's tools will never dismantle the master's house. They may allow us temporarily to beat him at his own game, but they will never enable us to bring about genuine change" (112). Here Lorde speaks to tactics of mar-ginalized groups to appropriate strategies of domination in their freedom struggles. African-centered scholars view Eurocentric ways of knowing, whether manifested in public school organization and practice (Ladson-Billings 2003; Ladson-Billings and Tate 1995), methods of ascertaining truth (Collins 2000), or attitudes toward Black family life and culture (Hilliard 1998), as integral in maintaining the domination of Black people (Akoto 1994; Ani 1994). In this way, Eurocentric ways of knowing can be considered to be "the master's tools" and as such, ineffective tools for Black liberation.

At question here is whether critical multiculturalism is tainted by its Eurocentric origins or redeemed by its commitment to solidarity with the oppressed (Fischman 1999). Inspired by European critical theorists of the 1920s such as Herbert Marcuse and also informed by the class analysis of Karl Marx and the conceptualizations of power and hegemony articulated by Michel Foucault and Antonio Gramsci, respectively (Fischman 1999; Kincheloe and Steinberg 1997), critical multiculturalism is based on the conceptualizations of European theorists and, at least in some respects, represents the interests of its creators (Asante 1991; Shujaa 1994). While utilizing Eurocentric theory to understand relations of domination should not, in and of itself, prevent a coalition between African-centered and critical multicultural scholars, the fact that theorists such as Peter McLaren, Joe Kincheloe, and Shirley Steinberg "went to the European theater for conceptual systems within which to ground their critical theorizing, when there existed here in the [Black] American experience conceptual systems of social critique that preceded by at least two decades" (Gordon 1995, 59–60). Their chosen theories do at least suggest a devaluing of African-centered knowledge at some level.

Critical multiculturalists emphasize the importance of highlighting subjugated knowledge in order to fracture the hold of dominant ways of knowing on the masses. Yet Gordon's (1995) point must be emphasized. Critical multicultural scholars credit Black scholars such as W. E. B. Du Bois, Michael Dyson, James Banks, Gloria Ladson-Billings, Cornel West, and bell hooks as informing their theory, but these scholars do not gain prominence in most critical multicultural work. Given the stated goals of critical multiculturalism, the centrality of Antonio Gramsci's notion of hegemony in critical multicultural theory seems misplaced. Without using the term hegemony, Carter G. Woodson (1933/1990) articulated this same concept when he wrote of the racial socialization process through which Blacks were miseducated into believe in their own inferiority and that because of mental enslavement, Blacks would participate willingly in their own oppression. Because critical multiculturalists work to uncover suppressed knowledge and empower the marginalized (including marginalized Blacks), the utilization of Woodson's (1933/1990) work would have seemed more relevant to their liberatory projects, especially those involving Black people, than the work of Gramsci. This seeming lack of meaningful inclusion of Black voices in critical multicultural theory suggests a tendency toward subordinating Black ways of knowing in favor of Eurocentric ones. Clearly then, a fundamental task which must precede any serious dialogue and/or coalition between African-centered and critical multicultural scholars is to take seriously Lorde's (1984) warning of using the "master's tools" for the liberation of marginalized people. While coalition building between African-centered and critical multicultural scholars appears feasible in theory, the practical aspects of such encounters may be much more difficult to bring to fruition given the above concerns.

Given the tensions and challenges to dialogue and coalition building discussed above, one might wonder what hope realistically exists for the social justice project explored in this chapter. Hope exists in the steadfast commitment of African-centered scholars to the holistic education of Black youth and to Black liberation, even if liberation requires change.

Shujaa (1994) expresses both hope and recognition of the need for change when he discusses the future of Afrocentricity. He writes:

> Afrocentricity is one of those rare and fundamental concepts that is so powerful that the task of determining its meaning belongs to the people. Its interpretations will change as history is produced by the movements of African people through time and space and with the construction of new realities reflecting African life. (375)

Hope also exists in the commitment of critical multiculturalists to social justice and, just as importantly, to constant self-reflection to root out their own hegemonic tendencies. This hope is expressed in the following passage by Peter McLaren.

> My whiteness (and my maleness) is something I cannot escape no matter how hard I try . . . in living my own life as a traitor to whiteness, I cannot become lazy by failing to interrogate the epistemological, political, and ethical assumptions of my own practice. If all whites are racists at some level, then we must struggle to become anti-racist racists. We must always rethink our positionalities, platforms, and affiliations without defaulting the main game, which is to resist and transform the market system based on the maximization of profits. After all, it was this system that enslaved millions of Africans in the United States and still disproportionately exploits people of color worldwide. (Peter McLaren as interviewed in Fischman 1999)

If critical multiculturalists such as Peter McLaren allow their theories to be genuinely informed by the insights and experiences of African-centered scholars, and African-centered scholars are willing to do the same, the social justice project described in this chapter could possibly become a reality.

Conclusion

A coalition between African-centered scholars and critical multiculturalists holds potential for strengthening both disciplines and facilitating social change through the creation of new forms of knowledge and new strategies of acting for social justice. The dialogue and resulting coalition proposed here has potential for resisting cultural domination by infusing African-centered thought with more flexible understandings of identity and by increasing opportunities for Black students to benefit from African-centered pedagogy. This project also would benefit critical multicultural scholars by allowing them to rethink some of their conceptualizations that apply to Black life and the political and psychological reasons for asserting collective Black identity. Through a process of respect, mutual dialogue, and willingness to change, African-centered scholars and scholars of critical multiculturalism can inform each other and further the cause of Black educational liberation.

If the experiences of Blackness in the United States, which exemplify elements of modernity and postmodernity (Ladson-Billings 2003), can be understood symbolically (West 1982) and ideologically (Hill 1999) as representative of the postmodern condition of alienation, despair, and yearning (hooks 1993 and 2003) then work to liberate Black America can serve as a model from which other social justice projects can be informed (Collins 2000). By examining key concepts of African-centered pedagogy and critical multiculturalism as well as tensions and points of commonality among each, this chapter has utilized a womanist perspective to explore the potential of a dialogical encounter between African-centered and critical multicultural thought. A coalition between African-centered and critical multicultural scholars was proposed to enhance the theoretical precision of African-centered scholarship and critical multiculturalism, expose African-centered scholarship to a broader audience, and facilitate the provision of African-centered pedagogy to Black youth in public schools. It was argued that by producing these outcomes, a coalition between African-centered scholars and critical multicultural scholars will facilitate Black educational progress and consequently, Black liberation.

Works Cited

Akoto, Agyei. 1994. "Notes on an Afrikan-centered pedagogy." In *Too much schooling, too little education: A paradox of black life in white societies*, ed. Mwalimu J. Shujaa, 319–40. Trenton, NJ: Africa World Press, Inc.

Anderson, Victor. 1995. *Beyond ontological blackness: An essay on African American religious and cultural criticism*. New York: Continuum.

Ani, Marimba. 1994. *Yurugu: An African-centered critique of European cultural thought and Behavior*. Trenton, NJ: Africa World Press, Inc.

Asante, Molefi. 1996. "Afrocentric theory rooted in proven facts: Attackers deny obvious to bolster racist notions." *The Philadelphia Tribune* 113, 7-A.

Asante, Molefi, and Diane Ravitch. 1991. "Multiculturalism: An exchange." *The American Scholar*, 267–76.

Banks, James A. 1989. "Multicultural education: Characteristics and goals." In *Multicultural education: Issues and perspectives*, 2–26. Boston: Allyn and Bacon.

———. 1997. *Educating citizens in a multicultural society*. New York: Teachers College Press.

———. 2001. "Approaches to multicultural curricular reform." In *Multicultural education: Issues and perspectives*, 4th ed, ed. James Banks and Cherry McGee, 225–46. New York: Wiley and Sons.

Bush, Lawson. 2004. "Access, school choice, and independent black institutions: A historical perspective." *Journal of Black Studies* 34:386–420.

Cannon, Katie. 1995. *Katie's canon: Womanism and the soul of the black community.* New York: Continuum.

Carruthers, Jacob. 1994. "Black intellectuals and the crisis in black education." In *Too much schooling, too little education: A paradox of black life in white societies*, ed. Mwalimu J. Shujaa, 37–56. Trenton, NJ: Africa World Press, Inc.

Collins, Patricia Hill. 1996. "What's in a name? Womanism, black feminism, and Beyond." *The Black Scholar* 26:19.

———. 2000. *Black feminist thought: Knowledge, consciousness, and the politics of empowerment.* 2nd ed. New York: Routledge.

Comer, James P., and Alvin F. Poussaint. 1992. *Raising black children: Two leading psychiatrists confront the educational, social and emotional problems facing black children.* New York: Plume.

Delpit, Lisa. 1995. *Other people's children: Cultural conflict in the classroom.* New York: New Press.

———. 1998. "Ebonics and culturally responsive instruction." In *The real Ebonics debate: Power, language, and the education of African-American children*, ed. Theresa Perry and Lisa Delpit, 17–26. Boston: Beacon Press.

———. 2006. "No kinda sense." In *The institution of education*, 5th ed., ed. H. Svi Shapiro, Kathe Latham, and Sabrina Ross, 255–64. Boston: Pearson.

Du Bois, W. E. B. 1935. *Black reconstruction in America*: New York: Harcourt Brace.

Fischman, Gustavo. 1999. E. "Peter McLaren: A call for a multicultural revolution." *Multicultural Education* 6 (4): 32–34.

Foster, Michelle. 1997. *Black teachers on teaching.* New York: New Press.

Giddings, Geoffrey. 2001. "Infusion of Afrocentric content into the school curriculum: Toward an effective movement." *Journal of Black Studies* 31:462–82.

Gill, Walter. 1991. "Jewish day schools and Afrocentric programs as models for educating African American youth." *Journal of Negro Education* 60:566–80.

Gordon, Beverly. 1994. "African-American cultural knowledge and liberatory education: dilemmas, problems, and potentials in postmodern American society." In *Too much schooling, too little education: A paradox of black life in white societies*, ed. Mwalimu J. Shujaa, 57–80. Trenton, NJ: Africa World Press, Inc.

———. 1995. "The fringe dwellers: African American women scholars in the postmodern era." In *Critical multiculturalism: Uncommon voices in a common struggle*, ed. Barry Kanopol and Peter McLaren, 59–88. Westport, CT: Bergin & Garvey.

Gorski, P. C., and Ed Change. 1999. "A brief history of multicultural education." Available at www.edchange.org/multicultural/papers/edchange_history.html.

Hill, Renee Leslie. 1999. "Disrupted/disruptive movements: Black theology and black power 1969/1999." In *Black faith and public talk: Critical essays on James H. Cone's black theology and black power*, ed. Dwight N. Hopkins, 138–49. New York: Orbis Books.

Hilliard, Asa G., III. 1992. "The meaning of KMT (Ancient Egyptian) history for contemporary African American experience." *Phylon* 49 (1–2): 10–22.

———. 1995. *Teacher education from an African American perspective.* ERIC Document # ED393798. eric.ed.gov/ERICDocs/data/ericdocs2/content_storage_01/0000000b/80/25/dd/c8.pdf. Accessed November 28, 2006.

———. 2001. "'Race,' identity, hegemony, and education: What do we need to know now?" In *Race and education: The roles of history and society in educating African American students,* ed. William H. Watkins, James H. Lewis, and Victoria Chou. Boston: Allyn and Bacon.

———. 2004. "Beyond black, white, and brown: A forum." *The Nation,* May 3 issue. www.thenation.com/doc/20040503/forum. Accessed November 9, 2006.

hooks, bell. 1993. "Postmodern blackness." In *A postmodern reader,* ed. Joseph Natoli and Linda Hutcheon, 510–18. New York: State University of New York Press.

———. 2003. "Greed: simply love." In *The institution of education,* 4th ed., ed. H. Svi Shapiro, Susan B. Harden, and Anna Pennell, 491–98. Boston: Pearson Publishing.

Institute for Independent Education. 1991. *On the road to success: students at independent neighborhood schools.* Washington, DC: Institute for Independent Education.

Jay, Michelle. 2003. "Critical race theory, multicultural education, and the hidden curriculum of hegemony." *Multicultural Perspectives* 5 (4): 3–9.

Kifano, Sabira. 1996. "Afrocentric education in supplementary schools: Paradigm and practice at the Mary McLeod Bethune institute." *The Journal of Negro Education* 65:209–18.

Kincheloe, Joe, and Steinberg Shirley. 1997. *Changing multiculturalism: New times, new curriculum.* Philadelphia: Open University Press.

King, Joyce E., and Thomasyne L. Wilson. 1994. "Being the soul-freeing substance: A legacy of hope in AfroHumanity." In *Too much schooling, too little education: A paradox of black life in white societies,* ed. Mwalimu J. Shujaa, 269–94. Trenton, NJ: Africa World Press, Inc.

Kohn, Alfie. 2000. *The case against standardized testing: Raising the scores, ruining the schools.* Portsmouth, NH: Hienemann.

———. 2006. "Test today, privatize tomorrow: Using accountability to 'reform' schools to death." In *The institution of education,* 5th ed., ed. H. Svi Shapiro, Kathe Latham, and Sabrina Ross, 363–76. Boston: Pearson.

Kozol, Jonathan. 2006. "The shame of the nation: The restoration of apartheid schooling in America." In *The institution of education,* 5th ed., edited by H. Svi Shapiro, Kathe Latham, and Sabrina Ross, 227–38. Boston: Pearson.

Kunjufu, Jawanza. 1996. *Restoring the village, values, and commitment: Solutions for the black family.* Chicago: African American Images.

Ladson-Billings, Gloria. 1997. *The dream keepers: Successful teachers of African-American students.* San Francisco: Jossey-Bass.

———. 2003. "New directions in multicultural education: Complexities, bound-aries, and critical race theory." In *Handbook of research on multicultural education*, 2nd ed, ed. James A. Banks and Cherry McGhee Banks, 50–65. San Francisco: Jossey-Bass.

Ladson-Billings, Gloria, and William F. Tate. 1995. "Toward a critical race theory of education." *Teachers College Record* 97 (1): 54–64.

Lee, Carol D., and Kofi Lomotey. 1990. "How shall we sing our sacred song in a strange land? The dilemma of double consciousness and the complexities of an African-centered pedagogy." *Journal of Education* 172 (2): 45–62.

Lee, Jaekyung, and Gary Orfield. 2006. *Tracking achievement gaps and assessing the impact of NCLB on the gaps: An in-depth look into national and state reading and math outcome trends.* www.civilrightsproject.harvard.edu/research/esea/nclb_naep_lee.pdf. Accessed January 15, 2007.

Liu, Goodwin. 2006. "How the federal government makes rich states richer." *Funding Gaps.* The Education Trust. www2.edtrust.org/NR/rdonlyres/CDEF9403-5A75-437E-93FF-EBF1174181FB/0/FundingGap2006.pdf. Accessed January 15, 2007.

Lomotey, Kofi. 1992. "Independent black institutions: African-centered educa-tion models." *The Journal of Negro Education* 61:455–62.

Lorde, Audre. 1984. *Sister outsider: Essays and speeches.* Berkeley, CA: Crossing Press

Madhubuti, Haki. 1994. "Culture work: Planting new trees with new seeds." In *Too much schooling, too little education: A paradox of black life in white societies*, ed. Mwalimu J. Shujaa, 1–8. Trenton, NJ: Africa World Press, Inc.

Marable, Manning. 2000. "Black studies, multiculturalism and the future of American education." In *A turbulent voyage: Readings in African American studies*, 3rd ed, ed. Floyd W. Hayes III, 24–34. Lanham, MD: Rowman & Littlefield.

May, Stephen. 1999. *Critical multiculturalism: Rethinking multicultural and antiracist education.* Philadelphia: Falmer Press.

McIntosh, Peggy. 2003. "White privilege: Unpacking the invisible knapsack." In *The institution of education*, 4th ed., ed. H. Svi Shapiro, Susan B. Harden, and Anna Pennell, 165–70. Boston: Pearson Publishing.

McLaren, Peter. 1994. "White terror and oppositional agency: Towards a critical multiculturalism." In *Multiculturalism: A critical reader*, ed. David Theo Golderg, 45–74. Cambridge, MA: Blackwell

———. 1995. *Critical pedagogy and predatory culture.* New York: Routledge.

Murrell, Peter C. 2002. *African-centered pedagogy: Developing schools of achievement for African American children.* New York: State University of New York Press.

Murtadha, Khaula, and Daud M. Watts. 2005. "Linking the struggles for educa-tion and social justice: Historical perspectives of African American leadership in schools." *Educational Administration Quarterly* 41 (4): 591–608.

National Center for Education Statistics. 2003. *Digest of education statistics tables and figures.* nces.ed.gov/programs/digest/d05/tables/dt05_038.asp. Accessed February 20, 2007.

——. 2006. *Characteristics of schools, districts, teachers, principals, and school libraries in the United States: 2003–04 schools and staffing survey.* nces.ed.gov/pubsearch/pubsinfo.asp?pubid=2006313. Accessed February 20, 2007.

Newfield, Christopher, and Avery Gordon. 1996. "Multiculturalism's unfinished business." In *Mapping multiculturalism,* ed. Avery F. Gordon and Cristopher Newfield, 76–115. Minneapolis: University of Minnesota Press.

Njuguna, Kabugi. 1997. "Independent black schools, another voice, another choice." *The new crisis.* www.findarticles.com/p/articles/mi_qa3812/is_199710/ai_n8781016. Accessed February 5, 2006.

Orfield, Gary. 2001. *Schools more separate: Consequences of a decade of resegregation. Executive Summary.* www.civilrightsproject.harvard.edu/research/deseg/separate_schools01.php. Accessed January 15, 2007.

Potts, Randolph. 2003. "Emancipatory education versus school-based prevention in African American communities." *American Journal of Community Psychology* 31:173.

Rashid, Kamua. 2005. "Slavery of the mind: Carter G. Woodson and Jacob H. Carruthers: Intergenerational discourse on African education and social change." *The Western Journal of Black Studies* 29 (1): 542–46.

Ravitch, Diane. 1990. "Multiculturalism: E Pluribus Plures." *American Scholar* (Summer): 337–54.

Richardson, Elaine. 2000. "Critique on the problematic of implementing Afrocentricity into traditional curriculum: 'The powers that be.'" *Journal of Black Studies* 31:196–213.

Schlesinger, Arthur. 1991. "The disuniting of America." *American Educator* (Winter): 21–33.

Shelby, Tommie. 2005. *We who are dark: The philosophical foundations of black solidarity.* Cambridge, MA: Belknap Press of Harvard University Press.

Shujaa, Mwalimu J. 1994a. "Afrocentric Transformation and Parental Choice in African-American Independent Schools." In *Too much schooling, too little education: A paradox of black life in white societies,* ed. Mwalimu J. Shujaa, 362–76. Trenton, NJ: Africa World Press, Inc.

——. 1994b. "Education and schooling: You can have one without the other." In *Too much schooling, too little education: A paradox of black life in white societies,* ed. Mwalimu J. Shujaa, 13–36. Trenton, NJ: Africa World Press, Inc.

Shujaa, Mwalimu J., and J. D. Ratteray. 1988. "Expanding 'schools of choice' for African Americans: Independent neighborhood schools in New Jersey." In *Blacks in New Jersey 1987 report. Crisis in urban education,* ed. New Jersey Public Policy Research Institute, 39–50. Absecon: New Jersey Public Policy Research Institute

Sleeter, C. 1996. *Multicultural education as social activism.* Albany: State University of New York Press.

Smith, Linda T. 1999. *Decolonizing methodologies: Research and indigenous peoples.* London: Zed Books.

Solórzano, Daniel. 1997. "Images and words that wound: critical race theory, racial stereotyping and teacher education." *Teacher Education Quarterly* 24:5–19.

———. 1998. "Critical race theory, racial and gender microaggressions, and the experiences of Chicana and Chicano Scholars." *International Journal of Qualitative Studies in Education* 11:121–36.

Solórzano, Daniel, and Miguel Ceja, and Tara Yosso. 2000. "Critical race theory, racial microaggressions and campus racial climate: the experiences of African-American college students." *Journal of Negro Education* 69 (1/2): 60–73.

Tate, William F. 1997. "Critical race theory and education: History, theory, and implications." In *Review of Research in Education* 22, ed. Michael Apple, 195–247. Washington, DC: American Educational Research Association.

Teasley, M., and E. Tyson. 2007. "Culture wars and the attack on multiculturalism: An Afrocentric critique." *Journal of Black Studies* 37:390–409.

Thomas, Linda E. 1998. *Womanist theology, epistemology, and a new anthropological Paradigm.* www.hartfordhwp.com/archives/45a/256.html. Accessed May 17, 2005.

Ukpokodu, Omiunota. 2003. "Teaching multicultural education from a critical perspective: Challenges and dilemmas." *Multicultural Perspectives* 5 (4): 17–23.

Walker, Alice. 1984. *In search of our mother's gardens: Womanist prose.* San Diego: Harvest Books.

Weiner, Ross, and Eli Pristoop. 2006. "How states shortchange the districts that need the most help." *Funding Gaps.* The Education Trust. www2.edtrust.org/NR/rdonlyres/CDEF9403-5A75-437E-93FF-EBF1174181FB/0/FundingGap 2006.pdf. Accessed January 15, 2007.

West, Cornel. 1982. *Prophesy deliverance!: An Afro-American revolutionary Christianity.* Philadelphia: The Westminster Press.

———. 1993a. "Black culture and postmodernism." In *A Postmodern Reader*, ed. Joseph Natoli and Linda Hutcheon, 390–97. Albany: State University of New York Press.

———. 1993b. "Black theology of liberation as critique of capitalist civilization." In *Black theology a documentary history. Vol. 2. 1980–1992*, ed. James H. Cone and Gayraud S. Wilmore, 410–26. New York: Maryknoll.

Williams, D. S. 1993. *Sisters in the wilderness: The challenge of womanist god-talk.* Maryknoll, New York: Orbis Books.

Williams, Heather A. 2005. *Self-Taught: African American education in slavery and freedom.* Chapel Hill: University of North Carolina Press

Woodson, Carter G. 1933/1990. *The miseducation of the Negro.* Washington, DC: Associated Publishers.

The Performance Gap 　　　　　　　　　　　　　　　**5**
Stereotype Threat, Assessment, and the
Education of African American Children

ERIC A. HURLEY

> *The current state of Negro education can only be understood*
> *by studying the forces effective in the development of Negro*
> *education.*

> —CARTER G. WOODSON[1]

The Problem

THE PERFORMANCE GAP BETWEEN Black and white Americans on academic assessments of all types has been the focus of such a volume and consistency of scholarship, policy, fiscal expenditure, news, and other discourse that, were it not so important an issue, it might rightly be considered "overdone." Indeed there are people whose lives are personally touched in one way or another, who find it boring, rightly or not. Here then are a few statistics that the reader may find boring, troubling, or both. In the most recent data for which they were available in time for this publication, the Black-white gap in mathematics and reading achievement appeared at every grade studied (1–12) (NCES 2006). In 2001, the National Center for Education Statistics (NCES) reported that African American students at the ages of nine, thirteen, and seventeen had scored lower than their white counterparts on standardized tests of mathematics consistently for three decades. Similar long-term gaps between Black and white students were reported for reading scores as well. Such an accounting of these trends could go on and on. Further, I can think of no more compelling illustration of their repercussions than the fact that in this country fourth-grade reading scores are used to project the number of prisons that should be constructed in preparation for those children's eighteenth birthdays[2] (Edelman 2007).

In Historic Context

Black social scientists have weighed in on issues in Black education from the beginning—literally. Francis Cecil Sumner, who became the first Black Ph.D. in psychology in 1920, published several papers in which he sought to address difficulties in the education (Sumner 1926, 1927a) and test performance (Sumner 1927b) of African American students. Indeed fourteen of the first twenty-five Black authored doctoral dissertations in psychology (1920–1946) concerned pedagogical or testing issues in the education of African Americans (Guthrie 1986).

At one time it was widely believed that segregation and the concurrent inequality of resources were the primary impediments to Black progress broadly and especially in education. That is to say, at one time it was widely if not universally[3] acknowledged that underachievement among African American students is but one symptom of the diseases that are racial prejudice, discrimination, and oppression in the United States.

Psychologists Kenneth and Mamie Clark, both trained at Howard and Columbia universities, were key figures in the fight to end segregation in education. It is unfortunate that, in service of their noble work helping to dismantle Jim Crow, the Clarks also participated in psychology's long-standing tradition of "proving" that there is something wrong with African American people. In their case a pathological self-hatred supposedly manifested in small children's preference for a doll that looked white rather than like themselves (Clark and Clark 1947, 1950). Subsequent research has rethought the appropriateness of those kinds of conclusions being drawn from those kinds of data (Baldwin 1979; Garfinkle 1959; Spencer 1999). However, the legacy of that scholarship lives on in their original conclusions, not in the critiques. First, in that *Brown v. the Topeka Kansas Board of Education* was decided significantly on the psychological evidence provided by the Clarks (1954) and secondly, in that their "doll studies" endure in the public mind even today as "evidence" that there is something pathologically wrong with African American people. As recently as late 2006, teen Kiri Davis generated nationwide attention with her documentary *A Girl Like Me* in which she imitated the Clark and Clark doll studies before a video camera. The footage made national news, was widely distributed on the Internet and in theaters, and reignited debate over the Black self-hatred thesis.

The *Brown* decision outlawed segregated schools and though no dream of integration was ever fully realized and what progress was made has not been sustained (Orfield, Frankenberg, and Lee 2003), the end of legal discrimination and the introduction of related policies were seen by many as the full extent to which white America could be held responsible for the educational difficulties facing Black Americans. When those difficulties did not disappear during the next several decades, an explanatory vacuum opened up. In the time since, a wide and contentious array of explanations have been cast into that vacuum from social science laboratories, but also from armchairs, and every possible fount of ideas in-between.

During and in the midst of the commotion, the mental testing movement, which had been building momentum since Louis Terman's 1916 publication of the portable IQ test, reached a fever pitch. Among its first orders of business was to dutifully quantify Black underperformance in a way that lent the appearance of objectivity to claims that—given universal access to public education—Blacks themselves are responsible for their difficulties in education as in society (Jensen 1973). It was on IQ tests that a Black-white performance gap was first evident as a stable phenomenon and where it was first vigorously debated. Indeed the arguments made by Black psychologist Martin David Jenkins disputing the validity of IQ testing (Jenkins 1943; Witty and Jenkins 1936) are very much the same ones made today. Its manifestation on other kinds of standardized tests have more recently come to the fore and the search for explanations and solutions has been ongoing.

It is worth noting that standardized testing, and mental measurement in general, is problematic in its own right but as related specifically to race is troubling mainly in that the performance gap reflects the alarming disparity between groups in U.S. public education.

The Stereotype Threat Model of Underperformance

From the beginning, Black psychologists were quick to wade into the discussion and debate about the performance gap. They have proposed a variety of influential explanations, which are often debated as if in competition. Among them the oppositional culture (Ogbu 1987), cultural integrity (Boykin 1986), and, of interest here, stereotype threat models are distinguished, if only for having captured the attention of scholars, policymakers, and the general public. A relative newcomer, Claude Steele's stereotype threat model joins the long heritage of Black thought and debates concerning the education of African American children. Though new in some important ways, the model also has much in common with other work in that tradition.

A Stanford University psychologist, Steele (2003) has written that he and Joshua Aronson were seeking a way to explain the persistent racial gap in grades among students who were equally well prepared for college. A series of seminal studies published in 1995 laid the foundation for the model, set in motion one of the most well-known and well-researched trends of the ensuing decade (Steele and Aronson 1995), and propelled Steele to iconic status among psychologists and among Black scholars in a variety of fields. Termed stereotype threat, the phenomenon, now considered a basic social psychological process, goes like this: among people who are capable at and ego-identified with a skill, and if there is an existing (or fabricated in the experiment) negative stereotype about their group's ability on that skill relative to some other group, then, if you describe a difficult test of the skill as diagnostic of natural ability they will perform less well than they would if the same test were described as non-diagnostic.

The associated theoretical model suggests that the threat of confirming negative stereotypes about the intellectual ability of African Americans somehow undermines the testing performance of African American students (Steele and Aronson 1995). The phenomenon has been commonly, though controversially, associated with the performance gap and efforts to close it, in the popular media (Chandler 1999; Cohen, Garcia, Apfel, and Master 2006; Wax 2004) and academic press (Brown and Day 2006; Helms 2005; Jencks and Phillips 1998). The controversy generally revolves around how much of the performance gap the stereotype threat may account for, with some suggesting that stereotype threat may be a/the key factor. Others suggest that while it may exacerbate the problem, stereotype threat should be viewed as a separate phenomenon from the performance gap. Critical to linking stereotype threat with the performance gap is the assertion that negative stereotypes about the intellectual abilities of African Americans are so pervasively available that Black test takers are automatically primed to ponder and feel threatened by them in testing situations (Steele and Aronson 1995).

This chapter analyses the stereotype threat model in order to examine its strengths and weaknesses in describing and as a guide for efforts to close the achievement gap, and more broadly for its contribution to the discourse on what it means to be Black in the United States. The analysis considers the theoretical, scientific, and practical merit of the stereotype threat proposal. The analysis also contemplates sociopolitical factors that would come into play should the nation earnestly pursue strategies for closing the performance gap that are premised on the reasoning of the stereotype threat model. Toward making this analysis, the chapter is organized around discussion of the following critical questions: (1) Why exactly do Black children underperform on standardized tests (proximal mechanisms)?; (2) Who/what is held responsible for the conditions that engender Black children's poor performance (distal mechanisms)?; (3) What are the empirical evidence supporting the theoretical model?; (4) What types of solutions does the nature of the model suggest?; (5) How plausible/realistic are the solutions proposed?; (6) What does the model contribute to the broader and popular discourse on Blackness and race relations in the United States? Without asserting that these are the only ones worthy of consideration, I wish to suggest at the outset that any description of, or prescription for, issues in Black education should be vetted against at least these six critical questions. By framing the analysis of *this* model around these six questions I hope to bring readers to a deeper and more critical understanding of the nature and scope of stereotype threat than is available in the popular discourse. I also hope to persuade the reader that our failure to consider such questions has repeatedly and will continue to undermine *any* efforts to alleviate the educational difficulties facing Black children. The question review is followed by a commentary and conclusion.

Exactly Why Do Black Children Underperform on Standardized Tests and Other Assessments?

This first question means to assess the models' description of mechanisms in the immediate schooling and testing environments that lead to children's underperformance. Contrary to the commonly held view that African American children and their families have negative attitudes toward learning and high achievement, the stereotype threat model suggests that many African Americans do in fact value learning and education and that many do significantly define their identities based on academic competence. It locates the mechanism of underperformance neither in children's failure to engage the learning process nor in their failure to learn. The stereotype threat model instead asserts that poor performance among African American students is either cognitively or motivationally associated with pervasive negative stereotypes about the intellectual abilities of African American people. Cognitive explanations suggest that thinking about such stereotypes, and about the possibility that their performance might confirm them, occupies some portion of a student's mental capacity. This is said to leave fewer cognitive resources for the problem solving needed to succeed on the assessment at hand (Stangor, Carr, and Kiang 1998). Another explanation suggests that anxiety over the same issues reduces students' accuracy and efficiency in problem solving (Osborne 2001). Others have suggested that stereotype threat causes Black students to actually doubt their own abilities and that this doubt (rather than anxiety or preoccupation) is what undermines their problem solving efforts (Steele and Aronson 1995). Motivational interpretations include that the fear of confirming stereotypes leads students to reduce their efforts because they perceive their efforts as unlikely to be fruitful (Baumeister 1995) and/or as a protective mechanism, in order to create plausible deniability (Croizet and Claire 1998; Stone, Lynch, and Sjomeling 1999).

The debate over which specific process(es) is/are responsible continues unresolved, yet all have in common the notion that whatever skill-level students arrive possessing, their reaction to their perception of threat undermines their ability to demonstrate those skills during standardized assessments of various types.

Who/What Is Held Responsible for Black Children's Poor Performance?

On this second question some writers and laypeople cling to the fatigued notion that Black children are either innately unable to meet the demands of schooling (Herrnstein and Murray 1994; Rushton and Jensen 2005) or develop an inability to do so as a result of their pathological home and community environments (Cosby and Poussaint 2007; Ferguson 2005; McWhorter 2000). Both perspectives have been widely and repeatedly discredited but linger nonetheless (see Boykin 1986; Kozol 1991, 2000; Ryan 1971; and White 1970).

Like others emerging from a more egalitarian perspective, the stereotype threat model identifies the current and historical occurrence of political and structural violence in U.S. Black-white relations as the main distal cause of underperformance among African American students. It holds that African Americans are aware of stereotypes describing them as less capable on an array of academic and other mental tasks. The model suggests that African American students cannot help but acknowledge that their performance on such tasks will be judged in relationship to these stereotypes, either singling them out if they do well or confirming negative stereotypes if they do not. As a result, Black students find themselves (at a highly inopportune moment) in a troubling identity conflict. This is a conflict that compels them to reexamine their relationship with an important in-group, in order to either distance themselves from, or bear the burden of uplifting, or suffer the guilt of bringing-down the race. The additional pressure is said to have a negative impact on their performance through one or more of the mechanisms described above.

What Empirical Evidence Supports the Model?

Stereotype threat presents an intuitively compelling and evocative narrative describing the mechanisms that lead to underperformance among African American children. Like several other explanations that have been offered, the model describes ways in which, even in school, children are not exempt from the tensions that contaminate adult inter-group relations in the broader United States (contrary to what the optimists among us might like to hope). The foci of the related empirical work help to clarify that the model is otherwise distinct from others. The third question asks for an assessment of the empirical evidence supporting the model. I will not attempt a comprehensive summary, but will highlight studies that are representative of the available evidence and that are most germane to the discussion at hand.

Stereotype threat has from its introduction been an empirically demonstrated phenomenon. Indeed the empirical evidence of the phenomenon has consistently outpaced psychologists' ability to explain it. The basic research paradigm is well illustrated by the original studies. High ability Black and white college students were given a difficult verbal test. Half of the Black and half of the white participants were lead to believe that the test was diagnostic of intellectual ability and the other half were told that the test was being used to examine problem solving but was not diagnostic of intellectual ability. Black students who believed that the test was diagnostic of intellectual ability performed significantly worse than did those who believed the test was non-diagnostic and worse than white students in both conditions. Black and white participants for whom the test was presented as non-diagnostic scored equally well.[4] Whites students scored equally well in both conditions.

The phenomenon has been replicated many times among African Americans (see Steele, Spencer, and Aronson 2002, for a review) and extended to other groups including Latinos on tests of intellectual ability (Gonzales, Blanton, and Williams 2002), women on tests of math ability

(Oswald and Harvey 2000), and people from low-income backgrounds on tests of verbal ability (Croizet and Claire 1998). The phenomenon has been observed among white men on tests of intellectual ability, where the comparison group is Asians—presumably there exists a stereotype that white men's math abilities are poor relative to those of Asian people (Aronson, Lustina, and Good 1999), and even advantaging Blacks relative to whites on an athletic task (golf putting) framed as indicative of natural athletic ability, but disadvantaging them when the same task was presented as related to intelligence (Stone, Lynch, and Sjomeling 1999). A fascinating study by Shih, Pittinsky, and Ambady (1999) found that female Asian participants experienced stereotype threat on a difficult math task, or did not, depending on whether their gender or ethnic identity was made salient in the experimental procedures. Although the phenomenon was discovered and much of the data has been collected among college-age students, several studies have observed stereotype threat in middle-childhood (Ambady, Shih, Kim and Pittinsky 2001; Aronson, Lustina, and Good 1999; McKowan and Weinstein 2003; Muzzatti and Agnoli 2007), around the ages at which children are likely to become aware of negative stereotypes about their groups.

That the experimental phenomenon known as stereotype threat is real and relevant to school children is at this point beyond debate. Indeed it has achieved status as a general social psychological phenomenon that transcends its discovery among high ability African American college students. Particular to its origins though, it is widely believed that unlike contrived-for-research stereotypes, those relating to African Americans and intellectual ability permeate the conditions in which Black students are assessed at the various stages of their academic lives. It is in part because of this assumption that stereotype threat is commonly considered relevant to the performance gap. The narrative that connects them proposes that Black students, constantly aware of negative stereotypes about their abilities, are threatened on the variety of assessments that they undertake throughout their education. The original Steele and Aronson studies provided some evidence in support of this contention (1995), reporting that no explicit stereotype cues were needed to generate the effect among African Americans (study 1) and that Black students distanced themselves from stereotypically Black activities such as basketball, hip-hop, and jazz in the face of a relevant and threatening assessment (study 3).

Aside from the obvious parallel between the stereotype threat experimental procedures and those widely used in standardized test administration, there is relatively little evidence of a connection to educational assessment in real settings. Stricker and Ward (2004), seeking to test the generalizability of Steele and Aronson's (1995, study 4) finding that a simple inquiry about students' ethnicity evoked a performance decrement for African American participants, manipulated whether students were asked to report their race prior to taking actual standardized advanced placement tests. They reported no significant differential effects. Similarly, Cullen, Hardison, and Sackett reported that an analysis of the relationships between standardized tests scores and performance indicators (SAT scores and course grades, Armed Services Vocational Aptitude Battery scores and technical proficiency, e.g., loading a machine gun) did not find evidence that stereotype threat exerted a systematic effect on the task performance of groups subject to the relevant stereotype (2004). Other studies have similarly failed to find evidence of stereotype threat in real-life situations (Cullen, Walters, and Sackett 2006; Mayer and Hanges 2003; McFarland, Lev-Arey, and Ziegert 2003; Nguyen, O'Neal, and Ryan 2003). The failure of a few studies to find evidence that stereotype threat explains racial group differences in real-world settings does not prove that stereotype threat plays no part in the performance gap. Indeed, that Stricker and Ward (for example) found no difference between groups might be because participants in the threat manipulation did not suffer from stereotype threat, but could also be because students in both conditions suffered from stereotype threat due to environmental factors outside the researchers' control, rendering their manipulation redundant. The price of better ecological validity in field studies is that there is a parallel increase in the risk that factors outside of researchers' control will affect the outcome of a study. Other researchers have tried to examine the relevance of stereotype threat in general to K–12 classroom environments.

Work concerning gender-based stereotypes for example has found some evidence that stereotype threat is relevant to classroom settings. Lummis and Stevenson (1990) found that as early as the first grade children start believing that boys are better at math than girls. In research by Huguet and Regner (2007), middle-school girls suffered a performance deficit in quasi-ordinary classroom circumstances on a test described as a measure of math ability. Ambady, Shih, Kim, and Pittinsky (2001) also found evidence of stereotype threat susceptibility among elementary and middle-school Asian American girls. Whether the findings of these studies can be generalized to race-based stereotype threat depends on how similarly gender and race dynamics may play out in classrooms. One potentially important difference is that the overwhelming majority of American classrooms are gender mixed but largely race homogenous. Thus girls are more likely confronted with the relevant stereotypes on a daily basis in school. The fact that there are more female than African American teachers in those classrooms is also likely to be relevant though it is difficult to predict just what impact it would have.

Another important question is whether stereotype threat can be linked with everyday activities in school. Indeed the model purports to explain underperformance only among the comparatively small population of high ability, high identified Blacks but makes no assertions that nationally Black and white students arrive at assessment situations equally well prepared. Since the students who are known to be vulnerable to stereotype threat cannot be assumed to represent the bulk of the performance gap, evidence that the same or similar mechanisms affect a broader range of students is needed. It stands to reason that some students not considered academically identified nor previously high achieving may attain that status due to stereotype threat-like insults to their progress in classrooms and on learning (rather than assessment) tasks all along. Along those lines, Ployhart, Ziegler, and McFarland (2003) distinguished *stereotype threat-specific*, that which occurs in and is restricted to testing environments and which undermines students' performance on those assessments, from *stereotype threat-general*, which is as a global sense of threat that individuals carry across situations and which may undermine African Americans' efforts on a variety of testing and non-testing activities. Stereotype threat-general is not thought to depend on students identifying with the relevant domain in the way the stereotype threat-specific does. Mayer and Hanges (2003) assessed each stereotype model using a questionnaire and found that both were predictive of performance but that they appeared to operate though different mechanisms. Threat-specific was associated with evaluation apprehension while threat-general was related to anxiety. However, the same study failed to find stereotype threat effects using an experimental manipulation that simulated a real-life employment testing situation.

It remains to be seen whether stereotype threat-general or something similar can help explain how Black children's learning is affected in day-to-day classroom activities and whether that line of explanations can help to explain portions of the gap that remains after accounting for resource and other inequities. For the time being, the evidence supports the recommendation by Cullen, Hardison, and Sackett (2004) for caution in generalizing laboratory findings to applied settings. More evidence linking stereotype threat with assessments relevant to the performance gap and/or explicitly linking stereotype threat with day-to-day classroom activities is still needed to justify claims that stereotype threat is a significant factor in the Black-white achievement gap.

What Types of Solutions Does the Nature of the Model Suggest or Imply?

Before addressing the fourth question I would draw the reader's attention to an important sub-question in this section, which is: on whom does the model, and related prescriptions for closing the performance gap, place the onus of change? For better or worse this question is separable from the issues of mechanism and responsibility discussed above and may be the determining factor in our discussions of practicality and contribution to the broader discourse on Blackness to be discussed later.

The prescriptions of the stereotype threat model share some similarities with other models, especially in implying that the best solution would be for the United States to eradicate racism, in this case the racism-driven myths about African American intellectual inferiority. Were those to disappear, so quickly would the threat they pose to African American test taking youth. Predictably, this grand solution is never meaningfully on the table. Regarded as straightforward and practical is the proposal to solve the problem by changing Black students' perceptions of the threat posed by these stereotypes. Stereotype threat researchers have theorized and confirmed in empirical research that stereotype threat effects can be reduced using any of several stereotype alleviation methods. These include simply warning students that they may be susceptible to stereotype threat (McGlone and Aronson 2007) or telling students that the task showed no racial differences on past administrations (Blascovich, Spencer, Quinn, and Steele 2001). Another type of strategy involves minimizing the salience of the negative stereotypes by having students reaffirm their self-integrity via a short writing assignment (Cohen, Garcia, and Apfel 2006). Presenting or having students self-generate/ponder positive role models prior to the assessment has also been found to alleviate stereotype threat (McIntyre, Paulson, and Lord 2003). A study by Rusty McIntyre and colleagues, for example, found that having participants read short biographies of positive role models alleviated stereotype threat and that the effects were cumulative (McIntyre, Lord, Gresky, Ten Eyck, Frye, and Bond 2003). Participants who read four such biographies performed better on a subsequent test than those who read three. Those who read three outperformed those who read two and so on. Another strategy for combating stereotype threat involves calling a student's attention to their other non-stereotyped identities (Gresky, Ten Eyck, Lord, and McIntyre 2005; Shih, Pittinsky, and Ambady 1999).

Yet another involves influencing students' beliefs about the nature of ability. A few studies have found that students who believe or have been convinced by an intervention that cognitive ability is expandable (versus fixed) are less susceptible to stereotype threat (Aronson, Fried, and Good 2002). Field studies have reported that such interventions lead to long-term improvements in GPA (Aronson, Fried, and Good 2002; Good, Aronson, and Inzlicht 2003).

Overall, the stereotype threat model and research implies that freeing students' from their perception of threat in various ways will allow them to live up to their potential on assessments (and otherwise). Educators are held responsible for creating the conditions for this change, however, responsibility for the critical change is placed on the students themselves.

Preface to Questions Five and Six

The remaining questions to be considered are different in kind from those that have preceded them. On the question of whether the implied or proposed solutions could be scaled up and would it help if they were, the relevant facts are considerably more disputable than those considered for the previous sections. The same is especially true on the question of what the model contributes to the broader discourse on Blackness, and as a result, analysis of both questions involves significantly more judgment and likely more controversy. These questions are of tremendous importance, however, despite that they are habitually overlooked in discussions about various difficulties facing Black America. They are dangerously absent from discussions about the performance gap as well. With those disclaimers and no pretense of objectivity, I offer the proceeding analysis of the two questions as they are related to stereotype threat.

Are the Proposed Solutions Achievable on the Scale Needed? If so, How Much Would They Likely Help to Close the Achievement Gap?

That the solution strategies from the stereotype threat model have been shown to benefit Black students in small-scale boutique interventions is only a first step. Since the performance gap is a national phenomenon, proposed solutions need to be judged in terms of their feasibility and likely effectiveness on a national scale. A "national scale" is one so large that it can be difficult to think about. I came closer to understanding how large a "national scale" is when I participated in a statewide evaluation of Texas schools several years ago. In the process I interacted with standardized test data from the nearly 9,000 elementary schools operating in Texas in 2001

(Hurley, Chamberlain, and Slavin 2000). Imagine. Using a very conservative estimate of 6 teachers per school each with 10 African American students, trying to permanently modify the activities of 54,000 teachers in those schools or of over half a million children. If you managed to close the performance gap in the 9,000 Texas schools (which would be a prize-worthy victory) you still would not have made a dent in the national problem. In 2006, Standard and Poor's (2006) issued a press release congratulating the *eight* Texas schools that managed to *narrow* and the *one* Texas school that managed to *close* the achievement gap between their Black and white students.

It should be clear that the question of whether a solution strategy could be reasonably implemented on a national scale is an important one. Equally important is the related question of whether, if you did manage to scale-up, the proposed solutions would definitely and meaningfully help to close the performance gap on that large scale. Answering that question necessitates consideration of factors not typically regarded as germane to education.

Evaluation of the practical utility of stereotype threat proposals depends significantly on one's estimation of one such factor, the state of Black-white relations in the United States today. Suppose for a moment that the "stereotype threat" Black children perceive is only a remnant of times when non-Black Americans commonly believed that African Americans' were intellectually inferior, but that the "playing field" is considered level by Americans today. If this were true, students' fears, based on a misperception of the world around them, might be the main remaining reason that Black students do not perform up to their potential. Moreover, if those fears are based on *mis*perception, their *mis*perception may be correctable. In that scenario, scaling up the implementation of stereotype threat alleviation strategies that change the attitudes of African American students from "threatened" to "secure" would likely change large numbers of Black children's experiences during important assessments. In that scenarios as well, alleviating the "imagined" threat would perhaps have a significant positive impact on the performance gap, at least among students for whom stereotype threat is relevant.

Much of the discussion around the performance gap seems premised on this optimistic view of the societal level backdrop against which we seek to solve this serious problem. However, if the playing field is not level in today's United States, other issues demand consideration.

For example, scholars of the model credit Black children with *correctly* identifying negative stereotypes about their abilities. A variety of other scholars have argued that racism is still pervasive in the United States and in U.S. education (Kozol 2000; Mickelson 2003, to name just two) and that negative stereotypes about African Americans remain prevalent among members of the dominant and other groups (Devine and Elliot 1995; Wittenbrink, Judd, and Park 1997). There is evidence for example that white Americans tend to believe that individual failings are the primary cause for African Americans' difficulties but blame structural barriers for similar problems faced by other ethnic groups. A recent study found that white Americans relied on "lack of motivation" to explain Black inequality but were more likely to offer "no chance for education" in explaining Hispanic inequality, despite the similar socioeconomic circumstances of the two groups (McDonald 2001). Another study reported that in a sample of predominantly white (89 percent) math teachers, respondents were more likely to attribute the minority-white achievement gap to student characteristics such as differences intellectual ability, motivational levels, and work ethic, than to explanations related to politics and policy or to curriculum factors (Bol and Berry 2005). Uhlenberg and Brown (2002) reported that white and Black teachers perceive the performance gap itself differently. White teachers tended to name students, parents, and home environments as the largest contributing factors, while Black teachers tended to cite teachers, schools, and the educational system. These are a few among various indications that African American students suffer from stereotype threat because they *correctly* identify the stereotypes by which they *will* be judged. We should acknowledge these truths even if we regard students' reactions as self-defeating.

Acknowledging that Black students may be correct in their assessment of the conditions under which they are expected to perform casts an unflattering light on attempts to change their perception. It hardly seems reasonable to trick them into false beliefs about their situation or to disarm their defensive coping strategies while leaving the threat for which they developed them intact. Moreover it seems doubtful that any such effort, no matter how well designed or well funded, could compete on a national scale with the accurate information students receive continuously in their everyday experience of being Black in America. It is here that William Ryan's (1971) classic analysis of universalistic and exceptionalist depictions of social problems can aid our own analysis of the performance gap.

Ryan defines *exceptionalist problems* as those that occur unpredictably as the result of individual defects, accidents, or uniquely unfortunate circumstances. Exceptionalist problems, because they are unpredictable, must be addressed via interventions directed at those who suffer them. By contrast, *universalistic problems*, though they affect individuals, are the byproduct of imperfect and inequitable social arrangements that systematically *create* unfortunate circumstances among particular segments of a population. Because they are systematically created, they are predictable and preventable and are best ameliorated via interventions directed at their causes, that is, *those imperfect and inequitable social arrangements.* Thirty-five years ago, Ryan accused American academic scholars and policymakers of habitually and effortfully framing the universalistic problems faced by various disenfranchised groups in exceptionalist terms. Doing so encourages solution proposals that minimize discomfort for anyone with some say in the level of discomfort they will feel in the process of dealing with social issues. Using the case at hand as an example, framing problems in education this way justifies prescribing and promoting "resilience" among "at-risk" students. It is more comfortable to endorse resilience strategies if one is not responsible for the harmful conditions that put students at risk and against that which they need to be resilient. Stereotype threat alleviation strategies offer an exceptionalist prescription for what is pretty certainly a universalistic problem.

A secondary benefit of assigning responsibility for the performance gap to student characteristics rather than infrastructural factors is that students who do succeed despite their expected shortcomings can then reasonably be described as *exceptional.* It is definitely possible to convince *some* students that they are (or can become) exceptional in this sense; that they can transcend the problems that hinder African Americans as a group. This is the thinking behind resilience-oriented educational interventions. It is not entirely misdirection, even the most willfully oppressive social structures make room for exceptions, so there is certainly room in a society that at least pretends equal opportunity. Students who can take advantage of those opportunities should. Again using the case at hand as an example, changing some Black student's attitudes from threatened to trusting is akin to cultivating resilience and would likely advantage those few students. It is important to keep in mind, however, that, by definition, such exceptionalist solutions cannot meaningfully impact the overall problem, which is universalistic in nature. Further, such strategies may ultimately do more to maintain the larger problem of our national performance gap, by reifying myths about equal opportunity, than they do to close it.

What Does the Model Contribute to the Broader and Popular Discourse on Blackness and Race Relations?

The final question, the question of what the model and associated solution proposals contribute to the broader discourse on Blackness is one that has too often been overlooked in the African American struggle for social justice. At the beginning of this chapter I referenced the role Kenneth and Mamie Clark played in the fight against Jim Crow. Though it is beyond the purview of this chapter to make a detailed analysis, the Clarks' research can be criticized for what it contributed to the broader discourse on Blackness in the United States. The famous doll studies, which helped to dismantle legalized segregation, did so by "demonstrating" that African American children suffer from a pathological self-hatred (said to be the result of the evils of segregation). That this was a pyrrhic victory would have been true even if the dream of integration had actually been realized (and if it was a good idea.)[5] This self-hatred myth has haunted the discourse on Blackness ever since reappearing in academic (Cokley 2002; Cross 1991) and popular discussions (Kimberley 2005; Page 2003) despite, as mentioned earlier, being widely criticized and reevaluated (Spencer and Markstrom-Adams 1990; Spencer 1999).

There are many other examples of well-meaning interventions that do more to undermine society's image of African Americans than they do to help the particular problem, which, with genuine humanitarian zeal, they seek to solve. In my courses related to these issues I have become fond of telling students that genuinely humanitarian actions, when paired with a presumption of Black inferiority of any kind, will always amount to racist oppression cloaked in pity. Another early example of this is the "talented tenth" thesis which, while trying to give the most resourced among us a sense of responsibility, also implies the untalented 90 percent. In the 1960s and 1970s there were programs that shipped Black children out to the suburbs to live with white families during the school week and/or brought nice white ladies into the homes of Black families with infants several days a week. Both of these worked toward ameliorating so-called cultural deprivation among African Americans, but mostly serving to etch the image of "culturally deprived Black families" into the American mind. More recently, an array of Black and white public figures, apparently certain that Black language is something shameful and deficient, spoke out against and ultimately caused the repeal of the Oakland, California, resolution to acknowledge the integrity of Ebonics in their language curriculum (Crochan

2000). This despite that the Linguistic Society of America, among other bodies, issued statements affirming the integrity of African American language traditions and affirming the linguistic and pedagogical soundness of the school board's plan (1997).

In a nation whose public discourse habitually portrays African Americans as the root of their own and many of society's other problems, we should not ourselves sign-off on any idea that helps to maintain and extend the inferiority myth that is the foundation of American racism. For that reason it is important to consider what any model that purports to explain the behavior of African American people and any strategy that hopes to address problems faced by Black Americans contributes to this broader discourse.

An especially toxic contribution to the discourse on Blackness came with the introduction of two terms to the mental health lexicon. Drapetomania and Dysaethesia Aethiopica, often cited as examples of scientific racism, are terms for mental disorders said to be particular to enslaved Blacks (Cartwright 1851). They are of another era, but nicely illustrate the point at hand. The symptoms of Drapetomania include the uncontrollable urge to escape bondage and those for Dysaethesia Aethiopica include a tendency to destroy (master's) property, create disturbances, and resist work. Because it seems obvious in retrospect that the people "suffering" from these "disorders" were in fact defending their very humanity in those actions, it sounds outrageous to problemitize, much less to pathologize, their behavior. Concerning the discourse on Blackness, however, defining the resistance behavior of enslaved people as mental illness contributed justification for a range of Draconian interventions under the banner of prevention and rehabilitation. Today we instantly recognize that if anyone in that situation was suffering from mental illness (and in need of prevention and rehabilitation), it was the oppressors. We can accuse or excuse those among the enslaved who did not much resist, but we must certainly acknowledge that given the circumstances those who resisted had exactly the right idea and that there was no need, nor justification, for any attempt to change their attitudes (though perhaps their methods could have used some improvement). Unto today, where the popular and academic discourse problemitizes, pathologizes, or otherwise blames African American children for their own dire predicaments, it justifies a range of inappropriate, impotent, and even destructive preventative and remedial interventions while excluding others that might actually help. Framing the problem in exceptionalist terms also grants educators, policymakers, and philanthropists license to the identity "trying to close the achievement gap" without requiring them to earnestly pursue the kinds of solutions that might actually close the achievement gap but which would definitely make them and a lot of other people uncomfortable in the process.[6]

Perhaps worst of all, victim blame becomes self-affirming as the time and resources spent on impotent exceptionalist solutions accumulate to the point where negative characterizations of Black culture offered by the likes of Cosby (Cosby and Poussaint 2007), McWhorter (2000), and Ferguson (2005), and accusations of genetic inferiority leveled by Social Darwinists Herrnstein and Murray (1994), Rushton and Jensen (2005), and others *appear* to gain credibility.

So what does the candidate model contribute? Like most other proposals the stereotype threat model identifies universalistic structural factors that help to produce the performance gap, but because the solutions that have emerged from stereotype threat scholarship ultimately portray African American children as that which is in need of (or most expedient to) change, this acknowledgement is inconsequential. In placing the primary burden of change on Black children, in problematizing their perceptions, attitudes, or reactions, the model ultimately contributes to the broader discourse on Blackness in America yet another version of the myth that there is something wrong with African American people.

In identifying this key shortcoming, I do not in any way mean to suggest that the stereotype threat model or any earnest attempt to explain the plight of Black school children is without value. Instead I mean it as a caution. Invested parties must learn to see this and other conceptual models for the value they bring in documenting the effects of inequality, but must not get distracted by the empty promises of what seem to be expedient solutions based on them. Indeed in the case of stereotype threat, this shortcoming is not even native to the model but is in the timidity of those of us who seek to address the problems that the model alerts us to.

Commentary and Conclusion

What we learn from the stereotype threat model adds another element to our understanding of the performance gap and its causes. The model alerts us to the fact that high identified, high-achieving students, whom we might have believed were immune, are also vulnerable to the toxic effects of structural racism in education and society. Stereotype threat vulnerability may be best interpreted as a latent cost of the disassociation, assimilation, or code switching strategies that many high-achieving African American students adopt in order to succeed under the circumstances in which they find themselves. This contribution helps us to appreciate the breadth of the problem and highlights the need for systemic change. It raises the question of whether so-called at-risk students might be better described as canaries in the coalmine, signaling the more general threat.

Even in this brief explication we begin to see that neither the stereotype threat nor any other single model can or should expect to adequately explain or solve the entire problem of underachievement among African American children. We should realize that such models contribute most when they bring us closer to a critical mass of evidence that the issues behind the performance gap are not separable from the broader issue of inequity in the United States and will never be addressed until and unless we address those. We must recognize that each of the dollars and each hour that policymakers, educators, and the general public contribute in the millions toward "solutions" that are misguided, piecemeal, and otherwise predictably doomed to failure, moves the nation closer to concluding that these problems are unsolvable. When African American scholars and leaders, by our participation, lend the appearance of credibility and objectivity to those same wrongheaded efforts, we may inadvertently contribute to what will *seem* like a critical mass of evidence that African American children are ultimately unreachable through education and thus principally unable to ever fully meet the demands of citizenship. I am pretty sure that is not a contribution we mean to make.

This chapter analyses the stereotype threat model order to examine its strengths and weaknesses in describing and prescribing remedy for the performance gap. The focus here has been on that one influential model as an important case in point, but I hoped also to make an argument, by demonstration, that all such proposals should be vetted against the kinds of difficult but key questions posed here. Perhaps less to determine their value or lack thereof, and more because such examination stands, while we harvest what is of value from them, to help us remain grounded in a clearheaded awareness of their limits.

Especially in the last twenty years, efforts to address Black children's educational difficulties have become increasingly systematic and comprehensive, both theoretically and in their emphasis on scientific research as the benchmark for validity. This development is heartening. In a growing climate of evidence-based reform, it is critical that Black social scientists and educators take leadership in the discourse on how best to improve the educational futures of Black children. The growing body of evidence from this and other influential models demonstrates the kind of willful self-determination called for by Carter G. Woodson (1933), Joseph White

(1970), and other leading Black thinkers who understood that by definition, African Americans are best equipped to provide the information and insight needed to guide school reform efforts directed toward African American children. In that regard Claude Steele and the many others who have dedicated their energy to these issues are to be commended.

I close with a final caution. Black educational scholars (and others) have known all along that the climate in many schools that serve African American communities is and has been noxious and undermining to Black children. This and other models have merit in that they enrich our documentation of race-based structural violence and its effects. However, if they fail to challenge pervasive negative views of what it means to be African American, or if they fail to insist that real causes of the performance gap be addressed, and when they lead us to accept the false compromise of exceptionalist solutions, they in fact add not so much that is new to the discussion.

Notes

1. See, Woodson (1933).
2. Eighteen is the age of criminal responsibility in most U.S. states.
3. In that era there were also those who believed that African descended people were racially oppressed because they occupy a lower step on the evolutionary ladder and that this lesser evolution also made them principally incapable of taking on the responsibilities of citizenship, including academic success. Nonetheless, most understood that racism and oppression were critical contributors to the difficulties facing Black Americans.
4. Scores in the original studies were adjusted to account for differences on the SAT for all Black-white comparisons. However, subsequent studies have employed samples with similar scores and found the same pattern (Blascovich, Spencer, Quinn, and Steele 2001; Croizet and Claire 1998; Good, Aronson, and Inzlicht 2003).
5. The wisdom of integration as a strategy for guaranteeing Blacks equal access to the resources and opportunities for social mobility is debatable, however in characterizing Black communities as inherently inferior and to be escaped, the strategy set in motion a tremendous brain and resource drain on Black business, social, educational, and other institutions. The effects of that drain on the overall status of predominantly Black communities are well documented. Kunjufu has made these arguments in detail.
6. I feel obliged to comment on the distinction there is to be made between *blame* and *responsibility* as related to this discussion. The arguments presented herein do not mean to imply that African Americans bear no responsibility for improving their own life (or educational) conditions. All humans have that responsibility.

Nor do they imply that no African Americans undermine their own prospects by engaging in negative behavior. Humans from all groups do that as well. Yet I would argue that in general, African Americans already bear their share and more of responsibility for improving their prospects and would, as they have historically, respond to conditions that genuinely favor striving with impressive industry. This brings us to the critical distinction between blame and responsibility. Focusing *blame* on African Americans for problems in their current circumstances has the effect of freeing everyone and everything else from any sense of their own culpability. Since victims, if I can be allowed that term for a moment, are the only group that retains responsibility for remedy whether they are at fault or not, freeing everyone else from blame has the effect of shifting *all of the responsibility* for change to African Americans. Moreover, released from *blame*, everyone else is free to take *no responsibility*, and worse to feel philanthropic when they do lift a finger in aid. Philanthropist is not, in my view, the right term for a person who helps to solve a problem they helped to create.

Works Cited

Ambady, S. N., A. Kim, and T. Pittinsky. 2001. "Stereotype susceptibility in children: Effects of identity activation on quantitative performance." *Psychological Science* 1 (12): 386–90.

Aronson, J., C. B. Freid, and C. Good. 2002. "Reducing the effects of stereotype threat on African American college students by shaping theories of intelligence." *Journal of Experimental Social Psychology* 38:113–25.

Aronson, J., M. J. Lustina, and C. Good. 1999. "When white men can't do math: Necessary and sufficient factors in stereotype threat." *Journal of Experimental Social Psychology* 35 (1): 29–46.

Baldwin, J. A. 1979. "Theory and research concerning the notion of black self-hatred: A review and reinterpretation." *Journal of Black Psychology* 5 (2): 51–77.

Baumeister, R. 1995. *Self and identity: An introduction.* In *Advanced social psychology,* ed. A. Tesser, 51–97. Boston: McGraw Hill.

Blascovic, J., S. Spencer, D. Quinn, and C. Steele. 2001. "African Americans and high blood pressure: The role of stereotype threat." *Psychological Science* 12:225–29.

Bol, L., and R. Q. Berry III. 2005. "Secondary mathematics teachers' perceptions of the achievement gap." In "Building an infrastructure for equity in mathematics education," special issue, *The High School Journal* 4:32–45.

Boykin, A. W. 1986. "The triple quandary and the schooling of Afro-American children." In *The school achievement of minority children,* ed. U. Neisser. Hillsdale, NJ: Lawrence Erlbaum.

Brown, R. P., and E. A. Day. 2006. "The difference isn't black and white: Stereotype threat and the race gap on raven's advanced progressive matrices." *Journal of Applied Psychology* 91:979–85.

Cartwright, S. A. 1851. "Report on the diseases and physical peculiarities of the Negro race." *The New Orleans Medical and Surgical Journal*, May 1851, 691–715. Reprinted in *Concepts of health and disease in medicine: Interdisciplinary Perspectives*, ed. A. Caplan, H. T. Engelhardt Jr., and J. McCartney. 1980. Boston: Addison-Wesley.

Chandler, M., writer and director. 1999. *Secrets of the SAT* [Television series episode]. In *Frontline*, executive producer M. Sullivan. Boston: WGBH.

Clark, K. B., and M. P. Clark. 1947. "Racial identification and preference in Negro children." In *Readings in social psychology*, ed. T. M. Newcomb and E. L. Hartley. New York: Holt, Rinehart & Winston.

———. 1950. "Emotional factors in racial identification and preference in Negro children." *Journal of Negro Education* 19:341–50.

Cohen, G. L., J. Garcia, N. Apfel, and A. Master. 2006. "Reducing the racial achievement gap: A social-psychological intervention." *Science* 313 (5791): 1307–10.

Cokley, Kevin O. 2002. "Testing Cross's revised racial identity model: An examination of the relationship between racial identity and internalized racialism." *Journal of Counseling Psychology* 49 (4): 476–83.

Cosby, B., and A. F. Poussaint. 2007. *Come on, people!: On the path from victims to victors*. Nashville, TN: Thomas Nelson, 265.

Crochan, M. 2000. "History, linguistics, California's CLAD initiative and the Oakland public schools resolution on Ebonics: What are the connections." *World Englishes* 19 (2): 73–87.

Croizet, J., and T. Claire. 1998. "Extending the concept of stereotype threat to social class: The intellectual underperformance of students from low socioeconomic backgrounds." *Personality and Social Psychology Bulletin* 24:588–94.

Cross, W. E., Jr. 1991. *Shades of black: Diversity in African-American identity*. Philadelphia: Temple University Press.

Cullen, M. J., C. M. Hardison, and P. R. Sackett. 2004. "Using SAT-grade and ability-job performance relationships to test predictions derived from stereotype threat theory." *Journal of Applied Psychology* 89:220–30.

Cullen, M. J., S. D. Walters, and P. R. Sackett. 2006. "Testing stereotype threat theory predictions for math-identified and non-math-identified students by gender." *Human Performance* 19 (4): 421–40.

Devine, P. G., and A. J. Elliot. 1995. "Are racial stereotypes really fading? The Princeton trilogy revisited." *Personality and Social Psychology Bulletin* 21 (11): 1139–50.

Edelman, M. W. 2007. "The cradle to prison pipeline: An American health crisis." *Preventing Chronic Disease* [serial online] July 4 (3): A43. www.cdc.gov/pcd/issues/2007/jul/07_0038.htm.

Ferguson, R. 2005 *Toward skilled parenting and transformed schools inside a national movement for excellence with equity*. Kennedy School of Government, Harvard University. devweb.tc.columbia.edu/manager/ symposium/Files/71_Ferguson_paper.ed.pdf.

Garfinkel, H. 1959. "Social science evidence and the school segregation cases." *The Journal of Politics* 2 (1): 37–59.

Gonzales, P. M., H. Blanton, and K. J. Williams. 2002. "The effects of stereotype threat and double-minority status on the test performance of Latino women." *Personality and Social Psychology Bulletin* 28 (5): 659–70.

Good, C., J. Aronson, and A. Inzlicht. 2003. "Improving adolescents' standardized test performance: An intervention to reduce the effects of stereotype threat." *Journal of Applied Developmental Psychology* 24:645–62.

Gresky, D. M., L. L. Ten Eyck, C. G. Lord, and R. B. McIntyre. 2005. "Effects of salient multiple identities on women's performance under mathematics stereotype threat." *Sex Roles* 53 (9–10): 703–16.

Guthrie. 1986. *Even the rat was white. A historical view of psychology.* Boston: Allyn & Bacon.

Helms, J. E. 2005. "Stereotype threat might explain the black-white test-score difference." *American Psychologist* 60 (3): 269–70.

Herrnstein, R. J., and C. Murray. 1994. *The bell curve: Intelligence and class structure in American life.* New York: Free Press.

Huguet, P., and I. Regner. 2007. "Stereotype threat among schoolgirls in quasi-ordinary classroom circumstances." *Journal of Educational Psychology* 99 (3): 545–60.

Hurley, E. A., A. M. Chamberlain, and R. E. Slavin. 2000. "Effects of success for all on TAAS Reading: A statewide evaluation." *Phi Delta Kappan* 82 (10).

Jencks, C., and M. Phillips, eds. 1998. *The black-white test score gap.* Washington, DC: Brookings Institution Press.

Jenkins, M. D. 1943. "Case studies of negro children of Binet IQ 160 and above." *The Journal of Negro Education* 12 (2): 159–66.

Jensen, A. 1973. "Race, intelligence and genetics: The differences are real." *Psychology Today* 7 (7): 80–84, 86.

Kimberley, M. 2005. "Freedom rider: Black self-hatred at Harvard." *Black Commentator* 132. www.blackcommentator.com.

Kozol, J. 1991. *Savage inequalities: Children in America's schools.* New York: Harper Collins.

———. 2000. "An unequal education." *School Library Journal* 46 (5): 46–49.

Linguistic Society of America. 1997. *Resolution on the Oakland "Ebonics" issue.* Unanimously adopted at the Annual Meeting of the Linguistic Society of America Chicago, Illinois, January 3, 1997.

Lummis, M., and H. W. Stevenson. 1990. "Gender differences in beliefs and achievement: A cross-cultural study." *Developmental Psychology* 26 (2): 254–63.

Mayer, D., and P. Hanges. 2003. "Understanding the stereotype threat effect with culture free tests: An examination of its mediators and measurement." *Human Performance* 16 (3): 207–30.

McDonald, S. J. 2001. "How whites explain black and Hispanic inequality." *Public Opinion Quarterly*, 65 (4): 562–73

McFarland, L. A., D. M. Lev-Arey, and J. C. Ziegert. 2003. "An examination of stereotype threat in a motivational context." *Human Performance* 16:181–205.

McGlone, M. S., and J. Aronson. 2007. "Forewarning and forearming stereotype-threatened students." *Communication Education* 56 (2): 119–33.

McIntyre, R. B., C. Lord, D. Gresky, L. Ten Eyck, G. D. J. Frye, and C. Bond Jr. 2003. "A social impact trend in the effects of role models on alleviating women's mathematics stereotype threat." *Social Psychology* 10 (9): 116–36.

McIntyre, R., M. Paulson, and C. Lord. 2003. "Alleviating women's mathematics stereotype threat through salience of group achievements." *Journal of Experimental Social Psychology* 39:83–90.

McKowan, C., and R. S. Weinstein. 2003. "The development and consequences of stereotype consciousness in middle childhood." *Child Development* 74 (2): 498–515.

McWhorter, J. H. 2000. *Losing the race: Self-sabotage in black America.* New York: Free Press.

Mickelson, R. 2003. "When are racial disparities in education the result of racial discrimination? A social science perspective." *Teachers College Record* 105 (6): 1052–86.

Muzzatti, B., and F. Agnoli. 2007. "Gender and mathematics: Attitudes and stereotype threat susceptibility in Italian children." *Developmental Psychology* 43 (3): 747–59.

National Center for Educational Statistics. 2001. *The condition of education (NCES Report No. 2001-034).* Washington, DC: U.S. Department of Education Office of Educational Research and Improvement.

———. 2006. *The condition of education (NCES Report No. 2006-072).* Washington, DC: U.S. Department of Education Office of Educational Research and Improvement.

Nguyen, H., A. O'Neal, and A. M. Ryan. 2003. "Relating test-taking attitudes and skills and stereotype threat effects to the racial gap in cognitive ability test performance." *Human Performance* 16 (3): 261–93.

Ogbu, J. 1987. "Variability in minority school performance: A problem in search of an explanation." *Anthropology and Education Quarterly* 18, no. 4 (December 1987)

Orfield, G., E. D. Frankenberg, and C. Lee. 2003. "The resurgence of school segregation." *Educational leadership* 60 (4): 16–20.

Osborne, J. 2001. "Testing stereotype threat: Does anxiety explain race and sex differences in achievement?" *Contemporary Educational Psychology* 26:291–310.

Oswald, D. L., and R. D. Harvey. 2000. "Hostile environments, stereotype threat, and math performance among undergraduate women." *Current Psychology: Developmental, Learning, Personality, Social* 19 (4): 338–56.

Page, C. 2003. "Race-ethnicity and identity: Showing my color." In *Down to earth sociology: Introductory readings,* 12th ed., ed. J. Henslin, 331–39. New York: Free Press.

Ployhart, R. E., J. C. Ziegler, and L. A. McFarland. 2003. "Understanding racial differences on cognitive ability tests in selection contexts: An integrations of stereotype threat and applicant reactions research." *Human Performance* 16:231–59.

Rushton, J. P., and A. R. Jensen. 2005. "Thirty years of research on black-white differences in cognitive ability." *Psychology, Public Policy, and the Law* 11:235–94.

Ryan, W. 1971. *Blaming the victim.* New York: Pantheon Books.

Shih, M., R. Pittinsky, and N. Ambady. 1999. "Stereotype susceptibility: Identity salience and shifts in quantitative performance." *Psychological Science* 10:80–83.

Spencer, M. B. 1999. "Transitions and continuities in cultural values: Kenneth Clark revisited." In *African American children, youth and parenting,* ed. R. L. Jones, 183–208. Hampton, VA: Cobb and Henry.

Spencer, M. B., and C. Markstrom-Adams. 1990. "Identity processes among racial and ethnic minority children in America." *Child Development* 61 (2): 290–310.

Standard and Poor's. 2006. "77 Texas School Districts, 41 Schools Recognized by Standard & Poor's." SchoolMatters. The McGraw-Hill Companies, Inc. samrayburn. ednet10.net/TX%20news%20release%20(06).pdf.

Stangor, C., C. Carr, and L. Kiang. 1998. "Activating stereotypes undermines task performance expectations." *Journal of Personality and Social Psychology* 75:1191–97.

Steele, C. M. 2003. "Through the back door to theory." *Psychological Inquiry* 14 (3–4): 314–17.

Steele, C. M., and J. Aronson. 1995. "Stereotype threat and the intellectual test performance of African Americans." *Journal of Personality and Social Psychology* 69:797–811.

Steele, C. M., S. J. Spencer, and J. Aronson. 2002. "Contending with group image: The psychology of stereotype and social identity threat." In *Advances in experimental social psychology* 34, ed. M. Zanna, 379–440. New York: Academic.

Stone, J., C. I. Lynch, and M. Sjomeling. 1999. "Stereotype threat effects on black and white athletic performance." *Journal of Personality and Social Psychology* 77 (6): 1213–27.

Stricker, L. J., and W. C. Ward. 2004. "Stereotype threat, inquiring about test takers' ethnicity and gender, and standardized test performance." *Journal of Applied Social Psychology* 34 (4): 665–93.

Sumner, F. C. 1926. "The philosophy of Negro educating." *Educational Review* 71 (Jan.): 42–45

———. 1927a. "Earmarks of high grade intelligence." *The institute monthly,* May, 6–8.

———. 1927b. "Morale and the Negro college." *Educational Review* 73 (March): 168–72.

Terman, L. M. 1916. *The measurement of intelligence.* Boston: Houghton Mifflin.

Uhlenberg, J., and K. M. Brown. 2002. "Racial gap in teachers' perceptions of the achievement gap." *Education and Urban Society* 34 (4): 493–530.

United States District Court for the District of Kansas. 1954. *Brown et al. v. Board of Education of Topeka et al. District of Kansas.* Argued December 9, 1952. Reargued December 8, 1953. Decided May 17, 1954.

Wax, Amy. 2004. "The threat in the air: Is fear of 'stereotypes' really why blacks do poorly on tests?" *The Wall Street Journal*, final edition. www.opinionjournal .com/extra/?id=110004973.

White, J. L. 1970. "Toward a black psychology." *Ebony Magazine*, September, 44–45, 48–50, 52.

Wittenbrink, B., C. M. Judd, and B. Park. 1997. "Evidence for racial prejudice at the implicit level and its relationship with questionnaire measures." *Journal of Personality and Social Psychology* 72 (2): 262–74.

Witty, P. A., and M. D. Jenkins. 1936. "Intra-race testing and negro intelligence." *Journal of Psychology: Interdisciplinary and Applied* 1:179–92.

Woodson, C. G. 1933. "The miseducation of the Negro." Washington, DC: Associated Publishers. (1977 reprint.)

Katherine Dunham 6
Decolonizing Dance Education

OJEYA CRUZ BANKS

ALLED A LIVING LEGEND, the late Katherine Dunham was indeed one of the most prolific dancers, choreographers, educators, and passionate activists to emerge out of the Harlem renaissance. A pioneer of dance anthropology,[1] she developed a dance pedagogy inspired by her ethnographic research on the Caribbean dance forms of Haiti, Jamaica, Martinique, and Trinidad. Her fieldwork among the Afro-Caribbean people provided valuable insights and cultural material that grounded her career as an academic, dancer, choreographer, activist, and educator (Aschenbrenner 1978). As a choreographer, she brought movement and parts of the body not activated by European dance to the American concert stage; and as a dance researcher and educator she recovered important knowledge embedded in African dance of the diaspora to foster self-knowledge in African American communities and her students (Aschenbrenner 1978, 1981, 1999, 2002; Rose 1990; Perpener 2001). The purpose of her dance education[2] was about returning dance to "its roots in communal living" (Dunham as cited in Ashenbrenner 1999, 151) and drawing from the historical and cultural knowledge embodied in dance. She pioneered a contemporary dance fusion called Dunham technique, which combined African and European movement styles, and hence promoted ideologies of cultural pluralism (Manning 2004). Dunham's choreographies told stories of spiritual ritual, racial prejudice, and oppression.

After a fruitful career as a dancer, actress, and choreographer, she turned her focus toward education for radical humanism in East St. Louis. Awarded grants from the Rockfeller Foundation and Danforth Foundation in 1967, she began to lay the groundwork for a dance school called

Performing Arts Training Center (PATC), which commenced in 1969 and lasted until 1974 (Ashenbrenner 1981). Dunham's interest in East St. Louis developed during her visits to the city as a child, where she was introduced to the blues and developed an affinity with the area; when she began teaching at Southern Illinois University in Carbondale, she rediscovered the neighboring city of East St. Louis devastated by the 1960s riots. The urban center struggled with an alarming rate of high school dropouts, illiteracy, and poverty among the African American population.

This chapter explores the sociopolitical relevance of Dunham's Performing Arts Training Center for youth in East St. Louis and how its dance pedagogy participated in the process of decolonization. I argue her educational philosophy and curriculum decolonized the Black body through using African-derived dances as primary educational content, thereby challenging Eurocentric models of education and countering the psychology of racism and colonialism. This research draws from historical and contemporary literature on Dunham, personal reflections about participating in a Dunham technique seminar in East St. Louis, Illinois in July 2003, and highlighting a class I attended taught by Katherine Dunham herself. Using theories of dance grounded in dance anthropology and postcolonial theory, I examine how Dunham's dance education is involved in a dialectical relationship with the legacies of the ideologies and practices of colonialism.

I go on to argue Dunham's work in East St. Louis is "decolonizing dance education," a dance practice involved in decolonizing the body. As Tuhiwai-Smith (1999) writes, decolonization is involved in divesting the bureaucratic, psychological, linguistic, and cultural consequences of colonialism. While I see dance included in the cultural divestment of colonial power, Dunham community dance education demonstrates the importance of involving the physicality of the body in the process of decolonization. Dance conditions our cultural identities through activating certain kinesthetic knowledge that is based on distinct world epistemologies. As Castaldi writes, dance "offers an unique cultural space that asserts a polycentric model of cultural production . . . and negotiates new ethnic and aesthetic rules . . . that communicate with the past and tear loose the fabric of colonial culture" (Castaldi 2006, 203).

Dunham's dance pedagogy fused African qualities of movement with ballet and modern styles of moving, thereby fostering intercultural communication through creating a cross-cultural dance conversation. The pedagogy was a form of social activism in how she dignified African culture in the face of American racism and subverted colonial ideologies that have suppressed the Black body and its distinct expressions of humanity.

A Historical Biography

Dunham was born in Chicago, Illinois, in 1909 to Fanny June Giullaume and Albert Millard Dunham. Her parents were of multiethnic heritage and both were passionate musicians. Fanny was of French Canadian, North American, English, and African descent, and Albert was of Malagasy and West African ancestry. At age four, Dunham's mother died and her father took her and older brother Albert Jr. to live with their Aunt Lulu on Chicago's Southside. During their stay with their father's relatives, Dunham was exposed to the performing arts of dance and theater. This was when Dunham became fascinated with the arts and developed a passion to be a performer. The children later returned to their father and his new wife (Ashenbrenner 2002; Perpener 2001).

In high school, Dunham joined a dance club and became determined to study ballet. Although Dunham had limited experience with dance, she was praised for her charisma as a performer in high school. Dance became a focal practice for her in college. In 1929, when Dunham moved to the windy city to attend the University of Chicago, she began studying ballet with Mark Turybill, Olga Speranza, and Ruth Page. Speranza was very influential dance mentor, who introduced Dunham to many dancers of diverse cultural styles such as Spanish, Balinese, Javanese, and East Indian. Dunham also became active in the local modern dance scene (Ashenbrenner 2002; Perpener 2001).

She quickly developed as a dancer and began teaching children and adults. This is when Dunham started exploring choreography. After her students starting performing recitals and promising students emerged, she formed a company named Ballet Negre, which was forced to disband because it had no long-term funding. The repertoire was mostly modern and ballet; she did not incorporate African movement into her teaching or choreography until after she embarked upon anthropological investigations in the Caribbean (Ashenbrenner 2002; Perpener 2001).

Applied Dance Anthropology

The University of Chicago was a vital place for Katherine Dunham becoming what Ashenbrenner (2002) describes her as "the anthropologist, the artist, the interpreter of African traditions, the social philosopher" (17), and I would add the community activist. The university's interdisciplinary atmosphere encouraged her to link the study of social-cultural anthropology to dance. She studied under seminal anthropologists such as Robert Redfield, Melville Herskovits, Edward Sapir, A. R. Radcliffe Brown, and Fay Cooper Cole. Redfield was Dunham's favorite mentor and he encouraged Dunham to combine her dance with anthropology studies even when she felt she had to do one or the other. To avoid the dichotomy, Dunham realized she needed to "study dance in a society in which it had a more central role than in the U.S." (Ashenbrenner 2002, 43).

Fay Cooper Cole introduced Dunham to Herskovits, who had done work in Haiti. He agreed to help her prepare for research in Haiti. Together, they developed a plan of study and a research proposal for the Rosenwald foundation and Dunham received a grant from them in 1935. She went to Haiti and also other Caribbean countries to study the social function of dance. She used her perspective as an anthropologist and dancer for collecting data.

Dunham's (1946, 1947, 1969) research found dance to be a vital practice for expressing the emotions of the religious rites and rituals of the vodun tradition. She found, "dance movements, music and language are powerful ingredients of the ceremony" (Ashenbrenner 2002, 73). She discovered dance was a physical cleansing in the vodun culture. In other words, the movement can take you on a spiritual journey in which you vent negative emotions such as nervousness, frustration, despair, and confusion. The fluid motion and hypnotic character of vodun movement can take a dancer to a deeply soulful, meditative physic place; it can replenish and soothe the body, mind, and spirit. Dunham said, "dance creates harmony with self and others" (in Ashenbrenner 2002, 76).

In the research process, she found her passion and dance skills provided her with a deep appreciation for the vodun Haitian culture. Dancing exalted her body to a "superior state" of being (78). Through dance, she learned to respect vodun and preserve much of its essential content through the execution of the movement. It was through her own personal study of the Haitian dance that she found the most profound understanding of the social function of dance. Her viewpoint as a dancer gave her a discernment about how the emphasis of certain body parts discloses something about culture (Ashnebrenner 2002). The vocabulary of bodies in motion marks distinct expressions of cultural identities.

Her experiences in the Caribbean attuned Dunham to the various African belief systems that respect ancestral spirit and value the ability of dance to be a healing practice, and a repository of cultural vitality for Haiti and other Afro-Caribbean people. The insights she gathered in Haiti helped her to see something missing for African Americans living in the United States. She knew the cultural resonance between African culture and African Americans need to be asserted.

After returning to the United States, Dunham began exploring the fusion of the Afro-Caribbean dance with ballet and modern movement in her teaching and choreography. She began highlighting African philosophies embodied in the movement and over the years of teaching, choreographing, and performing, she developed Dunham technique, a dance education rooted in the African cultures and spiritualities she studied in the Caribbean. She brought this cultural information to the people of East St. Louis in the mid-1960s, where she observed an economical and cultural depression caused by a lack of awareness of rich heritage, sense of inferiority, and sparseness of opportunity and achievement (Ashenbrenner 1981, 61). Dunham's dance education was doing what Daniels (2005) calls social medicine, "that is which is instrumental to community cohesion" (271) and provides individuals access to their higher consciousness. Dunham knew the cultural knowledge embodied in dance was a social and political force that had the potential to heal the apathy, anger, and hopelessness she observed in the youth.

Performing Arts Training Center: The Mission, the Civil Rights Movement, the Philosophy, the Curriculum, and the Students

Dunham opened the Performing Arts Training Center in 1969. The political nature of the school is explicitly stated in her mission statement. The schools strove to "motivate and stimulate unchallenged young people of East St. Louis through the arts" (Dunham 1969, 261) and provide an interdisciplinary educational experience and a cultural awakening in the community. She brought her former dance company members to East St. Louis to teach at the school. Together with Dunham, they immersed youth into the study of dance and its related subjects: theater, culture, and language. Her performing arts school offered a pedagogy that emphasized cultural fusion, spiritual growth, and community development (Redmond 1976).

The decade the PATC was established reflected a 1960s political landscape that was volatile with racism, but that also galvanized the Black power movement and responses from impassioned artists and cultural workers such as Dunham. Hence, the relevance of PATC cannot be divorced from the socio-political context, because the school arose out of the aftermath of the Jim Crow laws and the civil rights era. The United States at that time was a nation of blatant racism, economic glass ceilings, and educational injustices for Black people. Martin Luther King Jr., Malcolm X, and John F. Kennedy were assassinated and deep frustrations absorbed Black communities in the United States.

Dunham started to make keen observations of the social malaise and used her school to counteract the institutionalized racism, internal racism, and deep-seated insecurities that Woodson (1933) wrote about in his book *Miseducation of the Negro*. Dunham knew how imperative it was to restore the emotional and spiritual health of the young people of East St. Louis. Her school used the performing arts to assist youth in acquiring a cultural perspective that nourished socially responsible attitudes and life practices.

Dunham believed in teaching dance with an anthropological orientation (Asehnbrenner 1981, 145). She was known for her ability to communicate profound cultural insights through artistic expression (147). As a dance anthropologist, she understood dance to reflect culture. Dunham stated, "Dance is a social act, not merely a technique to be learned and thus should return to its roots in communal living" (Ashenbrenner 1981, 151). In her travels to the Caribbean and Africa, she found dance to be important to community ritual and celebration of their ancestors; she knew dance to bring about a common humanity, dignity, and compassion (Dunham 1946, 1947, 1969).

She wanted to move East St. Louis toward a cultural autonomy that provided the people the freedom to choose cultural alternatives that were empowering (Ashenbrenner 1981). The school often served young militant men, who were turning to gang violence and uncontrollable rage to cope with the depressed environment they lived in. Dunham states,

> It is a special challenge to be here . . . this city has been torn apart through the apathetic mentality induced by being on dole. . . . The inability for socialization and finally the riots . . . its our aim to socialize the young and old through culturalization, to make the individual aware of himself and his environment and to create a desire to be alive. (Ashenbrenner 1981, 61)

Dunham had the reputation as a calm but powerful teacher, whose passion often went beyond the doors of PATC. For example, she took a group of young men to visit her dear friend in New York, the distinguished Eric Fromm a well-known social theorist. Dunham requested he talk to them about alternatives to destructive violence (Ashenbrenner 1981; Dunham 1998). Her love for her students also got her put in jail for inquiring about one of her students' arrest. Her vigor for teaching extended beyond the classroom into the everyday trials of community life in East St. Louis. What the youth learned at PATC culminated into community dance performances featuring Dunham's choreography, and some of the students even toured the United States with Dunham performing at highly prestigious events.

The Performing Arts Training Center became a venue for mentoring youth and helping them overcome alienation, experience achievement, and acheive self-mastery through dance (Dunham as cited in Ashenbrenner 1981). The dance education Dunham offered taught the young people about their cultural histories and personal lives, and gave them an expressive art form that helped them construct valuable meaning in their lives.

In *Katherine Dunham: Dancing a Life*, Ashenbrenner (2002) interviews many of the Dunham students, some who have gone on to become certified Dunham technique teachers and master teachers. These renowned and exceptional teachers who studied with her in East St. Louis are Theodore Jamison, Keith Williams, Michael Green, Ruby Streete, and others from all over the country, including Penny Godboldo, Alicia Pierce, Halifu Osumare, Sarah Marshall, and Patricia Wilson, just to name a few. Master teachers of the Dunham technique are Vanoye Atkins, Albirda Rose, Glorie Van Scott, Ruth Beckford, Darrel Braddix, Theodore Jamison, Ruby Streete, and April Barry. The Dunham teaching legacy is not just technique but also, as Rose (1990) calls it a "way of life." The technique is an embodiment of a life philosophy and a way of being and perceiving the world.

Dunham Dance Technique: The Origins and Inspiration for the Pedagogy

> I am only interested in dance as an education, a means of knowing peoples, and I want students who want to learn and have a desire to develop people and tastes. . . . I believe that a person who dances should know why they dance, and to do so they must have an historical background. (Dunham as cited in Roberts 2005, 47)

Dunham developed a movement method and philosophy called the Dunham technique after her dance research in the Caribbean. In 1935 she received the Rosenwald grant to study African dance in the Caribbean, and she particularly fell in love with Haiti. Dunham became fascinated with the vodun religion and became initiated into its practices, and later became a vodun priestess (Rennart 1995). The Haiti experience had a great influence on the Dunham technique. Once she returned to the United States, she completed her bachelor's degree in anthropology and continued to pursue her career in dance. Word of her talent as a dancer and choreographer began to spread and she was commissioned to work with the Negro Federal Theater Project, and later she established the Dunham Dance Company.

The purpose of her technique was to create a dance with "an authentic base for Black people" (Dunham 1998, 351). Evolving over time, the Dunham technique is a fusion of ballet, modern, and African diasporic dance. Her work spearheaded contemporary fusion technique, and in particular an Afromodern dance style and philosophy.

Ashenbrenner (1981, 2002) states that Dunham stressed the fundamental African mode that characterized Haitian dance in her technique. Haitian dance became the theoretical basis of her technique; however, she blended the African aesthetic with ballet and modern dance. Dunham technique "stressed non-balletic use of the body that emphasized Afro-Caribbean movements—pelvic contractions, hip isolations, and undulating back movements . . . she also incorporated standard classical ballet movements such as tendus, developpes, and ronde de jambs" (Perpener 2001, 155). Over the years, she began to codify her technique and today there are distinct warm-up exercises, bar work, floor progression, and choreographic repertoire that make the Dunham technique what it is today (for a detailed discussion of Dunham technique see Rose 1990).

Since the 1980s, there have been annual summer Dunham seminars in East St. Louis, where young and old, beginner to advance dancers come and study with Dunham, her protégés, and certified Dunham teachers. This is where most people, including myself, were first introduced to the Dunham technique, family, and legacy.

Reflections of the Dunham Seminar of June 2003 in East St. Louis

Dunham is one of the spearheads of dance anthropology and the methodology of dance ethnography. This area of study understands dance to be a form of cultural knowledge and engages fieldwork that looks at the body as a window into the mental, emotional, and spiritual lives of human beings (Sklar 2001; Thomas 2003). Dance ethnography involves collecting data through participant-observation, field notes, and dancing. To study dance is to study culture, and dancing can enable one to acquire an emic perspective of the people we study.

Participants[3] of the Dunham seminar learn about this. The seminar involves intensive dance workshops, lectures, and discussions on Dunham history, education, and activism. Every day, students took two beginning-level Dunham technique classes, along with two other African and African Diaspora dance classes that have influenced the Dunham technique, such as Ghanaian, Haitian, Guinean, and Afro-Cuban dance classes. All of the dance classes were accompanied with live percussion from professional musicians; the music played in her classes was traditional and contemporary renditions of Nigerian, Haitian, and Cuban rhythms. The beats of the drums set the tone of the class and guided the timing of movement. The sound of congas, batas, and djembe drums permeated the rooms. Each breath and each movement correlated to the rhythms played. Dunham's technique follows the polyrhythmic timing of the drums and can be characterized as curvilinear, unlike ballet, the dominant European dance form. Dunham's movement includes contractions, angulations, isolations, circular hip motions, and syncopated footwork. Her movement reclaimed an African sensibility and approach to dance. The seminar was a cultural immersion and was rigorous physically and emotionally. The seminar lasted two weeks long and concluded with a community performance.

In 2003, Ruby Streete and Michael Green were the primary instructors for beginning-level Dunham technique classes. Mrs. Streete and Mr. Green had unique approaches to teaching, although there was great continuity between their pedagogies. Most classes began with students standing in parallel position, looking straight ahead, and pressing our shoulders down away from necks. As we engaged the abdomen, our tailbone grew long, and we took deep inhalations and exhalations. Breathing in Dunham technique is important to centering the mind, body, and spirit. The warm-up focused on "getting into our bodies" and disciplining the mind to become fully committed to the body conditioning and dance exercises. As we stood they would ask us to imagine an invisible circle that contained our positive energy. This exercise sought to interrupt the negative influences such as sabotaging thinking patterns, and low self-esteem that ultimately detracts one from the pure, honest, heartfelt dancing. These Dunham exercises taught a dancer about dedication, devotion, and detachment.[4] These three principles of Dunham technique were philosophical concepts for helping a dancer filter out distractions that hinder one from embodying the spirit of dance.

Dunham, in her nineties, taught two master classes herself. Her pro-tégé, Theodore Jamison, demonstrated for her. He and Dunham led the class with the warm-up starting on the floor, which then culminated into progressions across the floor. The classes with Dunham had the spiritual intensity of a ceremony. She had away of purifying the room and a danc-er's body with her words and through the movement exercises she chose for us. Dunham (1998) said, "dance commands your distinct energy and should bring about autohynopsis."

The intricacies of Dunham's movement stimulated the body's senses in a way that brought upon a feeling of a higher self. Her technique is a tool for creating cultural experiences that deepen your sense of humanity. Her pedagogy involves a sort of psychological restructuring of the body and mind.

She taught her pupils that dance is your church if you allow it to cleanse, empower, and educate the mind, body, spirit. Eugene Redmond, a well-known East St. Louis poet and friend of Dunham, wrote about her epistemological approach to dance. Redmond wrote, "body sermons, drum lectures, song sagas, gesture thoughts, and love prayers, are all vibrant elements of the Dunham cosmos. The ontology of a people, she believes, is seen in what they do and especially in the way they dance . . . in the expanded sense of the word" (quoted in Dunham 1976, 269).

Dunham developed a technique that enlivened an Afro-Caribbean cul-tural ethos. The technique is a form of cultural and ideological production in the way she challenged the reproduction of dominant culture in the United States with a dance education informed by cultural knowledge of the African Diaspora. Dance to her is not just movement but an expression of cultural and community soul.

Dunham's technique is a physical journey that can invoke a conscious-ness informed by African ritual life. Dunham technique is a passport into a cultural domain that decolonizes the body from the mental and psycho-logical consequences of the Atlantic slave trade and racist belief systems. A technique created to affirm an authentic African cultural perspective that dignified Black identity, her pedagogy countered the sociopolitical context of white supremacy and Black racism that was going on at the time. Dun-ham technique was a form of protest to the racist ideologies and oppression of African culture in the United States. Her dance pedagogy celebrated an African epistemology that reclaimed what African Americans in the United States lost during the period of enslavement. The pre-slavery criteria that African people used to define themselves—the languages, ancestral land,

and cultural expressions such as song, music, and dance—were literally stripped from them. Dunham's technique and approach to teaching countered the denigration of this heritage and revitalizes an African ethos.

Implications of Dunham's Decolonizing Dance Education

I call Dunham's applied dance anthropology *decolonizing dance education*, a dance praxis involved in the process of decolonizing the body through choreography, pedagogy, and community activism that challenges ideologies of race and colonial oppression inscribed upon the Black body. Historically, the social practice of dancing and drumming has been vital to the cultural expressions of African people. Her dance education rescued the social function of dance for humanizing and nourishing African American people. Dunham used dance to promote social change and mobilize identities based on cultural difference and promote multicultural orientations. Lepecki (2004) would say Dunham created "dances of subversive performance" (70), that is, dance that addresses an epistemological tension and moves counter to the way Black dance has been legislated or controlled by dominant political systems. Dunham's work provides us a historical context for understanding how dance can participate in cultural politics and be in a dialectical relationship with the problems of society. Dunham's dance education decolonizes the Black body by recovering dignified stories of African history, spiritual, and secular life with the dancing body. Her technique was encoded with valuable cultural knowledge with a mission to reeducate and enrich African American identity. Dunham understood dance to be a continuum of the cultural energy and a life force of humanity. She used dance as tool for reversing the ideological anatomy of colonial and racist representation in the body and mind.

Dunham's technique teaches one about dance as ritual and cultural energy. Through her movement, you can access what Daniels (2005)[5] calls "embodied knowledge," "knowledge found within the body, within the dancing and drumming body—rich and viable and should be referenced among other kinds of knowledge" (4–5). She goes on to say dance can be involved in a ritual community service that feeds the physical and social body (5).

Dunham technique instructs one to rise above the ordinary and dance for spiritual and artistic expression. As Daniels (2005) argues, dance houses

theoretical, emotional, aesthetic, and spiritual information, and a repository for belief systems (64–65). Dunham's pedagogy "educates from the
body" (Daniels 2005, 265). An example of this is her focus on quieting the
mind in order to give voice to the body. Dunham's principles teach one to
be more receptive to the flow of kinetic sensations. Dunham's technique
grooms a body awareness that fosters a spiritual consciousness and method
for perceiving the world.

In conclusion, Dunham's dance education demonstrates how artists
use dance as a form of political voice and action. Her utilization of dance
shows the body to be a powerful tool for self- and collective actualization
and determination. For Dunham, dance is a physical and intellectual practice in which identity is constructed and culture is produced. The dance
knowledge she collected from the Caribbean became a political tool for
reinventing the Black body with dignity. Roberts (2005) states,

> Through her research, fieldwork and experience in Haiti and other Carib-
> bean islands, Dunham would retrieve cultural and historical knowledge to
> re-educate dancers and audience. Based on this knowledge, she developed
> Dunham Technique and created dance for the concert stage. She wanted
> to declare Black people's humanity, which had been destroyed under
> segregation by the twin forces of alienated and [cultural] deracination. For
> mostly White audiences, she used such knowledge to speak truth to White
> dominating power by having a mostly Black dance company perform
> dance-stories derived from American and Diasporic Black culture. She
> challenged the notion that U.S. history was not a shared history and the
> widely held racist notions that Blacks were not human and were without
> culture, history, intelligence, dignity or greatness. (43–44)

Dunham's decolonizing dance education demonstrates the body to be a cultural force for affirming diversity and challenging deep-seated colonial/racist
ideologies in education and in the wider social context. Dunham centralized
the dancing body and its cultural expressions to recuperate cultural identities
lost, and address the years of miseducation of African Americans. Her dance
education sought to re-educate her students with the cultural knowledge
that informed Dunham's technique. Her technique was developed to be a
social resource for the mental, emotional, and spiritual health of the communities she served. Her dance education is humanizing and hence, decolonizing, because her work divested the ways in which we deny diversity and
cultural knowledge acquired and expressed in the body, and invested in the
valuable embodiments of humanity that we register when we dance.

Notes

1. Dunham was awarded many honorary doctorates from many prestigious universities for her contribution to the field of dance anthropology. See Ashenbrenner (2002).

2. Dunham worked in formal and informal educational sites.

3. The author of this paper participated in the Dunham dance seminar and studied primarily with Ruby Streete and Michael Green the year of 2003.

4. Dunham discussed these principles in her dance class in at the Dunham seminar in East St. Louis in 2003.

5. Daniels's (2005) work concentrates on the Caribbean Basin and considers three African-derived religious dance systems: Haitian Vodou, Cuban Yoruba, and Bahian Candomble. These are dance cultures that greatly influenced Dunham's dance pedagogy.

Works Cited

Ashenbrenner, J. 1978. "Anthropology as a lifeway: Katherine Dunham." In *Katherine Dunham: An anthology of writings*, ed. V. Clark and M. B. Wilkerson, 186–91. Berkeley: University of California Press.

———. 1981. *Katherine Dunham: Reflections on the social and political contexts of Afro-American dance*. New York: Cord, Inc.

———. 1999. "Katherine Dunham: Anthropologist, artist, humanist." In *African American Pioneers in Anthropology*, ed. I. Harrsion and F. Harrison, 137–53. Urbana: University of Illinois Press

———. 2002. *Katherine Dunham: Dancing a Life*. Urbana and Chicago: University of Illinois Press.

Castaldi, F. 2006. *Choreographies of African identities: Négritude, dance, and the national ballet of Senegal*. Urbana: University of Illinois Press.

Daniels, Y. 2005. *Dancing wisdom: Embodied knowledge in Haitian vodou, Cuban yoruba, and Bahian candomble*. Urbana: University of Illinois Press.

Dunham, K. 1946. *Journey to Accompong*. New York: H. Holt

———.1947. "Dances of Haiti." *Acta Anthropologica* 2 (4): 1–64.

———. 1969. *Island Possessed*. Urbana: University of Chicago Press.

———.1998. "Interview with Katherine Dunham." In *Ain't but a place: An anthology of African-American writing on St. Louis*, ed. G. Early, 350–54. Columbia: University of Missouri Press.

Lepecki, A. 2004. "Introduction: Presence and body in dance and performance Theory." In *Of the Presence of the Body*, ed. A. Lepecki, 1–9. Middletown, CT: Wesleyan University Press.

Manning, S. 2004. *Modern dance, negro dance: Race in motion*. Minneapolis: University of Minnesota Press.

Mazer, G. 1976/1978. "Katherine Dunham." In *Katherine Dunham: An anthology of writings*, ed. V. Clark and M. B. Wilkerson, 168–83. Berkley: University of California Press.

Perpener, I. J. O. 2001. *African-American concert dance: The Harlem renaissance and beyond*. Urbana: University of Illinois Press.

Redmond, E. B. 1976/1978. "Cultural fusion and spiritual unity: Katherine Dunham's approach to developing educational community theatre." In *Katherine Dunham: An anthology of writings*, ed. V. Clark and M. B. Wilkerson, 265–70. Berkley: University of California Press.

Rennart, R. 1995. *Profiles of great black Americans*. Nashville, TN: Chelsea House Publishers.

Roberts, R. M. 2005. "Radical movements: Katherine Dunham and Ronald K. Brown teaching toward a critical consciousness." Doctoral diss., City University of New York.

Rose, A. 1990. *Dunham technique: A way of life*. Dubuque, IA: Kendall/Hunt Publishing.

Sklar, D. 2000. Reprise: "On dance ethnography." *Dance Research Journal* 32 (1): 70–77.

Thomas, H. 2003. *The body, dance and cultural theory*. New York: Palgrave Mac-Millern Press.

Tuhiwai Smith, L. 1999. *Decolonizing methodologies: research and indigenous peoples*. New York: Zed Books Ltd.

Woodson, C. 1933. *The miseducation of the Negro*. Washington, DC: Associated Publishers.

ADVANCING THE RACE: AFRICAN AMERICAN EDUCATION AND SOCIAL PROGRESS   III

Live the Truth

Politics and Pedagogy in the African American Movement for Freedom and Liberation[1]

DANIEL PERLSTEIN

7

THIS CHAPTER EXAMINES THE INTERWOVEN political and educational ideas of the African American movement for freedom and liberation of the 1960s and 1970s. During those decades, the Student Nonviolent Coordinating Committee (SNCC) and the Black Panther Party formed the militant vanguard of efforts to imagine new modes of teaching and learning. Both groups insisted that the elimination of racial oppression required the development of a new consciousness within the African American community, leading both to create alternative schools for Black youth. Moreover, close ties united the two groups and their educational projects (Pearson 1994, 85–94, 152, 162–63). While SNCC's freedom schools and the Black Panthers' liberation schools had short existences and directly touched only a small fraction of Black students, they epitomized the movement's visionary commitment to emancipatory education. Although other organizations, notably the NAACP, may have had greater impact on educational policy, none embodied more fully the pedagogical ideals of the African American struggle for social justice.

In their educational projects, SNCC and Panther activists developed, abandoned, recreated, and again abandoned open-ended, progressive approaches to the study of social and political life.[2]

The continuities and shifts in activists' educational visions mirrored the continuities and evolution of the movement as a whole. Like the broader civil rights movement of the early 1960s, SNCC's freedom schools were shaped by a liberal faith that America's democratic institutions could fully accommodate Black aspirations for equal citizenship. "The basic thesis of democracy," as W. E. B. Du Bois suggests, is "that the best and only ultimate authority on an individual's hurt and desire is that individual himself" and that "life, as any man has lived it, is part of that great reservoir of knowledge without which no government can do justice" (Du Bois 1973, 119). Commitment to this liberal democratic synthesis of individual autonomy and collective self-determination led SNCC organizers to envision freedom schools in which self-actualizing learners defined and shaped their world.

Such progressive approaches, as Horace Mann Bond argues, presuppose "an elastic, democratic social order in which there are no artificial barriers set against the social mobility of the individual" (Bond 1935, 167). Over the course of the 1960s, activists became increasingly convinced that racial oppression was an essential element of American life and not a Southern deviation from the American Creed. As faith in America's democratic potential declined, the freedom school pedagogy of open ended-inquiry gave way to explicit instruction that aimed at revealing to students the nature of oppression. The Black Panther liberation schools embodied this new pedagogy.

To be sure, the line separating liberal and revolutionary activism—and the pedagogical practices they engendered—was never absolute. The SNCC freedom schools *and* the Panther liberation schools envisioned a new, humanizing education as both a goal of the movement and a prerequisite for social transformation. Moreover, even if freedom schools reflected what historian Robert O. Self calls "the movement in its most overtly liberal phase," radicalism was not only liberalism's antithesis but also its "constant companion" (Self 2006, 18). Just as freedom schooling constituted a critique of liberalism no less than an expression of it, Panther liberation schools always included elements of experiential learning along with teachers' expositions of political critique. In short, movement educational projects highlight both the differing ideological sources of Black pedagogical thought and a shared commitment to replacing brutalizing schools with an emancipatory form of education.

SNCC and Progressive Pedagogy

A new politics, infused with pedagogy, emerged at the outset of the 1960s, a politics announced by lunch counter sit-ins and represented organizationally by the founding of the Student Nonviolent Coordinating Committee. Like the more established civil rights organizations, SNCC sought to achieve racial integration and to win equality for African Americans. In addition to protesting racial injustice, however, the young SNCC activists sought to live their beliefs. The sit-ins derived their power from protesters' ability to reconstitute the meaning of their own humanity, while they also demanded the abolition of unjust laws. In their own words, SNCC activists viewed the freedom struggle as an arena in which Blacks would "learn in order to do and to discover who they are" (Perlstein 2002, 252).

As activists worked to expand their protests into a mass movement, they engaged poor southern Blacks in the same project of self-discovery and social transformation to which they had committed themselves. No less than the activists themselves, SNCC's Charles Sherrod maintained, the masses of Southern Blacks were "searching for a meaning in life" (Carson 1981, 57–58). Although activists "wanted to end segregation, discrimination, and White supremacy," SNCC's Charlie Cobb explained, "the core of our efforts was the belief that Black people had to make decisions about and take charge of the things controlling their lives. . . . Most of us organizing soon learned that our main challenge was getting Black people to challenge themselves. Stated another way, people would have to redefine themselves" (Cobb 1999, 134). This commitment to a politics of self-discovery, self-expression, and self-determination imbued SNCC's work with pedagogical concerns.

Far from repudiating American society, SNCC activists, as historian Clayborne Carson argues, wanted to solidify their entry into it (Carson 1981, 13). The movement, in the words of activist Jimmy Garrett, was "for the Black people, a search for acknowledgment of presence and a desire for recognition" (Garrett 1969, 8). Activists' hopes depended upon America's capacity to live up to its professed ideals. "Through nonviolence," SNCC proclaimed in its 1960 statement of purpose, "mutual regard cancels enmity. Justice for all overthrows injustice. The redemptive community supersedes systems of gross social immorality. . . . Integration of human endeavor represents the crucial first step toward such a society" (Perlstein 2002, 252). No mere tactic, nonviolence reflected both the desire for full participation in a reformed America and a belief that America would recognize Black rights.

By 1963, Mississippi had become the focal point of SNCC's work. Even among Southern states, Mississippi was extreme in its resistance to racial justice. Local authorities sanctioned a murderous campaign to maintain white supremacy, while imposing brutal punishments on Blacks who exercised their rights. To crack the closed society of Mississippi, a SNCC-led coalition of civil rights groups organized the 1964 Freedom Summer. Enlisting privileged whites, SNCC hoped, would "bring America to Mississippi," compel the United States government to protect activists, and demonstrate the possibility of interracial fellowship (Guyot 1996). Hundreds of white volunteers answered SNCC's call, working as political organizers and teaching in freedom schools.

Freedom schooling reflected both SNCC activists' critique of Jim Crow public schooling and their vision of the movement. Although organizers condemned Mississippi's stark racial disparities in educational resources and attainment, they were even more critical of the "complete absence of academic freedom," which "squash[ed] intellectual curiosity" and rendered poor Blacks and whites unable to "question the system of oppression which keeps them . . . in the [cotton] fields." Because of seg-regation, activists charged, "Negroes and Whites aren't allowed to know each other." How, they demanded, "can a people who are separated from their fellow men live the truth?" (Perlstein 1990, 303).

At the same time as SNCC activists believed that Black conscious-ness was distorted by segregation, they were convinced that Blacks could draw from their experience an understanding of the nature and promise of American society. In contrast to the "disciplined and organized and ideo-logical" old left organizing that preceded it and Black nationalist struggle that would follow, the Mississippi movement, Charlie Cobb argues, was "spontaneous" (Cobb 1996). In 1963, Cobb proposed the creation of free-dom schools in order to help "young Negro Mississippians . . . articulate their own desires, demands and questions" (Perlstein 2002, 253).

SNCC's commitment to students exploring their own experience and articulating their own desires reflected a dual conviction that American society was not irretrievably alien to students and that they could satisfy those desires within it. "The value of the Freedom School," Freedom Summer volunteers learned, "will derive from what the teachers are able to elicit from the students in terms of comprehension and expression of their experiences" (Freedom School Curriculum 1991, 7). To "train people to be active agents in bringing about social change," teachers were instructed to begin by having students describe the schools that they attended. The Freedom School Curriculum included a dozen sample questions such as, "What is the school made of, wood or brick?" (1991, 9). Students were then asked to compare Black schools with white ones. Similarly detailed questions focused on housing conditions, employment, and medical care. Organizers explained to freedom school volunteers,

> We have attempted to design a developmental curriculum that begins on
> the level of the students' everyday lives and those things in their envi-
> ronment that they have already experienced or can readily perceive, and

builds up to a more realistic perception of American society, themselves, the conditions of their oppression, and alternatives offered by the Freedom Movement. It is not our purpose to impose a particular set of conclusions. Our purpose is to encourage the asking of questions, and the hope that society can be improved. (9)

For activists, then, the act of questioning was not just a step in a process of intellectual growth but also a repudiation of subordination and a prerequisite to democratic citizenship.

While the freedom school curriculum reflected SNCC's politics, it also drew on both earlier movement educational projects and the liberal tradition in white American educational thought. At the Highlander Folk School, SNCC organizers and other grass-roots activists analyzed their shared experiences in order to devise collective solutions to their problems. This reliance on learners' experiences and problems was directly influenced by John Dewey, with whom Highlander founder Myles Horton corresponded for many years. "If ideas, meaning, conceptions, notions, theories, systems are instrumental to an active reorganization of the given environment," Horton would say, quoting Dewey, "they are reliable, sound, valid, good, true" (Perlstein 1990, 306–8).

SNCC also worked with movement adult literacy and voter education leader Septima Clark. In Clark's citizenship schools, participants discussed the problems they encountered in daily life, analyzed the political forces that created them, and learned skills necessary to address them. Clark traced her method in part to Teachers College, where she had studied in 1930, when the influence of progressive educators was at its height. There, she "found out how to use the expressions of the children to teach them the words that they used every day" (Clark 1986, 115). Like Horton, Clark enlarged the frequently apolitical pedagogy of mainstream, white American progressivism, promoting individual transformation in a movement context that fostered genuine problem solving through collective action.

SNCC recruited a wide array of Black and white activists in addition to Horton and Clark to help plan the freedom schools. The Mississippi curriculum reflected contributions from educators who had helped organize earlier freedom schools in Prince Edward County, Virginia (established after local authorities responded to the *Brown* decision by shutting down the public schools) and in Boston (established during a school boycott demanding the integration of that city's schools). Others who helped with freedom school curriculum development included Bayard Rustin, Ella Baker, Michael Harrington, and Staughton Lynd (Perlstein 1990, 2002).

In the summer of 1964, about forty freedom schools served between two and three thousand students. The schools were usually located in church buildings; classes often met outside in a circle under a tree. As one group of volunteers reported, a typical school day started

> at 9:00 AM with singing and current events. Students are divided into classes according to age level and interest—ages run from 4 to 25 years. But all students take citizenship in the morning. The class includes Negro History, Mississippi politics and composition. Students can choose dance, drama, art, auto mechanics, guitar, games or sports for the second hour. School closes from noon to 2 PM although it is open for those who bring bag lunches. Afternoon classes are many of the same subjects plus other special classes. One of the staff, a professional teacher, teaches a play-writing class three times a week, and debate and journalism each once a week. (Perlstein 1990, 316)

In the afternoons and evenings, students and teachers often engaged in political work such as voter registration or picketing. At the same time as the schools blurred the line between school and (political) life, they wedded politics and self-expression. Across Mississippi, freedom schools combined the civic curriculum centering on the movement with literary studies, journalism, creative writing, foreign languages, and other expressive endeavors. This combination both represented SNCC's commitment to self-expression as a basis for political action and reflected a desire to offer disenfranchised Black youth the best of conventional American schooling.

The politics and pedagogy of the freedom schools were embodied in a widely celebrated lesson taught by SNCC activist Stokely Carmichael. Carmichael began the class by writing four pairs of sentences on a blackboard. "I digs wine" was matched with "I enjoy drinking cocktails"; "The peoples wants freedom" with "The people want freedom"; and so on. "What do you think about these sentences?" Carmichael asked.

"'Peoples,'" Zelma answered, "isn't right."

"Does it mean anything?" Carmichael persisted.

"Peoples," Milton acknowledged, "means everybody" (Stembridge n.d., 1–2). Conventionally incorrect usage, students affirmed in answer to Carmichael's continued questioning, was widely spoken and understood in their community.

Students' inquiry into nonstandard English legitimized demands for the full citizenship of those who spoke it. At the end of the hour-long lesson, it was left to a student rather than to the teacher to draw the conclusion that rules about what constitutes correct English are used to reproduce an unjust social order. "If the majority speaks" nonstandard English but it has lower status than proper English, a student named Alma explained, "then a minority must rule society" (2).

For Carmichael, teaching consisted entirely of asking a series of questions. SNCC activist Jane Stembridge observed that Carmichael "trusted" students' understanding of political and social life and their ability to articulate that understanding. He "spoke to where they were" and relied on "the movement of the discussion" to deepen analysis (3). Activists publicized Carmichael's lesson because it epitomized SNCC's pedagogical ideal.

Freedom Summer, historian Vincent Harding suggests, represented the movement's view that "human beings are meant to be developmental beings; that we find our best identity and purpose when we are developing ourselves and helping to develop our surroundings" (Harding 1998, 137).

The hope that Blacks could participate fully in American democratic life was a precondition for activists' pedagogy, as for their politics. The freedom schools, according to SNCC's Charlie Cobb, reflected "traditional liberal concepts and approaches to education." Although the schools did not "grapple with the deeper flaws in education and society," they contributed "to expanding the idea . . . that Black people could shape and control at least some of the things that affected their lives" (Cobb 1999, 137).

Political Shifts and Pedagogical Changes

In the years that followed the Mississippi Freedom Summer, the trust—in America and in students' understanding—that infused SNCC's activism began to dissipate. Declining faith in integration was in part ironic testimony to the movement's success in raising Black consciousness. "Young Black people," activist Jimmy Garrett observed, "began to see that the inequalities placed upon them by American society were not individual inequities taking place at odd moments, but rather a group activity against a group of people regardless of their education or economic status. They began to see that there were continuous activities by the White community to shut them out of the major society" (Garrett 1969, 8).

The movement's successes were not, however, the only source of activists' disenchantment. Freedom Summer began with the disappearance of civil rights workers Michael Schwerner, Andrew Goodman, and James

Chaney, and activists' "Running Summary of Incidents" included literally hundreds of acts of violence, ranging from threats and arrests to bombings and murders. At the same time as the unrelenting campaign of white supremacist violence scarred activists, their very reliance on the presence of white volunteers to attract national attention testified to the enduring power of American racism. According to activist Dave Dennis, organizers had come "to Mississippi looking for the dissimilarities" between the South and the American mainstream. During and after the summer, however, continuous violence and the refusal of the federal government or even of white liberal leaders to fully support equal rights, together with interracial tensions among activists in Mississippi, increasingly convinced organizers that "the only difference is that the political oppression and control in Mississippi is much more conspicuous, much more overt" (Perlstein 2002, 256). "What you could see at the end of '64," Charlie Cobb echoed, "was that Mississippi really was part of the U.S." (Cobb 1996).

Matters came to a head at the 1964 Democratic Party national convention in Atlantic City. Much of the Freedom Summer had been dedicated to organizing the Mississippi Freedom Democratic Party among Blacks excluded from the segregated regular Democratic Party. MFDP representatives petitioned to replace the all-white Mississippi delegation in Atlantic City. "If the Freedom Democratic Party is not seated," Mississippi activist Fannie Lou Hamer told the convention in a riveting speech, "I question America" (Lewis 1998, 279). "How could we not prevail?" SNCC's John Lewis would still wonder decades later. "The law was on our side. Justice was on our side. The sentiments of the entire nation were with us" (278). President Johnson, however, was not on the activists' side. Seeking to appease segregationists, Democratic Party leaders refused to seat the integrated and integrationist MFDP delegation. For Lewis and countless other activists,

> this was the turning point of the civil rights movement. . . . Until then . . . the belief still prevailed that the system would work, the system would listen. . . . Now, for the first time, we had made our way to the very center of the system. We had played by the rules, done everything we were supposed to do. [We] had arrived at the doorstep and found the door slammed in our face. (282)

Moreover, past successes in dismantling Jim Crow offered activists little guidance in challenging the deeply rooted system of racial and economic oppression manifest in Northern ghettos. There, government agencies, business groups, and labor unions combined to promote the growing comfort of white citizens and the growing alienation of Blacks. Meanwhile, the Northern school integration movement foundered in the face of opposition from white parents, real estate interests, and educators. Racism in schools, the legal system, housing, and employment continued to oppress Blacks despite the right to vote and the absence of segregation laws (Perlstein 2004).

The years following the Freedom Summer witnessed the eclipse of the civil rights movement's integrationist phase, a transformation announced by the electrifying demand for "Black Power," which SNCC's Stokely Carmichael popularized in 1966. The conclusion that America itself was hopelessly racist precluded political mobilization through a language of shared American values. Gradually, as the notion that one could live the truth while living in America receded, so too did the belief that students' open-ended exploration of their experiences could foster their understanding of themselves and of possible avenues for social change. A focus on self-discovery and self-expression among the voiceless was replaced by a desire to articulate a critique of society to the oppressed.

Bill Ware, the leader of SNCC's 1966 Atlanta Project, noted that Freedom Summer had "presupposed that Mississippi schools were so far below the national norm that freedom schools were needed to help bring Mississippi Negroes up to some kind of national norm" (Perlstein 2002, 257). Rather, Ware claimed, "our experience in this country . . . has taught [Blacks] that they are intrinsically inferior. . . . The lies that little Black children learn about themselves leave a crippling scar" (Perlstein 2002, 257). Whereas 1964's freedom school organizers enlisted white volunteers from across the United States to help plan and staff the freedom schools, the Atlanta group limited recruitment to local Black students.

Declining trust in white activists was matched by a declining interest in the study of American society and a declining sense that pedagogy should flow from students' experiences. When Washington, DC, SNCC activists planned a 1968 "liberation school," three of the four courses covered African history and culture (Perlstein 2002, 257). The transmission of information had become more important than students' exploration of their own experiences.

Veteran activist Jimmy Garrett embodied SNCC's evolving politics and pedagogy. Through the mid-1960s, Garrett had ardently embraced SNCC's integrationist vision as a vehicle for the empowerment of African Americans. A freedom school, he argued in a 1965 proposal to bring SNCC's educational program to Los Angeles, was "an area, atmosphere, situation—any place where young people, whether Black or White, rich or poor, come to deal with real questions as they relate to their lives," a place that lets "young people challenge not only the authority which stifles them, but also . . . challenge themselves" (Perlstein 2002, 258). Then, in 1965, came the Watts "riot," a six-day rebellion in which thousands of Blacks participated and to which authorities responded with massive military force.

Garrett remained committed to African American empowerment, but he now argued for Blacks to "build their own institutions" (Orrick 1969, 80). In 1966, Garrett left SNCC's Los Angeles office and headed to San Francisco State College. There, he led the campaign to create the first Black Students Union (BSU) in the United States. Garrett and the San Francisco State BSU, together with a group from nearby Merritt College that included Black Panthers Huey Newton and Bobby Seale, spearheaded the struggle to establish the first Black studies programs at American universities (Hine 1992, 12; Smith et al. 1970, 131; Garrett 1998–1999, 161). Although Garrett drew on the Mississippi freedom school curriculum in imagining Black studies, the new program abandoned SNCC's trust in students to decide what was of value in their culture. Rather, the goal of Black studies, argued SNCC veteran Mike Thelwell, was the "the rehabilitation of . . . a culture and a heritage they have been taught to despise" (Thelwell 1969, 704, 712).

Garrett's growing skepticism about integrating Blacks into American society shaped his educational efforts. No longer did he see Black and white students as united by common yearnings. "Black people are not western," he argued in 1969. "They are westernized. In much the same way as one might get simonized. We are painted over with Whiteness." Black children failed in school, Garrett claimed, "because the information that [they] receive is alien to them, dealing almost completely with White culture." BSU programs, he declared, sought to "build Black consciousness" by teaching elementary, secondary, and college students "their history and values as a People" (Orrick 1969, 80, 87; Garrett 1969, 8).

As activists concluded that Black oppression was a permanent feature of American society, they lost faith that Black students could draw from their American experience an understanding of their real needs, desires, or identity. A progressive pedagogy that trusted students to discover the truth gave way to one in which students were informed about politics and culture. Whatever one labels the alternative to progressive pedagogy— teacher-centered, traditional, and direct instruction are popular terms—its essential characteristic is that a predetermined body of information or skills that students lack is delivered to them. Such an approach won increasing support among Black activists.

Black Power, Revolution, and Direct Instruction[3]

San Francisco State's BSU worked closely with the Black Panther Party. Jimmy Garrett's grim drama of racial conflict, *And We Own the Night*, was first performed at a 1967 Panther rally. Fellow SNCC veteran Stokely Carmichael was among the featured speakers at the play's premiere. Like Garrett, Carmichael had renounced the optimistic integrationism and open-ended pedagogy of SNCC's early years (Garrett 1969, 69; Perlstein 2002, 259).

Whereas Carmichael's 1964 lesson on African American vernacular had legitimized claims for full citizenship in a fully democratized America, in 1968 he viewed Blacks as "a colonized people" and used Black English to justify a separatist politics:

> We are an African people, we have always maintained our own value system. . . . Take the English language. There are cats who come here from Italy, from Germany, from Poland, from France—in two generations they speak English perfectly. We have never spoken English perfectly. . . . Never did, never will, anyhow they try to run it down out throat, we ain't gonna have it. (1971, 113–14)

Carmichael's new understanding transformed his educational project. No longer did Carmichael trust students to draw political understanding from their experience. "The honky," he maintained, "has channeled our love for one another into love for his country—his country." Meanwhile, the victims of colonization "have been so dehumanized, we're like a dog that the master can throw out of the house, that the master can spit on, and whenever he calls, the dog comes running back" (113, 120–21).

Carmichael worked to transmit to students a Black humanity that was not dependent on the dominant white American society. "The first stage" of the liberation struggle, he argued,

> is waking up our people . . . to the impending danger. So we yell, Gun! Shoot! Burn! Kill! Destroy! They're committing genocide! until the masses of our people are awake. Once they are awake, it is the job of the revolutionary intelligentsia to give them the correct political ideology (185, 190).

Carmichael and Garrett, together with countless other Black activists, found a model of revolutionary commitment in the Black Panther Party. Advocating a synthesis of Marxism and nationalism, the Panthers espoused the need to replace rather than reform American institutions. No less than early SNCC protesters, the Panthers lived their beliefs. Public displays of weaponry and militant confrontations with the police did not merely demand an end to the colonial occupation of the Black community; they announced a new standard of Black manhood. So too, "survival programs" both suggested a radical critique of America's refusal to serve the needs of the poor and prefigured what living in a humane society might be like. "More than any other group of the 1960s," historian Clayborne Carson argues, "the Black Panther Party inspired discontented urban African Americans to liberate themselves" (Carson 1995, ix). In the eyes of SNCC activist Julian Bond the group represented the "standard of militance, of just forcefulness, the sort of standard we haven't had in the past" (xix).

A commitment to transmitting their revolutionary analysis led the Panthers to use a banking language in their educational proposals. The group's 1966 program demanded "education for our people that exposes the true nature of this decadent American society" (Newton 1996, 121). The main purpose of "the vanguard party," Panther founder Huey P. Newton explained, was to "awaken . . . the sleeping masses" and "bombard" them "with the correct approach to the struggle" (Newton 1972, 15–16). "Exploited and oppressed people," argued Panther leader Eldridge Cleaver, needed to be "educating ourselves and our children on the nature of the struggle and . . . transferring to them the means for waging the struggle" (Williamson 2000, 6, 9–10, 13).

Political education classes became a central Panther activity, through which Party leaders and theoreticians could "disseminate" their ideas to the cadre (Hilliard and Cole 1993, 143, 161). Simultaneously, the Panthers relied on public lectures to educate the community about Panther ideology. "Imagine people living in a cave," Huey Newton explained:

> At the end of the cave shines a light. Now one person among them knows the light is the sun. The rest are afraid of the light. They've lived in darkness and think that the light is some kind of evil. Now let's say the person who knows about the light tells them it's not evil and tries to lead them out of the cave. They'll fight and probably overpower and maybe even kill him. Because all they know is darkness, and so quite logically they would be fearful of the light. So instead he has to gradually lead them toward the light. Well,

it's the same with knowledge. Gradually you have to lead people toward an understanding of what's happening. (Hilliard and Cole 1993, 121)

Like progressive education, the transmission of political theory required consideration of the intellectual steps through which students gained understanding. Still, the Panthers did not believe they could rely on Blacks living in darkness to discover the path to liberation. It was up to their teachers to light the way.

No less than SNCC's earlier commitment to eliciting students' own questions, the Panthers' commitment to teacher-centered inculcation transformed Black consciousness. "I had been taught only to revere White people," former Panther Regina Jennings would recall. "Panther teachers . . . taught us from an Afrocentric perspective, whereby the needs and interests of African people determined our perception of the world. The void I used to fill with drugs was now filled instead with a pure and noble love for my people" (Jennings 1998, 259–60).

As the Panthers expanded their educational program, they began to teach children as well as adults. Here too their goal was to transmit revolutionary ideology to Blacks living in an environment so oppressive that it precluded their discovering the truth. Among the Party's most prominent educational programs was a network of "liberation schools" through which the Panthers taught children "about the class struggle in terms of Black history" (Perlstein 2002, 262). First established in 1969, the Panther liberation schools were perhaps the closest counterpart from the late 1960s to the freedom schools of 1964. Both had an ephemeral existence, but both epitomized the political and pedagogical values of the most dynamic African American activism of their day. Together, the two programs therefore illuminate the evolving relationship of politics and pedagogy.

By the late 1960s, Black activists across America had long documented the pervasive inequalities of public schooling. Like SNCC, however, the Black Panthers recognized that Black students' material deprivation was less brutalizing than the psychic and ideological damage of oppression. The public school system was "completely controlled by the power structure," a *Black Panther* article claimed, because "those who can control the mind can control the body" (The Black Panter Party 1971, 1).

First-hand experience reinforced the Panthers' critique. At Oakland Technical High School, Huey Newton was branded a troublemaker and prohibited from talking in class. When he nevertheless raised his hand to ask a question, his teacher reminded him that he was not allowed to speak.

Newton then "stood up and told him it was impossible to learn anything if I was forbidden to ask questions. Then I walked out" (Newton 1995, 45). When David Hilliard's six-year-old son misbehaved at school, his first-grade teacher locked him in a classroom closet (Hillard and Cole 1993, 199–200). "The power structure," Panthers concluded,

> allowed Black people to go to school but totally controlled . . . the amount and type of education. . . . The method and process of teaching are . . . designed to fit the individual into the present oppressive system. The student is taught that obedience to school rules is primary, and knowledge secondary, or unnecessary. (Perlstein 2002, 263)

Whereas SNCC had once embraced a pedagogy of open-ended inquiry, the Panthers applauded explicit, direct instruction in revolutionary analysis. "Black people and other poor and oppressed people must begin to seek an education, a true education that will show them how those in power wage outright war against us," the Party argued. "Our eyes must be opened to the social brutality" (Perlstein 2002, 262). At the high school level, Panther leader Bobby Seale elaborated,

> we will probably teach more about revolutionary principles. At the grammar school level we will . . . teach little Black kids about how to identify not only a White pig, but also a Black pig. . . . We're going to be talking about downing the class system, cultural nationalists and capitalists, both Black and White, who are the same: exploitative. (Peck 2000)

The first liberation school opened in Berkeley, California, on June 25, 1969. There, elementary- and middle-school students were taught to "march to songs that tell of the pigs running amuck and Panthers fighting for the people." Employing a curriculum "designed to . . . guide [youth] in their search for revolutionary truths and principles," the Panthers taught their students "that they are not fighting a race struggle, but, in fact, a class struggle . . . because people of all colors are being exploited by the same pigs all over the world" (Perlstein 2002, 262).

Panther liberation schools spread as the group formed chapters across the United States. While the schools often offered remedial instruction and supplemented formal lessons on ideology with studies of African American and African culture, informal discussions, and field trips, the transmission of political theory and analysis constituted the core of schools (Hopkins 2005, 54).

At the Panthers' San Francisco Liberation School, "everything the children do is political. . . . The children sing revolutionary songs and play revolutionary games." The entire curriculum contributed to students receiving a clear and explicit ideology. Teachers avoided lessons "about a jive president that was said to have freed the slaves, when it's as clear as water that we're still not free." Instead, students learned the origins and history of the Black Panther Party and could "explain racism, capitalism, fascism, cultural nationalism, and socialism. They can also explain the Black Panther Party Platform and Program and the ways to survive" (Perlstein 2002, 262).

In Chicago, a Panther free breakfast program offered an occasion to teach children about the source of their troubles. Akua Njeri (1991) and her fellow activists "explained to the children that we are not the people out there committing a crime. . . . The police are the ones who are committing the crime because they just snatch us up at whim, particularly African men, and beat us up. . . . We let the young brothers and sisters know what the real deal was" (15).

Black children went to school "and learned nothing," Njeri argued, "not because they're stupid, not because they're ignorant. . . . We would say, 'You came from a rich culture. You came from a place where you were kings and queens. You are brilliant children. But this government is fearful of you realizing who you are. This government has placed you in an educational situation that constantly tells you you're stupid and you can't learn and stifles you at every turn'" (15–16). In the Panthers' eyes, the public schools of Northern cities were no different from Jim Crow schools in the segregated South. Activists' use of direct instruction was needed to counter the brutalizing impact of American schools and society.

In 1971, the Panthers built on the liberation school pedagogy with the establishment of an elementary school for the children of Party members. Like the liberation schools, Oakland's Intercommunal Youth Institute sought "to relieve the disabled minds and, subsequently, the disenfranchised lives of this country's poor communities" (Newton n.d.). In addition to providing academic classes, the IYI offered instruction in the ideology of the Party, together with fieldwork "distributing the Black Panther newspaper, talking to other youths in the community, attending court sessions for political prisoners and visiting prisons." Unlike at public schools, an IYI student reported to *Black Panther* readers, "at this school we don't have to salute the flag." Instead, "over here they teach us about what the pigs are doing to us" and about "philosophy, ideology, dialectical materialism, and stuff like that" (Perlstein 2002, 263). Whereas SNCC's preferred image of the freedom schools portrayed teacher and students sitting in a circle, the Panthers portrayed disciplined IYI students sitting in rows or marching in the Panther uniforms.

Community Organizing and
Progressive Pedagogy

Gendered concerns about the brutalizing impact of racism on Black men played a central role in the Panthers' politics and pedagogy. America, Huey Newton charged, treats the Black man as "a thing, a beast, a nonentity." Refusing to "acknowledge him as a man," society reduced him to "a constant state of rage, of shame, of doubt" (Newton 1972, 80–81). Armed self-defense and teacher-centered approaches to education challenged gendered images of Black subservience.[4]

Within a few years of the Party's founding, however, the Panthers' politics and approach to education began to shift. As a brutal government campaign jailed or killed much of the Panthers' male leadership, women, many from relatively privileged backgrounds, played an increasingly prominent role in Party activity (Matthews 1998, 277–78). The Party, as David Hilliard (1993) has put it, became "a split organization," its militant displays of Black manhood degenerating into macho thuggery while its community service programs encouraged grassroots organizing, the "two halves operating in completely separate spheres" (363). Deferring revolutionary aspirations, activists gradually returned to community organizing and rediscovered progressive teaching methods.

The opposing tendencies in Panther activism—a declining capacity to articulate revolutionary demands and a growing capacity to foster grassroots activism—reshaped the Panthers' educational ideas, and a commitment to progressive pedagogy reappeared. "All you have to do is guide [children] in the right direction," explained Panther teacher Val Douglas. "The curriculum is based on true experiences of revolutionaries and everyday people they can relate to. . . . The most important thing is to get the children to work with each other" (Perlstein 2002, 264).

In Intercommunal Youth Institute (IYI) classrooms, student-centered learning steadily supplanted the inculcation of Panther ideology. In language echoing Deweyan pragmatism and the Mississippi freedom schools, the Panthers justified the teaching of "the basic skills—reading, writing, math, science"—by arguing that such study enabled students to "begin to define the phenomena around us and make all phenomena act in a desired manner" (Perlstein 2002, 264–65).

At the IYI, the Panthers encouraged students to "openly criticize all areas" of school activity and allowed them to "make most of the decisions in reference to activities that take place. . . . The purpose for this is to give each one the opportunity to make decisions, to do things for themselves, and to put things into practice." Activists contrasted the IYI, where students were "regarded as people whose ideas and opinions are respected," with public schools, where children who questioned the dominant ideology were "labeled troublemakers" (Perlstein 2002, 264).

For a few years, historian Craig Peck (2000) notes, the IYI mixed "vestiges of prior Panther ideological training" with "progressive educational modes" (19). At the same time that students learned liquid and dry measures by baking brownies, they learned English by writing to political prisoners. The Panthers' mix of progressive and transmissive pedagogies mirrored the ambiguity of their politics. As they swayed between revolution and reform, the Panthers were undecided as to whether the Black community had the capacity to articulate its own demands or had to depend on a vanguard to reveal the truth about its situation. "We know that because the People, and only the People, are the makers of world history, we alone have the ability to struggle and provide the things we need to make us free. And we must . . . pass this on to all those who will survive" (Perlstein 2002, 265).

Whatever the merits of the IYI curriculum, the Panthers' political evolution precluded their maintaining the institute's delicate educational balance. As Craig Peck (2000) argues, the very opening of the IYI reflected a profound shift away from revolutionary aspirations toward toward reformist electoral politics (11). By 1973, the Panthers acquired a new, larger home for the Oakland school and assigned to it a central role in the Party's new focus on local electoral campaigns. In its brief existence, the institution's mission changed from the training of future Panthers to the establishment of a "progressive" school that could model a "humane and rewarding educational program" for poor urban youth (Perlstein 2002, 265).

IYI pedagogy shifted increasingly from the inculcation of revolutionary political theory to open-ended lessons reminiscent of the earlier freedom schools. "The goal of the Intercommunal Youth Institute (IYI)," the Party now explained, was to "teach Black children basic skills necessary to survive in a technological society and to teach children to think in an analytical fashion in order to develop creative solutions to the problems we are faced with" (The Black Panter Party 1973, 4). IYI students, *The Black Panther* now told readers, received "the greater portion of their education through direct experience" (The Black Panter Party 1974, 5). The school used field trips, including ones to the zoo, an apple orchard, Mount Diablo, and the trial of the San Quentin Six, to "teach the children about the world by exposing them to numerous learning experiences." Claimed IYI director Brenda Bay, "the world is [the students'] classroom."

Through "individualized instruction," the school helped children "analyze and interpret their experiences." "We're not here to teach our children WHAT to think," Panther leader Bobby Seale announced at a 1973 school ceremony. "We're here to teach our children HOW to think!" (Perlstein 2002, 265).

In 1974, the IYI was renamed the Oakland Community School (OCS), further distancing it from its revolutionary Panther roots. The OCS offered poor Oakland youth "individual attention in reading, mathematics, writing, and really, an understanding of themselves and the world," new school director Erika Huggins told educator Herb Kohl in a 1974 KPFA radio interview. Whereas, she argued, the public school "does not allow for the individual mind or personality," the OCS was "very concerned about children relating to their environment and to this world as it really is" (The Black Panter Party 1974, 4). In order for them to do so, the school relied on

> practical experience as a basis of our learning experience. That is, if we want to know what makes trees grow, then we won't go to a book about trees or have a science demonstration and just talk about trees. We might have the children go outside to see a tree or trees of various sizes or trees in various stages of development. We would see what makes them grow and what keeps them from growing and thereby try to understand what would be the best way to help a tree grow. (Perlstein 2002, 266)

Students built their vocabularies through "words we use around town" and "at home": library, physician, china, chair. They learned mathematics by going to the store and getting change. In words echoing classic American progressivism, OCS educators argued that through the use of concrete objects to teach arithmetic, "thought and action become one" (2002, 266).

To enable students to "draw their own conclusions," the OCS educator was expected to serve "primarily as a demonstrator and a reference." Teachers, the school's instructor handbook stressed, "do not give opinions in passing on information; instead, facts are shared and information discussed. . . . Conclusions are reached by the children themselves" (Williamson 2000, 11–12).

Echoing the progressive ideal of free personalities freely experiencing their world, OCS promised to treat children as "people who have personalities of their own and experiences of their own" (Perlstein 2002, 266). "In contrast to public school instruction, which consists mainly of memorization and drilling," The Black Panther now maintained, OCS "encourages the children to express themselves freely, to explore, and to question the assumptions of what they are learning, as children are naturally inclined to do." Whereas public school 'discipline' means a set of rules, punishments and rewards that are imposed by teachers and authority figures," Panther education now "emphasize[ed] internal discipline" (Perlstein 2002, 266).

Like the Panther's earlier liberation schools, the OCS reflected activists' egalitarian project of transforming the education and lives of poor Black youth. However, the political analysis underlying the school's pedagogy had shifted. The Panthers' flagship school now sought the expansion of liberal education practices and integration into mainstream American life rather than the abolition of an oppressive social order.

The Abandonment of Activism and the Eclipse of Progressivism

The Panthers' local organizing led to some influence in Oakland politics, but those limited successes could not compensate for the atrophied aspirations they embodied. Activists' embrace of mainstream progressivism therefore proved to be as tenuous as their earlier effort to transmit a revolutionary curriculum. By 1974, the Panthers criticized not only the repressiveness of public schooling but also its failure "to adequately teach English or grammar." At OCS, in contrast, students "recite[d] consonant blends" and studied word endings, diacritical marks, and alphabetization. By 1976, Panther leader Elaine Brown repudiated the OCS's ideological roots. "This is not a Black Panther school, per se," she told *Jet* magazine. "It's not a 'freedom school' or a 'liberation school' in the sense that we teach the children rhetoric." *Jet* supplemented Brown's views with descriptions of younger students learning "basic English —not 'Black English' or 'Ghetto English'"—and older students reading such unobjectionable works as *Animal Farm* and *Jonathan Livingston Seagull* (Lucas 1976; Perlstein 2002, 267).

By the end of the 1970s, Craig Peck notes, OCS "instructor handbooks reveal[ed] a minimal attention to Black and ethnic studies and, importantly, contain[ed] no references to the Black Panthers." Moreover, rote education in basic skills continued to supplant progressive methods of instruction. Whereas IYI language arts classes had once focused on the works of Black authors, teachers were now directed to stress "phonics . . . handwriting . . . and language mechanics." "In this country," the handbook argued, "language barriers have systematically been used to oppress Black and other poor people. . . . The ability to speak and read Standard English is essential" (Peck 2000, 28). Earlier Panthers might have observed that this claim confused the means through which oppression is reproduced with the forces that reproduce it. Gone were hopes of even modest social change and with those hopes went much of OCS's progressivism.

A social sciences unit on California's government suggests how much the Panthers' hopes for political transformation had narrowed. The unit plan called for students to state who "the current governor of California is and what his job entails." Whereas in an earlier era the Panthers articulated the state's role in policing the oppressed, the OCS instructor now evaluated students' ability to state, "The governor's job is to carry out the laws of the state and make life better for people living in the state" (25).

The conventionalism of the OCS curriculum reflected the Panthers' diminished sense of the capacity of Blacks to determine their individual or collective destinies. Instead of "trying to build a model school" or "provide a real education to Black kids," Panther chief Elaine Brown (1992) lamented,

> right now, I think, we're mostly saving a bunch of lives. . . . There's a nine-year-old boy who's been shooting heroin into his mother's veins before school every morning. Three kids from one family came to us with no shoes. . . . One of my own student's back was imprinted with permanent welts from being beaten so much. . . . [Keeping them away from] the snake pits of their neighborhoods . . . and keeping anybody from doing any more damage than has already been done . . . seems to clear the way to teach them . . . skills. (392–94)

OCS never completely abandoned its critique of racial and economic oppression or its progressive practices. "I love freedom, power, and community" one elementary student wrote on a drawing displayed on an OCS bulletin board. Similarly, the 1975 OCS Christmas pageant featured skits of "the upper middle-class and wealthy wallowing in their greed" and "Rudolf the Black Nose Liberator" (Perlstein 2002, 268). Educators employed peer tutoring, individualized instruction, and other progressive techniques. Moreover, just as the legacy of the Black Panthers continued to shape African America long after the Party had withdrawn from the vanguard of movement activism, so too it continued to shape education in what had been the Party's flagship school. Panther cadre were a continual presence at the school, which served a community-building function in Oakland no matter what its pedagogy. Still, as the radical hopes of the late 1960s faded, the school abandoned the idea that students could either make meaning of their world or be instructed so as to understand their oppression.

Conclusion

Although purported concerns about Black youth are central to current American school reform discourse, proposals to increase school choice, close the achievement gap, or equalize funding rarely question what Black youth need to learn. By comparison, movement educators and activists wrestled with fundamental matters. A "degenerating sense of 'nobodiness,'" Martin Luther King Jr. (1985) declared, constitutes the Black child's unique burden (435). "The Black child," veteran educator and civil rights activist Septima Clark echoed, "is different from other children because he has problems that are the product of a social order not of his making or his forebears" (Brown-Nagin 1999, 89). The primary task of African American education, W. E. B. Du Bois (1973) reasoned, was to "make men carpenters" rather than "to make carpenters men" (64). Black children, Harlem educator Merle Stewart echoed, needed education that would "creat[e] men and women out of the 'things' which they now are" (K. King 1971, 57). The freedom and liberation schools exemplified this struggle to recover Black humanity in the face of racism's brutalizing power.

The pedagogical projects of the African American movement for freedom and liberation varied with the evolving concerns of the movement as a whole. SNCC's most significant educational achievement reflected progressive ideals. The Black Panthers' greatest impact in transforming the consciousness of African America—that is, their most significant achievement as an educational agency—occurred in the years when their work was least informed by progressive techniques.

The history of movement schooling demonstrates that no one pedagogy embodies African American culture or inherently serves the cause of social justice. Despite their crucial differences, however, both SNCC and the Panthers confronted a dilemma at the heart of African American schooling and of political life. On the one hand, genuine education requires the active, authentic engagement of the learner. On the other hand, racism profoundly scars Black youth and circumscribes their capacity to know their authentic identities and interests. The pedagogical dilemma of African American education in turn reflects the political dilemma of African American life. How can one make real the democratic promise of self-discovery and self-expression within a system of racial oppression and repression that precludes self-determination? Faced with this dilemma, freedom and liberation schools reflected educational visions that were simultaneously contradictory and complementary.

In the final analysis, however, what distinguishes the movement schools from most of public education is not primarily the techniques they employed. Rather, at issue was whether curriculum and pedagogy would perpetuate racism and other forms of domination or would contribute to their elimination. Both the freedom schools and the liberation schools offered students an alternative to the ideologies of racial supremacy and economic oppression that surrounded them. Both thus conveyed a transcendent sense of possibility, of education that offered Blacks, individually and collectively, new ways of being.

The movement and its schools serve as a reminder that no curriculum project can fundamentally transform learning if it is not part of a process of transforming social relations as well. Any discussion of emancipatory educational methods for disenfranchised students that omits the centrality of social change omits an essential element of the educational process.

Notes

1. An earlier version of this chapter appeared as Daniel Perlstein, "Minds Stayed on Freedom: Politics, Pedagogy, and the African American Freedom Struggle," *American Educational Research Journal* 39 (2002): 249–77. Copyright © 2002 by the American Educational Research Association. Reproduced with permission of the publisher.

2. Within education, pedagogical progressivism and its contemporary descendent, constructivism, generally hold that knowledge is not a body of facts, skills, and interpretations to be transmitted to students but rather is actively constructed by learners as they interact with their environment (Bruner 1996, 19–20).

3. Unlike constructivism, direct instruction assumes the existence of a truth that is independent of the knower. A preset curriculum breaks this knowledge into components, which are presented to children in teacher-centered lessons (Bereiter and Engelmann 1966, 51).

4. The degree to which armed self-defense in part reflected dominant American notions of masculinity suggests the need to take neither nonviolence nor armed self-defense at face value but rather to situate their particular meanings within the movement's broader evolution. Just as armed self-defense is not reducible to masculinist politics, the movement's earlier embrace of nonviolence signified more than a commitment to pacifism. As historian Akinyele Umoja makes clear, nonviolent SNCC organizing in Mississippi often relied on the presence of armed Blacks (2003). Moreover, just as one could imagine a nonviolence that repudiated

American life, one could imagine a form of armed self-defense that sought entry into the American mainstream. Whatever the strategic choices made by activists, calls for nonviolence and armed self-defense reflected the movement's wider ideals and analysis of American life. In the early 1960s, faith in the movement's capacity to win the support of the liberal white public and federal protection of Black rights were central to nonviolent commitments. Later, calls for armed self-defense articulated a radical repudiation of American society. Thus, despite her "exasperation with chauvinism of Black Panther men," Panther leader Elaine Brown remained convinced that "sexism was a secondary problem. Capitalism and racism were primary" (Brown 1992, 357, 367).

Works Cited

Bereiter, Carl, and Siegfried Engelmann. 1966. *Teaching disadvantaged children in the preschool*. Englewood Cliffs, NJ: Prentice-Hall.

The Black Panter Party. 1971, March 27. *Educate to liberate*, 1.

———. 1973, September 15. *Youth institute opens*, 4.

———. 1974, January 5. *Youth institute's environmental studies project an educational Experience*, 5.

———. 1974, February 2. *Youth institute succeeding where public schools failed*, 4.

Bond, Horace Mann. 1935. "The curriculum and the Negro child." *Journal of Negro Education* 4:159–68.

Brown, Elaine. 1992. *A taste of power: A Black woman's story*. New York: Pantheon.

Brown-Nagin, Tomiko. 1999. "The transformation of a social movement into law? The SCLC and NAACP's campaigns for civil rights reconsidered in light of the educational activism of Septima Clark." *Women's History Review* 8:81–138.

Bruner, Jerome. 1996. *The culture of education*. Cambridge, MA: Harvard University Press.

Carmichael, Stokely. 1971. *Stokely speaks*. New York: Random House.

Carson, Clayborne. 1981. *In struggle: SNCC and the Black awakening of the 1960s*. Cambridge, MA: Harvard University Press.

———.1995 Forward to *The Black Panthers speak*, ed. Philip Foner. New York: Da Capo, ix–xviii.

Clark, Septima, with Cynthia Brown. 1986. *Ready from within: Septima Clark and the civil rights movement*. Navarro, CA: Wild Trees Press.

Cobb, Charles. 1996. "Oral history." John Rachal, interviewer. Mississippi Oral History Program. Hattiesburg, MS: University of Southern Mississippi.

———. 1999. "Organizing freedom schools." In *Freedom is a constant struggle: An anthology of the Mississippi civil rights movement*, ed. Susan Erenrich, 134–37. Montgomery, AL: Black Belt Press.

Du Bois, W. E. B. 1973. *The education of black people: Ten critiques, 1906–1960*. New York: Monthly Review.

Freedom School Curriculum—1964. 1991. *Radical Teacher* 40:6–34.

Garrett, James. 1969. "And we own the night: A play of blackness." *Drama Review* 12:61–69.

———. 1998–1999. "Black/Africana/Pan African studies: From radical to reactionary to reform." *Journal of Pan African Studies* 1:153–61.

Guyot, Lawrence. 1996. "Oral history." John Rachal, interviewer. Mississippi Oral History Program. Hattiesburg, MS: University of Southern Mississippi.

Harding, Rachel. 1998. "Biography, democracy, and spirit: An interview with Vincent Harding." *Callaloo*, Summer, 682–98.

Hilliard, David, and Lewis Cole. 1993. *This side of glory: The autobiography of David Hilliard and the story of the Black Panther Party*. Boston: Little, Brown.

Hine, Darlene. 1992. "The black studies movement: Afrocentric-traditionalist-feminist paradigms for the next stage." *Black Scholar* 23: 11–18.

Hopkins, Evans. 2005. *Life after life: A story of rage and redemption*. New York: Simon & Schuster.

Jennings, Regina. 1998. "Why I joined the party: An Africana womanist reflection." In *The Black Panther Party reconsidered*, ed. Charles Jones, 257–66. Baltimore: Black Classic Press.

King, Kenneth. 1971. "Attitudes on school decentralization in New York's three experimental school districts." Doctoral diss., Teachers College, Columbia University.

King, Martin Luther, Jr. 1985. "Letter from Birmingham jail—April 16, 1963." In *Afro-American religious history: A documentary witness*, ed. M. Sernett. Durham, NC: Duke University Press.

Lewis, John. 1998. *Walking with the wind: A memoir of the movement*. New York: Simon & Schuster.

Lucas, B. 1976. "East Oakland ghetto blooms with growth of Black Panther school." *Jet*, Feb. 5.

Matthews, Tracye. 1998. "'No one ever asks what a man's place in the revolution is': Gender and the politics of the Black Panther Party 1966–1971." In *The Black Panther Party reconsidered*, ed. Charles Jones, 267–304. Baltimore: Black Classic Press.

Newton, Huey. 1972. *To die for the people: The writings of Huey P. Newton*. New York: Vintage.

———. 1995. *Revolutionary suicide*. New York: Writers and Readers.

———. 1996. *War against the Panthers: A study of repression in America*. New York: Harlem River Press.

———. n.d. Statement by Huey P. Newton. *Dr. Huey P. Newton Collection*, Series 1, Box 59, Folder 6, Special Collections. Stanford University, Stanford, California.

Njeri, Akua. 1991. *My life with the Black Panther party*. Oakland, CA: Burning Spear Publications.

Orrick, William, Jr. 1969. *Shut it down! A college in crisis, San Francisco State College, October 1968–April 1969*. Washington, DC: National Commission on the Causes and Prevention of Violence.

Pearson, Hugh. 1994. *The shadow of the Panther: Huey Newton and the price of Black power in America*. Reading, MA: Addison-Wesley.

Peck, Craig. 2000. "From guns to grammar: Education and change in the Black Panther Party." Paper presented at the annual meeting of the History of Education Society, Oct. 19–22, in San Antonio, Texas.

Perlstein, Daniel.1990. "Teaching freedom: SNCC and the creation of the Mississippi freedom schools." *History of Education Quarterly* 30:297–324.

———. 2002. "Minds stayed on freedom: Politics, pedagogy, and the African American freedom struggle." *American Educational Research Journal* 39:249–77.

———. 2004. *Justice, justice: School politics and the eclipse of liberalism*. New York: Peter Lang.

Self, Robert. 2006. "The Black Panther party and the long civil rights era." In *In search of the Black Panther Party: New perspectives on a revolutionary movement*, ed. Jama Lazerow and Yohuru Williams, 15–55. Durham, NC: Duke University Press.

Smith, Robert, et al. 1970. *By any means necessary: The revolutionary struggle at San Francisco State*. San Francisco: Jossey-Bass.

Stembridge, Jane. n.d. *Freedom school notes*. Boston: New England Free Press.

Thelwell, Michael. 1969. "Black studies: A political perspective." *Massachusetts Review* 10:701–12.

Umoja, Akinyele. 2003 [1964]. "The beginning of the end of nonviolence in the Mississippi freedom movement." *Radical History Review* 85:201–26.

Williamson, Joy. 2000. "Educate to liberate! SNCC, Panthers, and emancipatory education." Paper presented at the annual meeting of the American Educational Research Association, Apr. 1–5, in New Orleans.

Black Schools, White Schools

8

Derrick Bell, Race, and the Failure of the Integration Ideal in *Brown*

NOEL S. ANDERSON

> *The Negro needs neither segregated schools nor mixed schools. What he needs is education.*

> —W. E. B. DU BOIS[1]

> *At best, the* Brown *precedent did no more than cast a half-light . . . enough to encourage its supporters but not bright enough to reveal just how long and difficult the road to equal educational opportunity would prove to be. Contending with that resistance [to desegregation efforts] made it unlikely that any of those trying to implement* Brown, *including myself, would stop to consider that we might be on the wrong road.*

> —DERRICK BELL[2]

Hypersegregated Nation

BLACK AND WHITE STUDENTS are living under "hypersegregated"[3] conditions, living and learning in virtually two separate Americas, and becoming increasingly isolated from one another. Across the nation, urban communities continue to hold the lion's share of under-resourced, low-performing schools with swelling populations of African American and Latino students, while rapidly growing suburban and exurban school systems continue to be a refuge for white students. Although Blacks within the middle class have become a presence in suburbs since the 1960s, it has not spurned large-scale racial integration within suburban communities either. Blacks tend to reside in Black, inner-ring suburban enclaves, and the schools often reflect this trend (Ascher and Fruchter 2001; Wamba and Ascher 2003).

Numerous factors contribute to the hypersegregation phenomenon. An amalgamation of historical antecedents, such as de jure (legal) and de facto (custom) segregation in housing, education, and employment; discriminatory public policy; and residential settlement in communities throughout the United States have fostered this circumstance. Since the 1940s and 1950s, mass urban migration and immigration changed the racial makeup of large metropolitan centers. Urban neighborhoods that were largely populated with whites (largely white ethnics) at the beginning of the century became increasingly diverse with the arrival of Blacks from Southern states, immigrants from the Caribbean, Latin America, and elsewhere by the post-WWII years.

Simultaneous with urban population growth was the precipitous sprawl of suburbs in the postwar period. Places like Levittown, Long Island, were touted as bastions of the American dream—seemingly safe, accommodating neighborhoods in which to raise families. Simultaneously, discriminatory practices such as redlining[4] by banks, mortgage lenders, and government agencies, including the Federal Housing Association (FHA) in the 1950s and 1960s, obstructed both urban home buying and Black residential settlement in suburban communities (Thabit 2003; Katznelson 2005). Consequently, whites fled to the suburbs in record numbers by the 1960s and 1970s, leaving behind Blacks, and increasingly Latinos, in overcrowded and poor urban communities (Clotfelter 2001).

When the *Brown* decisions were handed down in 1954 and 1955 (*Brown I* in 1954 determined segregated schools illegal and *Brown II*, as it is referred to, in 1955 called for lower courts to address desegregation with "all deliberate speed"), there was an intense, yet relatively brief movement to desegregate schools. In fact, the most aggressive K–12 desegregation movements occurred primarily during the 1960s and 1970s, resulting in some of the most integrated schools being located in the South throughout the 1980s (Friedman 2004, vii). However, a challenging and promising moment for desegregation efforts during the late 1960s and 1970s was quickly dashed. In the aftermath of what is referred to as the *Brown III* case in 1987, state courts began to strike down most school desegregation efforts (Orfield and Lee 2006). By the 1990s, virtually all elementary and secondary schools in the nation remained segregated, particularly in the North, which tended to have de facto segregation in schools. Friedman (2004) notes that "by the mid to late 1990s, Black students became the majority in large urban public school systems: over 90% of the students in public schools in Atlanta, New Orleans, San Antonio, Washington, DC and Richmond were minorities. In Chicago, 90% of public school students were minorities and in New York City the figure was 84%" (vii). Increasingly, Latinos have become the largest minority in schools systems nationwide, relegated to many of the same inferior schools where Black students attend (Anderson 2006). Even during the heyday of desegregation efforts in both the South and North, whites tended to respond by sending their children to private schools in greater numbers or moved out of the city to surrounding suburbs for better performing schools or to avoid districts with high interracial contact.[5] This symbiotic relationship between housing discrimination and educational segregation has created a gestalt of what funk musician George Clinton's song "Chocolate City" cleverly states are "chocolate cities, and vanilla suburbs."[6]

Under the weight of disappointment resulting from what has been referred to as a the new guise of Jim Crow, a small yet significant chorus of civil rights supporters assert that *Brown* was a failure, that it did not accomplish what it was designed to do, to totally abolish racial segregation in schools for good. Further, some maintain that the subsequent resigned acceptance of Black schools and white schools in America undermines the promise of *Brown*, and reinvigorates an antiquated system of racial apartheid in the United States (Kozol 2005; Williams 2006)

But should the hypersegregation in our nation's schools be concluded as a failure of *Brown*? Did we fall back on our laurels after *Brown* and simply miss a great opportunity to live out the "American creed," the vision of an egalitarian, racially integrated society? Or is it more complicated than that? Should *Brown*, as an important legal decision, be assessed in a more nuanced manner? Could it be viewed, simultaneously, as both a success and a failure, especially as it relates to the advancement of Black education?

African American legal scholar and civil rights attorney Derrick Bell posits that the *Brown v. Board of Education* decision was, indeed, successful in striking down the "separate but equal" legal doctrine that legitimized Jim Crow segregation. However, it has been rendered virtually irrelevant as a legal precedent to desegregate public schools around the country. For Bell, the public lament over a perceived "failure" of *Brown* fifty years later, is characteristic of a troublesome internal tension within civil rights discourse and Black educational thought, namely a supposed normative role of *Brown* and the daunting reality of the permanence of racism in the United States. Bell maintains that the racial integrationist idealism that shaped the *Brown* case and subsequent desegregation litigation, and fueled the larger civil rights movement, has run its course, and continues to impede strategies for achieving greater educational equity for Black children in a hypersegregated, post–civil rights era.

Focus of the Chapter

In this chapter, I examine Derrick Bell's legal writings, essays, and literary works to glean what he views as the limitations of the integrationist ideal in Black education. For clarity, I briefly situate Bell's life and work within the larger historical context that shaped the racial integration ideal in the civil rights movement, particularly as a legal strategy in the *Brown* case. Lastly, I conclude with an assessment of the limitations of Bell's formulations, particularly his reluctance to probe the deepening class division in Black communities and in Black education. Fundamentally, I argue that given the pervasive reality of hypersegregated schooling in the United States, Derrick Bell's work provides insight into how the failings of the integration ideal in *Brown* can, in fact, inform new, more creative strategies to advance educational equity and social justice in a post–civil rights era.

Derrick Bell: Critical Legal Scholar

Derrick Bell spent most of his career as a civil rights litigator. A first to integrate University of Pittsburgh Law School, Bell soon followed in the footsteps of civil rights attorneys such as Charles Houston, Robert Carter, and Thurgood Marshall when he worked with the NAACP Legal Defense and Education Fund as a litigator for school desegregation cases. Bell is also recognized for being the first African American professor to gain tenure at Harvard Law School, a position he left some years later after a very public protest against Harvard's resistance to providing tenure to a woman of color.

As a founder of the critical legal studies movement, Derrick Bell's examination of race and law is recognized in legal education circles. Yet Bell's astute insight on the political and social purpose of Black education, as well as his ideas for enhancing the material conditions of Black children in public schools, have been understudied. His writings examining school segregation, for instance, reflect the rigor of legal reasoning and the nuance of literary analysis and hard-hitting social criticism. His body of work, collectively, raises critical questions from simple answers about the legacy of *Brown*, questioning the very premise and underlying assumption of the power of legal decision to bring about social justice and emancipatory possibilities for Blacks within the United States. His ideas are a refreshing departure from staid discourse in the post–civil rights era. Provocatively he advances a thought about what possibly could have been *lost* in the zealous pursuit of an integration ideal. The post–civil rights era has largely been characterized as a glacial and fragmented movement toward full and equal rights. Since the civil rights gains of the 1960s, only portions of the Black population are afforded the chance to vie for opportunities that have historically benefited whites. Alarmingly, the growth in a Black middle class is also coupled with a greater portion of Blacks being under- or unemployed and living in resource-starved conditions in inner cities. This seemingly paradoxical relationship, thus, creates a tension of sorts: what distinguishes those who "make it" to the Black middle class from those who remain poor and are classified as the Black underclass? Bell attempts to grapple with this question as he both theorizes and historicizes the supposed failure of *Brown*, and uses the lens of race to make sense of the current application and rather high expectation of the groundbreaking legal decision in the larger pursuit of Black educational and social progress.

The *Brown v. Board* Case:
A Hallmark of Black Judicial Activism

Derrick Bell, in his early writings, observes that the school desegregation campaign under *Brown* represented, in fact, a hallmark moment in Black judicial activism, that the campaign to end "separate but equal" did not miraculously emerge with the 1954 *Brown v. Board of Topeka* case. In a signature article of the critical legal studies movement, *Serving Two Masters: Integration Ideals and Client Interests in School Desegregation Litigation* (1995), Bell observes that there has been a long line of legal attempts that sought to abolish the "separate but equal" doctrine as it applied to schooling. "Their [*Brown* cases] genesis can be found in the volumes of reported cases stretching back to the mid-nineteenth century, cases in which every conceivable aspect of segregated schools was challenged" (Bell 1995c, 6). As early as 1787, Prince Hall, a Black Revolutionary War veteran, advocated for Black public schools and petitioned the Massachusetts legislature to educate Black children. Through the early 1800s, coalitions of Blacks and liberal whites pushed for better quality and integrated schools in Boston (Bell 2004; Kluger 1975). Even after the Civil War ended in 1865 when "Jim Crow"[7] became the policy of the South, in 1881 (prior to the historic 1896 *Plessy v. Ferguson* Supreme Court decision that established segregation on railway cars), in the face of aggressive litigation, the Kansas Supreme Court departed from many other states by insisting that schools be integrated, arguing that "persons by isolation may become strangers even in their own country and by being strangers, will be of but little benefit either to themselves or to society" (Bell 2004). Even with such radical claims that segregated public schools were inferior, Bell (2004) observes that the response had been met by orders requiring merely facilities be made equal, yet remain racially separate. This nadir of racial segregation remained well into the twentieth century.

As Bell observes, it is useful to view the 1954 *Brown* decision as a tumultuous crescendo of over one hundred years of litigation to change the condition of segregation in the Southern and border states. With an increase in Black lawyers in the first half of the twentieth century, and a great many being trained at Howard University Law School (Black students tended to be barred from attending a great many public and private white law schools), the courts increasingly became an arena of choice to spar over Jim Crow laws, and the vehicle of jurisprudence became essential to advance what was becoming a larger, more visibly organized civil rights movement. Pioneering and courageous Black civil rights attorneys, namely Charles Houston, Constance Baker Motley, Spottswood Robinson, Robert Carter, William Hastie, James Nabrit, and future Supreme Court Justice Thurgood Marshall, became a vanguard for a reinvigorated Black judicial activism through the 1930s and 1940s. Howard Law School became the center of training for many leaders within this vanguard.

As early as 1929, Howard University's visionary president Mordecai Johnson tapped a talented thirty-four-year-old Harvard Law graduate and part-time instructor to transform the law school. In just six years, Charles Houston not only moved a fledgling law school to remarkable prominence but forever situated Howard Law School as a locus of Black judicial training and activism during the civil rights era. By the time the witty and affable Thurgood Marshall arrived, Houston "was Howard Law School," an institution unto himself, initiating a generation of young men into the rigor of legal training and immersing them into the paradox of civil rights law. Historian Richard Kluger, in his comprehensive analysis of the *Brown* cases, titled *Simple Justice*, observes how Houston was quite aware of the paradoxical nature of legal training for Negroes, particularly as it relates to civil rights law. Kluger writes:

> A law school for Negroes was different from a medical school for Negroes, or, say, an engineering school for Negroes. Hearts and lungs and glands worked the same way inside Negroes as in whites. And the principles of thermodynamics or the properties of the hypotenuse did not vary with the

color of man contemplating them. But the laws of the United States did not operate to provide equal justice for whites and blacks, and so it would not do just to learn about them in general and principle. Charles Houston set out to teach young Negroes the difference between what the laws said and meant and how they were applied to Black Americans. His avowed aim was to eliminate that difference. (Kluger 1975, 126)

Houston's indefatigable approach to legal instruction, which demanded of his students a monastic examination of case law, encyclopedic recall of legal principles, and impeccable standards for articulating and advancing a cogent legal argument in his classes, greatly influenced Marshall and his classmates at Howard Law. Houston both inspired and compelled his students to recognize the ways in which laws can paradoxically liberate as well as legitimate inequality for the Negro. He illustrated that laws bestow rights to citizens, but can also be used unjustly to deny rights. He was quite certain that these contradictions in laws could also be employed in the greater pursuit of social justice. Houston and his cohorts held a great deal of trust in the possibilities of law and liberal democracy. Never naïve to the reality that racism serves as an indelible stain on a supposed neutral system of legal jurisprudence, these attorneys were deeply rooted in a Black progressive liberal tradition that, since the Abolitionist periods, attempted to go against the grain to extend the rights and liberties of the U.S. democratic experiment to Black people.

The Black judicial activism flowing from Howard Law School was indeed part of the larger struggle for civil rights during this time period. It was intertwined with other forms of Black activism, viewed as one of many strategies needed to eradicate apartheid in the United States. Cornel West states that Black judicial activism was but a "wave in an ocean of Black resistance to white supremacy" (West 2001). Historian Robin D. G. Kelley in *Yo' Mama's Disfunktional!* (1997) asserts that the civil rights movement attacked the legitimacy and basis for white supremacy on three fronts: (1) the voting booth, (2) public spaces, and (3) public education. The right to vote, which was granted first to free Black males with the adoption of the Civil War amendments in the late 1800s, was summarily denied all Blacks in the states through discriminatory policies and outright intimidation and violence by organizations such as the Ku Klux Klan. The subsequent adoption and enforcement of the Voting Rights Act of 1965 began to change much of this. Further, the *Brown* case challenged public schools by illustrating the hypocrisy of a "separate but equal" ethos and by exposing the empirically flimsy and overtly racist foundation upon which the legal decision of 1896, *Plessy v. Ferguson* (hereafter referred to as *Plessy*) was substantiated. The *Plessy* decision established the provision of "separate but equal" on railway cars, but segregation policies infected all aspects of Southern life. Yet the *Brown* case had far-reaching implications beyond education, raising critical questions about the constitutionality and practicality of segregation of public spaces (i.e., parks, public buildings, and facilities). Ultimately, the *Brown* 1954 decision and the subsequent civil disobedience campaigns throughout the South sparked the adoption of the Civil Rights Act of 1964.

Indeed, the young men of Howard Law School, who would eventually argue the *Brown* case, held to an ideal promoted since the Age of Enlightenment and has characterized the liberal movement in the 1930s and 1940s, that the United States is the most promising (certainly among the youngest) of democracies, with great potential for incorporating the Negro. Essentially, they echoed a belief that America is an ever evolving enterprise that upheld universal equality of man and the acceptance of all individuals.

In his book *Silent Covenants* (2004), Bell states that early in his career he held these same ideals of Houston, Marshall, and others in the civil rights community, believing in the promise of the American democratic experiment. With the *Brown* case, he "believed with an almost religious passion that the Brown decision was the equivalent of the Holy Grail of racial justice" (3). Bell continues, "the Constitution is said to be America's civil religion. If Brown's revised reading of the Constitution were fully enforced in the public schools across the country, it would serve eventually to eliminate racial discrimination in all aspects of life" (3). Like others before him, Bell held fast the transformative potential of *Brown* as a legal racial remedy, a vehicle for extending equal rights to blacks through education. Importantly, this almost singular focus on integration as a legal and political tactic eventually became a civil rights ideal, taking on a life of its own. Racial integration became the unspecified benchmark by which Black social progress could be measured.

The Integration Solution:
The Legal Strategy in *Brown*

Bell's observations about the widely held belief in civil rights circles that *Brown* would help sweep away segregation in all areas of American life was central to the Legal Defense Fund's litigation approach in the historic case. "The goal of the NAACP campaign [to desegregate schools], as early as the 1930s, was a carefully planned one to secure decisions, rulings and public opinion on the broad principle instead of being devoted to merely miscellaneous cases" (Bell 1995c). These strategies, according to Bell, were intended to eliminate racial segregation, not merely in public schools but throughout society. Strategically, the NAACP focused on education because it presented the most absurd, morally reprehensible example of an oxymoronic "separate but equal" doctrine. Who would not be moved, so the prevailing thought went at the time, by the images and stories of maltreated school children learning under inferior situations? Bell argues that the "public schools were chosen because they presented a far more compelling symbol of the evils of segregation and a far more vulnerable target than segregated railway cars, restaurants, or restrooms" (Bell 1995c). The goal was to strike at the legal rationale for an unjust and unethical social arrangement. Hence, innocent children as hapless victims of adult transgressions and institutionalized bias would, in fact, provoke a greater clarion call for legal and social change than concerns of interracial dining or racially integrated travel accommodations.

Since its founding in 1909, the NAACP focused on racial justice concerns and utilized a great many strategies to address issues ranging from lynching to segregation. It even challenged the Supreme Court as early as 1917 to overturn residential segregation laws that emerged in Baltimore in 1910 and proliferated throughout the South thereafter (Kluger 1975). In 1939, when Thurgood Marshall took over the education desegregation campaign from Houston to become the leader of the newly established NAACP Legal Defense Fund (LDF), he continued the charge to challenge the "separate but equal" doctrine. Much of the civil rights litigation focusing on education during the 1930s and 1940s centered on pay equity concerns, fighting to ensure that Black teachers were getting paid the same wages as white teachers, as well as equal funding for segregated schools. Over time, Houston, Marshall, and the cohort of lawyers at LDF expanded their focus to higher education, centering their legal strategies on desegregating graduate and professional schools in the contentious states that upheld Jim Crow policies. Pivotal cases were won, resulting in the desegregation of graduate and professional schools in Missouri, and some Southern states.[8]

Hence, the *Brown* case is analogous to a tributary emerging from a larger river of lawsuits and court decisions regarding K–12 and higher education.[9] A potent force feeding the river was social science research, which will be discussed in greater detail later in this chapter. The position of the LDF was that segregated schools by their very nature and design were not and could not be equal. The argument was that Blacks were subordinated

to a second-class status under Jim Crow (denied even the right to deliberate or vote on whether they want or support the social arrangement of Jim
Crow) and that segregation coupled with a lack of Black political, social,
and economic power led undeniably to inferior schools (e.g., limited number of teachers, inadequate school facilities, scarce resources) (Anderson
and Byrne 2004; Payne 2004). For the LDF, the subordination of Blacks
in the South made it, a priori, impossible for Blacks to exercise their Constitutional rights and immunities as "equal citizens" in the United States.
Waldo Martin maintains that the LDF's stance was consistent with a long
line of integrationist stances. He states:

> The overriding objective of the NAACP lawyers' strategy was a gradual-
> ist approach of destroying over time the separate but equal fiction of Jim
> Crow by making its practice financially impossible as well as unlawful, to
> render Jim Crow unworkable by demanding that the separate worlds of
> Southern Blacks be made truly equal in every respect to that of Southern
> whites. (Friedman 2004)

Kluger (1975) observes that the lawyers at the LDF took a concerted
stance to shift their tactics from equalization cases, which they deemed too
long and arduous a process to argue state by state, court by court, toward
the total abolition of *Plessy*. It is useful here to point out that the LDF's
goal in *Brown* was not to argue, head on, the constitutionality of separate
but equal but to challenge the legality as it was applied throughout the
Southern states. One major component of the argument was that *Plessy*,
which established segregation on railway cars, did not and should never
apply to education. And, thus, by branching *Plessy* into schooling, a severe
and egregious misapplication of the statute resulted, limiting the rights and
legal protections of school children. This line of argument was simply one
approach to larger goal of eradicating separate but equal. In fact, Thurgood
Marshall likened "separate but equal" to the Southern Black Codes established during Reconstruction, the infamous predecessors to Jim Crow laws
(Amar 2005). With this stance, Marshall reasoned that by demonstrating
that separate but equal was not practiced legally in contentious states (not
only in the application of *Plessy* to public education but evident by the
inferior conditions of Black schools) and based on the mounting weight
of legal precedents in higher education cases, then the constitutionality of
Plessy as a doctrine would have to be reassessed, if not overturned. Yet
to demonstrate that separate but equal was not practiced legally in K–12
education throughout the Southern states would require: (1) evidence that
segregated schools were a violation of the equal protection clause under

the 14th amendment by not having separate and truly equal schools; (2) since Black children were somehow denied equal protection in segregated schools, they were injured or severely disadvantaged in someway under current segregated school conditions; and (3) require a series of representative cases from around the country that would illustrate the widespread injury. In sum, the LDF endeavored to show that there were egregious and observable violations of the "equal protection" clause of the 14th amendment for Black students in Southern states.

The NAACP and the LDF rejection of the longstanding strategy to concentrate on equalization of segregated public school facilities as a remedy was replaced by a zealous goal to desegregate all Jim Crow schools. Integrated schools became viewed as the only viable solution that Black children would receive the needed resources and quality education they deserved. Integrated schools, ipso facto, assured that Black students would receive the resources (i.e., books, supplies, and well-maintained facilities). The financial dimension of the *Brown* case should not be dismissed. Integrating schools after decades of uneven success in equalization cases served a pragmatic function as well. Yet, in time, integrating schools made the idea of an egalitarian education a more reachable goal. More importantly, the ultimate *end* was not simply racially integrated schools but an integrated society. Black and white students learning together, the reasoning went, would certainly begin erasing the demarcated racial lines that persisted in all other areas of society. This concept of full integration was not some display of utopian naiveté by those in the movement. Activists involved in the civil rights struggle were well aware of the arduous journey, the possible resistance, and the outright danger to this approach. The lynching tree as the ultimate arbiter of white justice had long been rooted in Black social memory and the use of violence to those advocating integration and social equality for Blacks had up to that time been inextricably woven into the fabric of American life. Nevertheless, an integration ideal as both a deeply democratic and moral as well as pragmatic endeavor fueled the goals and strategies of the LDF in the *Brown* case, and continued to shape the larger direction of the civil rights struggle.

"Sociological Jurisprudence": Social Science, Integration, and the *Brown* Case

As I highlight earlier, social science became a major factor in the formation of the argument in the *Brown* case. Specifically, race as a topic of study within social science was gaining wider recognition by the time the *Brown* case was being designed, and provided the basis not only for illuminating the deplorable conditions in Black schools but to also confirm that these unequal conditions negatively impacted the development and social advancement of Black children. The use of race in social science to fuel civil rights and social policy agendas was not new, however. W. E. B. Du Bois's path-breaking research examining Black communities in Philadelphia in the late 1890s pioneered the use of race in empirical studies. Devising a conceptual lens of race and political economy, Du Bois observed that Philadelphia Negroes were poor based on restricted access and racial discrimination in the urban industrial economy. He convincingly argued that the discriminatory practices visited upon Negroes were not arbitrary but "built into the everyday operations of the economy" (O'Connor 2001). *The Philadelphia Negro* not only distinguished Du Bois as an early scholar of empirical studies and forerunner of modern sociology, but the work informed generations of the value of using race as a variable in social science inquiry, to better understand the conditions of the Negro in modernity.

By the 1930s and 1940s, sociologist E. Franklin Frazier, as well as historians Rayford Logan and John Hope Franklin, political scientist Ralph Bunche, and economist Abram Harris, were a noted group of distinguished scholars at Howard whose research on the condition of the Negro was informed by Du Bois's earlier work. Baker (1998) points out, "Howard emerged as an important center for the study of the Negro during the New Deal era. During this period, Howard's faculty advanced a multidisciplinary discourse on race relations that demonstrated how economic and environmental processes prevented most Negroes from fully assimilating a 'legitimate culture'" (18). Yet unlike Du Bois, who acknowledged a distinct African influenced Black culture, Howard sociologists such as Frazier stressed the notion that Blacks needed to assimilate a legitimate culture that mirrored white society and this assertion became a key feature of the analysis and justification for integration. Emanating from the work of sociologists at the University of Chicago in the 1930s, and eventually supported by Frazier and others at Howard, was the formulation that Blacks have not fully evolved as a culture in the American context. Robert Park, a key member of the Chicago School (and one of Frazier's professors) and an early proponent of this theory, designed a cultural assimilation model that "posited that African Americans go through four phases of social evolution: competition, conflict, accommodation and finally assimilation" (Baker 1998). In this exhaustive schema, he theorizes that under the current segregated and discriminatory conditions, African Americans were being foreclosed from assimilating, to the detriment of the race and the larger cohesion of the United States (Park and Burgess 1967). Park's empirical works saturated the Howard circle and affirmed and bolstered its position on assimilation. This model also underpinned Myrdal's groundbreaking volumes *An American Dilemma* (1944), and also became the basis for the legal strategy later used in *Brown*.[10]

The "Dilemma" of Racial Segregation and the Integration Solution

An American Dilemma became the compass directing arguments on the socioeconomic injury of Blacks in the United States since slavery. It represented a scathing critique of race in the American context. Author and Swedish economist Gunnar Myrdal compiled research from various scholars and essentially re-presents the argument that Blacks, as a race, have been systemically marginalized from the American mainstream.

He discards antiquated notions of Black physical and mental inferiority, which was the charge of previous works of social science that shaped public policy[11] to argue, empirically, that the subjugation of Blacks is the product of slavery, racism, and systemic discrimination; and that this marginalization of Blacks posed a serious "dilemma" for America. He builds on the idea Frazier asserted some years earlier that Blacks have the potential to establish a legitimate culture just as whites have. It is important to distinguish here, however, that Frazier and eventually Myrdal made class distinctions in their works, noting the variation in the assimilation of culture between the Black middle class and the Black poor. For instance, E. Franklin Frazier in his text the *Black Bourgoisie* (1965), levies criticisms about the consumptive behaviors and accommodating predilections of the Black middle class. Yet, he fundamentally reinforces an underlying assumption that educated middle-class Blacks have come closer to fully assimilating into the American social mainstream than lower-class Blacks. The unassimilated populations of poor Blacks, Frazier asserts, in the black belt South and particularly in the urban North, were viewed as endemic of a larger pathology in the Black community, and, subsequently, this culture of pathology among poor Blacks came to characterize the "Negro problem" in America. Pathologies, Frazier argues, were reflected in high illiteracy rates, high crime, "matriarchal families," and high unemployment. But the belief was that these pathologies would diminish as opportunities for advancement and assimilation opened for Blacks.

O'Connor (2001) reasons that this assumption of the "Negro problem" as a cultural pathology among unassimilated Blacks in research and literature became a source of what remains an enduring and divisive debate" (100). Disturbingly, the supposed cultural divide between whites and Blacks formulated in social science research not only bolstered the rationale for eradicating legal barriers under *Brown* but led to the codification of the "Negro problem" as a quintessentially "poor Black" problem. As a consequence, this notion would remain an undercurrent of civil rights and Black social movements as well as continue to fuel social policy debates regarding the "urban underclass" and the "culture of poverty" many decades after the *Brown* decision.[12]

Although Myrdal's ideas fundamentally reinforced what Frazier and other Black scholars had advanced, *An American Dilemma* appealed to white audiences at the time. The attraction of the work is that Myrdal situates the racial dilemma in the preferences and prejudices of whites rather than in the economic and social structures that reinforce racism. His hard-hitting assertions and data illustrating the existence of an increasingly alienated black America are fundamentally softened by rhetorical pronouncements for better race relations that promote the common good and the American creed.

Further, Myrdal's work tapped into the postwar concerns about racial strife and the potential for communism to spread in Black communities, particularly in the Southern states. Derrick Bell reinforces the sentiment that the anti-communist fear pervasive in the United States during the Cold War period may have weighed a greater influence on the Warren Supreme Court than moral sympathies about the racial isolation and exclusion of Blacks from the social mainstream. He states that during the Cold War period after WWII, "the continuation of segregation posed a contradiction for self-proclaimed exemplar of freedom. American policy was geared to fighting communism abroad and subversive activities at home" (Bell 2004, 62).

When developing the *Brown* campaign, the LDF could not rely solely on legal precedent to win cases, given the past difficulty in proving injury under separate but equal conditions. Therefore the attorneys decided to employ their own "form of sociological jurisprudence by adopting the most authoritative science available: it presented *An American Dilemma* as Exhibit A" (Baker 1998). Initially Marshall and some within the legal team were skeptical of using any type of social science in the case, viewing it as "soft science" compared to the physical sciences. Yet LDF attorney Robert Carter was notably a proponent of using Myrdal's work, and was persuasive in convincing the LDF to incorporate Kenneth and Mamie Clark's controversial doll tests.[13] Carter expressed that the social science testimony and briefs were at the "heart of our case" in Brown (Carter and Franklin 2005). Kenneth Clark (1988) observed some years later in his work, *Prejudice and Your Child*, that "since they [LDF lawyers] could not demonstrate that racial segregation inflicted concrete, overt physical damage upon these children, they had to find evidence of psychological damage—that is, injuries to personality, the self esteem of these rejected children" (xx)

With the support of social science, the LDF attorneys endeavored to prove that Jim Crow was, by design, un-American, that Black children were injured by learning under unequal and segregated conditions, and that assimilation would pave the way to a uniform American value system and ensure full equality for all races. Indeed, social science, particularly direct references to Myrdal's findings in *An American Dilemma* and Clark's extensive work with Black children, would subsequently inform Chief Justice Warren's majority opinion in favor of desegregation in the *Brown* case.[14] Consequently, integration and assimilation became not only a legal goal but viewed as a necessity for the well-being and longevity of the Black populous. A social ideal for the mainstream civil rights movement, integration became the "crown jewel of the Civil Rights agenda" (Hill Collins 2006).

On the Wrong Road: Derrick Bell's Critique of the Integrationist Ideal

As a practicing civil rights attorney with LDF in the 1960s and 1970s, Derrick Bell handled the lion's share of school desegregation cases in the South. His work with clients as well as the mounting resistance he encountered within Southern courts to integrate schools led to a healthy skepticism of the potential of an integrationist idealism and more importantly an uneasiness with the concordant legal strategies emanating from the *Brown* decision. Bell states the LDF's unwavering approach to addressing school integration and other racial remedies became increasingly out of step with his clients interests in cases. In *Serving Two Masters* (1995) Bell observes that the social and political realities of Black people have shifted greatly since *Brown*, evident by the "increasing segregation at local and national levels and the waning support in the federal courts for desegregation initiatives" (5), rendering school integration an unrealistic goal and unreasonable benchmark for measuring Black educational improvement.

Citing cases in Boston, Detroit, and Atlanta, Bell states that

> where racial balance is not feasible because of population concentrations, political boundaries, or even educational considerations, there is adequate

legal precedent for court-ordered remedies that emphasize educational improvement rather than racial balance. For civil rights groups, racially balanced schools seem to have become a symbol of the nation's commitment to equal opportunity, not only in education but housing, employment and other fields. However, simply placing Black children in "white" schools will seldom suffice. Lawyers in school cases who fail to obtain judicial relief that reasonably promises to improve the education of Black children serve poorly both their clients and their cause. (Bell 1995c, 18)

Yet this focus on school integration continues to foreclose more pragmatic, albeit more complex solutions to improve the quality of education for Black children. He asserts that, in fact, "desegregation rather than improvement of education has become the moniker of civil rights" (Bell 1995c). Interestingly, civil rights groups tended to read the continued resistance to school integration by the courts and various communities as further evidence that this strategy is morally and legally just, on the right road, so to speak, to rupturing all forms of segregation.

In one of his exchanges with his fictional legal heroine, Geneva Crenshaw, in *And We Are Not Saved* (1987), Bell states: "the resistance to desegregation was so fierce and came from so many directions that any progress we [civil rights attorneys] made in overcoming it was simply accepted as a victory without much thought of how we prevailed. . . . We knew that we were right, that God was on our side" (108). He elaborates that "civil rights lawyers dismiss the new obstacles as legally irrelevant. Having achieved so much by courageous persistence, they have not wavered in their determination to implement *Brown* using racial balance measures developed in the hard-fought legal battles of the last two decades" (5). However, Bell maintains that this mounting resistance to and the subsequent reversals of desegregation remedies cloud the pressing needs and concerns of clients attending school under hypersegregated and inadequate educational conditions. For Bell, this integrationist ideal which continues to fuel desegregation legal strategies is deeply flawed and elusive on a practical level.

Interest Convergence and the Integrationist Ideal of *Brown*

As a critical legal theorist, Bell is primarily concerned with both revealing and challenging the orthodoxy of legal education and jurisprudence, and, most importantly, the racialized assumptions that underlie law. The notion that law is objective, value free, and neutral in its design and its application to real-world problems, particularly as it pertains to race, is continuously interrogated by Bell and others in the critical theory movement. For critical legal theorists, the veneer of fair-minded reasoning that shapes legal precedent as well as the supposed detached approach in legal training is shot through with race-, class-, and gender-based assumptions. Assumptions about white social privilege and the social value of Black life are deeply rooted in our nation's history and continue to mediate our daily social interactions. Bell, as one of the founders of the critical legal studies (CLS) movement, is unwavering in his analysis highlighting the permanence of race in America; how race, for instance, shapes much of constitutional law. Hence, when assessing the theoretical assumptions underlying *Brown*, he trains a critical eye on the foundational belief in civil rights discourse that racial equality is achievable through integration. He elaborates on this stance by questioning the notion that racially integrated schools represent evidence of racial equality and that, most importantly, equal educational opportunity for Black children can be adequately judged or measured by the level of integration in schools.

In order to raise these critical questions, Bell tends to employ literary theory, allegorical tales, and fictional alter egos, such as Geneva Crenshaw, a fearless civil rights attorney, to cause ruptures in widely held assumptions and perceptions about the normative role of civil rights laws and racial remedies. For instance, in *And We Are Not Saved* he weaves a myth of Black school children disappearing from a Southern town on the eve of the implementation of a court ordered desegregation plan. It is revealed in the conclusion that although Black students represented over half of the school going population in this fictional, racially segregated town, their vanishing does not alter the function of the town's school system. In fact, in anticipation of having to comply with the school desegregation mandates, white school officials prepared contingencies such as reallocating money to continue to uphold the social and educational benefits for whites. Neither does a proposed desegregation order, nor the absence of Black children from this town, impact the education of white students. This thought-provoking tale underscores Bell's skepticism about the viability of engineered racial remedies, such as court ordered desegregation plans, to bridge the entrenched racial divisions in the United States. The power to both create and ultimately execute a contingency plan by white officials, for Bell, is an allusion to the tenuous nature of racial plans that go against the entrenched interests of a white majority population. More importantly, in this tale, Bell unsettles a prevailing notion among a number of civil rights groups that the presence of white students where there are Black children is ipso facto evidence of "equal educational opportunity." This, for Bell, is spurious logic. He asserts, emphatically, that "there is no evidence that Blacks simply studying with whites have faired better educationally" (Bell 1995c). The widespread belief that school integration guarantees that Black students will receive the same education as whites is based on leaps of logic and speculation.

Importantly, Bell does not negate the idea that there may perhaps be some value in children of different races learning together. Moreover, his critique should not be misconstrued as promotion of a separatist or an orthodox Black nationalist standpoint. Bell still adheres to a liberal tradition, advocating reconciliation and comprise to political and social conflict. He maintains a belief that agitation of institutions and revealing forms of injustice by institutions can alleviate suffering of groups in the short term.

For certain, however, Bell shakes loose the long-held ideals that appear foundational in *Brown* that racial, even educational equality is achievable, through the social integration of whites and Blacks. To further counter this widely held view of the supposed failure of *Brown*, Bell theorizes that racial remedies tend to satisfy Black integrationist ideals (e.g., social integration in schools) only temporarily, due to what he terms an "interest convergence" with white society. Specifically, Bell's interest convergence theory holds that Black rights are recognized and protected when and only so long as policymakers perceive that such advances will further interests that are their primary concern (Bell 2004). He reasons that because of the permanence of racism in the United States and based on the ignominious legacy of chattel slavery, racial discrimination, and racial isolation, Black interests will always be negotiable, be open to reevaluation, and, in numerous cases, be rejected by whites.

Therefore, under the interest convergence theory any legal or political victories that promote Black interests and freedom must compliment the political will and interests of the majority white population. Black rights and interests, in order to have some longevity, must converge with or advance, not curtail in any significant way, white privileges. For Bell, the interest convergence formulation is inextricably linked to traditional liberal notions of "compromise" and "consensus" in matters relating to government and public affairs. Yet he departs somewhat from this stance and holds that all racial remedies, no matter how popular at a given point in history, are, in fact, expendable. Ostensibly, racial "compromise" and "consensus," for Bell, is a façade. Hence the idea and level to which social integration initiatives take place among Blacks and whites (i.e., the aftermath of *Brown*) is based on whether whites, because of their power as a majority, benefit in the long run or, more importantly, do not perceive to be losing rights and/or privileges in the racial enterprise.

Bell reinforces the existence of the interest convergence theory by historicizing it. In *Silent Covenants* (2004), he examines key events in U.S. history, dating back to the Emancipation Proclamation and the Civil War, when Blacks were granted rights and privileges (or not) by whites based on a convergence with the greater needs of the white majority and, by extension, American society. He states that these convergences materialize in the guise of "covenants," which are usually unwritten in this circumstance, most often unspoken agreements within society. Bell reasons that the silent agreements or silent covenants regarding race are fortuitous and can take on two forms: (1) an interest convergence covenant or (2) a racial sacrifice covenant. An interest convergence covenant is when a particular law or policy that overtly grants Black rights and interests by design supports or advances the interest of whites. In contrast, a racial sacrifice covenant is when Black rights and interests are jettisoned in order to resolve disputes between whites over a particular policy or law. Bell observes that these racial covenants, however fragile, comprise much of America's racial history.

Bell illuminates how both an interest convergence covenant and racial sacrifice covenant operate in the historic *Brown* cases. He argues that the decision to tackle the legal justification of school segregation was aligned with the larger goals of postwar America. An interest convergence covenant materialized when, as stated earlier, there was growing concern among President Truman and the U.S. government about the potential spread of communism in the Cold War period and greater focus on Black isolation and the potential for social unrest in the South. Communist fears led to questions of national security. Bell reasons that Truman and his administration were overly concerned that Blacks languishing under Jim Crow segregation would be a breeding ground for communist infiltration, that there would be growing Black resentment about freedoms and victories garnered abroad in WWII, and elusive equality in America. Bell states emphatically that this interest convergence covenant to extend rights to Blacks to maintain peace at home was reinforced by a liberal Warren Supreme Court. For Bell, *Brown* was also an anticommunist decision.[15]

However, the racial sacrifice covenant can also be observed, specifically, in the 1955 *Brown II*, "all deliberate speed" decision when the same court, fearing great resistance to desegregation efforts from the South and questions of court violations of states' rights under federalism, left it to the lower courts to design and implement desegregation efforts. As a result of this Supreme Court policy, lower courts were not given specific directives or timelines, or monitored to comply with the *Brown* decision. Subsequently, the desegregation of schools dragged on into the 1970s, resulting in some school districts closing down schools altogether, as in Prince Williams County, Virginia, to avoid school integration. Legitimated through legal rules, in this case, a racial sacrifice covenant occurred based on anticipated white resistance to the original *Brown* decision, resulting in the slow efforts to desegregate schools by the lower courts, for instance.

Bell maintains that both an interest convergence covenant and racial sacrifice covenant emerged in *Brown* to simply address the egregious issue of poor, undereducated Black school children and to not, necessarily address larger concerns of racial discrimination, and, more importantly, social integration. This is highlighted, Bell observes, by the fact that the very same court the following year after the *Brown* decision refused to even hear a case[16] that would challenge the Alabama law[17] barring marriage between Blacks and whites (see also Weinberger 1957, 437). Hence the notion that *Brown* would be the vehicle for social integration was met with the reality of racial fortuity in policy making.

Bell maintains that since *Brown*, desegregation efforts have faltered given the resistance by whites to desegregation, and support from the federal courts has waned with the disproportionate growth of Black populations in urban areas. Bell argues that civil rights lawyers, post-*Brown*, are out of step with this reality, to the detriment of their clients whose educational interests may no longer accord with the integration ideals of their attorneys. Unconditional integration appears irrelevant to the current conditions and dynamics within communities. Bell argues that traditional civil rights lawyers have viewed *Brown* as a moniker for desegregation and not education. Despite the reversal in desegregation efforts nationally, racially "balanced" schools are still held up as the epitome of social justice. Unfortunately, this somewhat romantic view of integration, for Bell, will continue to support antique and ineffective strategies to improve Black education.

Bell, the "Politics of Protest," and Limits of "Racial Reasoning"

As a civil rights "insider," someone who has been a part of the LDF and argued popular desegregation cases, Bell adds both a refreshing and nuanced look at the *Brown* issue, and the current state of Black public education. However, there are some limitations to his racial reasoning. Bell's critique of *Brown* and the integration ideal still leaves one with the question: If

Brown did not live up to its ideal, how do we then address the needs of Black children being educated in poor schools around the country? If we resign ourselves to the permanence of racism in the United States, what incentives do we have for agency, for transformation?

Bell reasons that Black resistance to historical injustices, in and of itself, is a useful, existential stance. He argues for Blacks fighting against and in spite of the permanence of racism, to adopt a *racial realism* that acknowledges the permanence of racism yet energizes folks to agitate institutions to alleviate suffering and despair. Racial realism for Bell is a philosophy that is influenced by scholars from the Legal Realist camp.[18] Legal Realists argue that laws are not neutral, value-free entities, but are inextricably linked to our conventional social norms or rather, reflect what we believe we ought to value as a society. These beliefs render laws a creation of social, moral, and political processes, not scientific, immutable, or infallible reasoning.

As a response, Bell calls for a type of "racial fortuity," or a more apt term may be, "protest politics" to respond to racial injustice. He posits that protest politics entails a realistic understanding of the permanence of racism in the United States coupled with a vigorous and informed resistance to injustice. Using the civil rights movement as a model, a protest politics incorporates direct action against institutions that limit rights and the interests of Black citizens, and a gradualist approach to expanding rights through institutions. For Bell, protest is an unapologetic way to create spaces for change. Further, it is an all encompassing term. He seems to collapse all versions and strategies under this broad umbrella. For instance, when assessing the power of sit-ins as a form of protest during the civil rights movement, he states,

> sit-ins taught us that a great many whites would not maintain discriminatory policies if the cost was too high. Employing tactics based on this knowledge will lift the sights, providing a bird's eye view of discriminatory situations and how best to address them . . . from this broadened perspective, [*sic*] we can recognize, understand, and thus be better able to cope with the various stages of racial subordination. (Bell 2004, 190)

Other than using this example of protest and information gathering that comprises the stages of nonviolent resistance Martin Luther King Jr. advocated in "Letter from Birmingham Jail" (1986). Bell is not exactly clear what this contemporary protest politics would look like.

He calls for holding institutions accountable for causing Black suffering as well as utilizing these same institutions to alleviate conditions. He also reveals his ambivalence about this enterprise when speaking of the courts to correct injustice. He states, "while the law functions as a tool of the dominating class, it must function so as to induce the dominant and dominated classes to accept the hierarchy . . . the very process of realizing a gain sought through the courts ultimately serves to deepen the legitimacy of the system" (Bell 2004, 188). He is seemingly calling for a historical "inside-outside" approach to making change in the United States, agitating institutions through visible protests and defiance campaigns as well as working within existing structures to make gradual social and political changes. Hence, Bell holds a traditional liberal stance in this regard, pushing, like others have before him, to extend rights to Blacks in all areas of American life. He is quite clear that racial reasoning should not curtail resistance.

However, he is also less forthcoming in his writings about the large class gulf in Black America that tends to stymie conversations about the supposed causes of Black underachievement and precludes useful strategies for collective action. For instance, a great number of prominent Black leaders within the middle class (and wealthy class) have subscribed to a "culture of poverty" analysis, and have publicly castigated poor Blacks for underachieving and, thus, failing *Brown*.[19] Invoking historic pleas for black self-help, these pundits have reframed the conversation away from structural inequalities to the behaviors of inner city dwellers. In fact, as I highlighted earlier, this growing Black class divide becomes prominent during the *Brown* case, illuminated by the burgeoning social science research at the time, and is still present today. Currently, Black academic underachievement and poor school performance are viewed, primarily, as quarantined to the inner city, and classified as just some of the many pathological conditions that plague ghetto communities. The rhetoric promoted is that whereas the Black middle class, throughout history, has embraced schooling as a value and as a vehicle for social and economic mobility, poor Blacks have turned away from literacy and educational advancement. Therefore, drastic and systemic changes in the behavior and culture of inner city Blacks, not simply structures, pundits argue, will go farther to advance this population. Indeed, if protest politics are still possible to address racism in the schooling of Black children, an interrogation of the class divide not only in America but particularly in Black America is greatly warranted.

On the issue of schooling, Bell is more reliant on existing models to advance the education of Black children. A politics of protest in education, for Bell, is one where there is a greater push for Black schools with curriculum and teaching centered on supporting excellence and positive racial identity. He situates contemporary Black schools within the long history of black communities developing and revering their own educational institutions. He observes that under Jim Crow, Black schools were resource starved and substandard compared to white schools. Yet there were also rich examples of Black teachers supporting and nurturing excellence among black children, encouraging literacy and numeracy for collective advancement in Black communities. He highlights recent examples of charter and independent schools that are centered in Black communities that promote learning as well as nurture the self-esteem of Black children. In reality, these innovations, however, will never satisfy the sheer demand for public education by the growing population of youth in Black communities. Yet for Bell, this is a positive development in the face of segregated realities, and something that needs to be expanded.

A most important feature of Bell's work is his examination of school finance as part of a new civil rights agenda. He asserts that the frontier in Black education centers on financial equity not school integration. He states,

> for years, advocates assumed that integration, on its own, would improve the educational prospects of Black children, but time proved that the persistent educational gap between Black and white students was only indirectly traceable to segregation. Instead, the root of the problem appeared to be the substantial disparities in the resources provided to Black students relative to white students. (Bell 2004, 160)

Bell observes that civil rights advocates realized that they now needed to concentrate on "desegregating the money" (161). He subsequently looks to decades of school finance litigation in places such as California and New York, for instance, as clarion examples of the push for greater resources in a hypersegregated climate. These, he argues, will help foster more effective schools for Black children, not simply an attempt to integrate classrooms.

Examined closely, the historic school desegregation struggles are as emblematic of conflict and competition over resources as they are about the quest for racial justice through education. During Jim Crow, white communities rebelled against attempts to share or redistribute financial resources, to create parity in educational budgets for Black and white school systems (Kluger 1975). Fast forward decades and many states and localities today continue to reject such things as equalization plans that require, for instance, the spreading of the uneven tax revenues across Black and white school districts such as the "Robin Hood" program in Texas.[20] In sum, concerns with school desegregation center on the mixing of money as well as about the mixing of races. Allocating the proper funding for Black or integrated schools has always been a contentious issue in the United States.

The realities of housing segregation coupled with increased standards and high-stakes testing in urban school systems around the country require more effective approaches to distributing financial resources to public education. Antiquated school finance formulas and policies need to be jettisoned for more appropriate fiscal arrangements that take into consideration demographic shifts, funding disparities between suburban and urban schools, and the needs of specific communities. Even in the face of growing white resistance to funding equity initiatives and legal cases across the country, Bell asserts that pushing for better and more resources will have a greater impact in the long run for the urban schools and the education of Black children.

Conclusion

In his writings, Derrick Bell provides a thought-provoking view on the *Brown v. Board* decision and the subsequent challenges with school desegregation in the post–civil rights era. He views the public lament over the supposed failure of *Brown* as centering more on the failure of an ideal than the actual Supreme Court decision. In fact, *Brown* did accomplish its goal, to strike down the "separate but equal" doctrine. Further, the decision had far-reaching implications beyond Black education, impacting the education of various discriminated groups in the United States. For Bell, the normative role of *Brown*, which was to fully integrate racial groups, has not been achieved.

The hypersegregation of black and white school children is caused by greater forces than the supposed failure of the 1954 Supreme court decision. It is fueled by a historical legacy of white supremacy and as Bell argues, "silent covenants" within white America that tend to go undiscovered and unchallenged. Yet in the twenty-first century, the issue is no longer simply Black and white. The increase in the immigration of other groups from around the world has complicated the simplistic Black/white binary. In segregated urban schools as well as in Southern communities, for instance, immigrants from the Spanish speaking countries are now learning alongside African and Black Caribbean students, young people whose parents may not have been in the country when *Brown* was handed down. Some may not even be aware of this historical case and its significance to public education.

This necessitates our rethinking who is included in the vague assertion of "Black education." As our nation grows more diverse, culturally and linguistically, Black education has become an even more complex term. Yet with this diversity is also the constant nagging reminder of the class inequalities in America. The relegation of poor young people to urban schools while the middle to wealthy classes have greater options and better quality schools will not go away anytime soon. More importantly, the growing number of young people, Black and white, who are born into households with an abundance of resources beyond human need, in fact, sheds light on the lack of educational freedom experienced by young people growing up in poverty. Class divisions, in fact, exacerbate the educational divide among and within groups. The new challenge is not simply integrated classrooms but establishing integrated public policies, integrated financial and educational resources, and integrated civic interests that support and enhance public education as a primary service in communities.

Notes

1. Du Bois (1935, 385).
2. Bell (2004, 19).
3. Hypersegregation is a termed used by scholars to capture the exacerbated spatial separation of people along racial, ethnic, and class lines in society.
4. Redlining is a practice whereas banks and mortgage lenders would draw red lines on neighborhood maps to indicate undesirable areas that would not be funded by those institutions. Those redlined areas tended to be populated by poor Blacks and people of color.
5. Orfield and Eaton (1997) in *Dismantling Desegregation* exhaustively capture the complex dynamics of resegregation and hypersegregation in the United States since *Brown*. Orfield chronicles the evolution of resistance to court-ordered and voluntary desegregation efforts in communities around the country. Also see Clotfelter (2001).
6. See Parliament (1975).
7. The term "Jim Crow" is based on the name of a minstrel character of the 1920s who performed in black face. It eventually evolved to describe a system of racial apartheid in the American South.
8. Kluger (2004), *Simple Justice*, does an excellent job chronicling the litigation leading to *Brown*.
9. The *Brown* case is comprised of five separate cases from Delaware, South Carolina, Kansas, Virginia, and Washington, DC.
10. Social scientists argue that the use of Park's work in civil rights and poverty studies would give rise to the culture of poverty thesis, promoting that some Blacks, particularly the middle-class Blacks, have adopted a legitimate culture and

social progress ethic while poor Blacks have not. This stance many believe has exacerbated divisions among middle-class and poor and working-class Blacks.

11. There is a long line of behavioral and social science dating back to the late nineteenth and early twentieth century that shaped social policy and legal discourse regarding African Americans. The *Dred Scott* decision (1857), which essentially dismissed the claim of Black citizenship and equal protection under U.S. law, was shaped by the racial theories of white superiority advanced by pseudoscientists such as Joseph Arthur Comte de Gobineau, *Essay on the Inequality of the Human Races*; Sir Francis Galton, *Heredity Genius: An Inquiry into Its Laws and Consequences* (1869); and Carl Brigham's *A Study of American Intelligence* (1923).

12. See works of William Julius Wilson (1980, 1990, 1997, 1999, 2006).

13. See Hurley's chapter in this volume.

14. Here . . . there are findings below that the Negro and white schools involved have been equalized, or are being equalized, with respect to buildings, curricula, qualifications, and salaries of teachers, and other "tangible" factors. Our decision, therefore, cannot turn on merely a comparison of these tangible factors in the Negro and white schools involved in each of these cases. We must look instead to the effect of segregation itself on public education. . . .

Today, education is perhaps the most important function of state and local governments. Compulsory school attendance laws and the great expenditures for education both demonstrate our recognition of the importance of education to our democratic society. . . . Today it is a principal instrument in awakening the child to cultural values, in preparing him for later professional training, and in helping him to adjust normally to his environment. In these days, it is doubtful that any child may reasonably be expected to succeed in life if he is denied the opportunity of an education. Such an opportunity, where the state has undertaken to provide it, is a right which must be made available to all on equal terms. . . .

To separate them [children in grade and high schools] from others of similar age and qualifications solely because of their race generates a feeling of inferiority as to their status in the community that may affect their hearts and minds in a way unlikely to ever be undone. . . . Whatever may have been the extent of psychological knowledge at the time of *Plessy v. Ferguson*, this finding is amply supported by modern authority. . . .

We conclude that in the field of public education the doctrine of "separate but equal" has no place. Separate educational facilities are inherently unequal. Therefore, we hold that the plaintiffs and other similarly situated . . . are . . . deprived of the equal protection of the laws guaranteed by the Fourteenth Amendment. See *Brown v. Board of Education*, 347 U.S. 483. (1954)

15. Earl Warren served as the Fourteenth Chief Justice of the United States and ruled in cases on legal status of racial segregation, civil rights, and separation between church and state.

16. See *Jackson v. Alabama*, 347 U.S. 888 (1954) and *Jackson v. State*, 37 Ala. App. 519, 72. So. 2d, 114, cert.

17. 1901: Miscegenation [Constitution]

Declared that the legislature could never pass any law authorizing or legalizing "any marriage between any white person and a Negro, or descendant of a Negro."

1940: Miscegenation [State Code]

Prohibited intermarriage and cohabitation between whites and blacks or the descendant of any Negro. Penalty: imprisonment in the penitentiary for two to seven years. Ministers and justices of the peace faced fines between $100 and $1,000 and could be imprisoned in the county jail for up to six months.

See www.jimcrowhistory.org/scripts/jimcrow/insidesouth.cgi?state=Alabama.

18. Oliver Wendell Holmes was an early proponent of Legal Realism. The Legal Realists were a radical departure from the traditional strict interpretivist stance in legal training. Rather than seeing law, particularly legal precedent, as a sound, and unchanging tool, Legal Realists argue that social milieu shapes the nature and relevance of law and legal reasoning.

19. See works of Patterson (1998), Williams (2006), and McWhorter (2003).

20. Known as the Texas "Robin Hood" Finance Law, "in 1949 the Texas legislature enacted the Gilmer-Aikin Act (Foundation School Program Act), 51st Legislature. . . . The purpose of the Gilmer-Aikin was to "guarantee to each child of school age in Texas the availability of a minimum Foundation School Program for nine full months of the year, and to establish the eligibility requirements." Such allotments, "based upon white attendance shall be utilized in white schools, and allotments based upon negro . . . shall be utilized in negro schools." See Wilson (2003).

Works Cited

Amar, A. R. 2005. *America's constitution: A biography.* New York: Random House.

Anderson, J., and D. N. Bryne. 2004. *The unfinished agenda of* Brown v. Board of Education. New York: Wiley Press.

Anderson, N. 2006. "Hostile takeover: Antiunionism and the neoliberal politics of urban school reform in New York." *Working USA: The Journal of Labor and Society* 9:225–43.

Ascher, C., and N. Fruchter. 2001. "Teacher quality and student performance in New York City's low performing schools." *Journal of Education for Students Placed At Risk* 6 (3).

Baker, L. D. 1998. "Unraveling the boasian discourse: The racial politics of culture in school desegregation 1944–1954." *Transforming Anthropology* 7 (1): 15–32.

Bell, D. 1987. *And we are not saved: The elusive quest for racial justice.* New York: Basic Books.

———. 1992. *Faces at the bottom of the well: The permanence of racism.* New York: Basic Books.

———. 1995a. "*Brown v. Board of Education* and the interest convergence dilemma." In *Critical race theory: The key writings that formed the movement*, ed. K. Crenshaw. New York: The New Press.

———. 1995b. "Racial realism." In *Critical race theory: The key writings that formed the movement*, ed. K. Crenshaw. New York: The New Press.

———. 1995c. "Serving two masters: Integration ideals and client interests in school desegregation." In *Critical race theory: The key writings that formed the movement*, ed. K. Crenshaw. New York: The New Press.

———. 2004. *Silent covenants:* Brown v. Board of Education *and the unfulfilled hopes for racial reform*. New York: Oxford University Press.

Brown v. Board of Education of Topeka, 347 U.S. 483 (1954).

Carter, R., and J. H. Franklin. 2005. *A matter of law: A memoir of struggle in the course of equal rights*. New York: The New Press.

Clark, K. B. 1988. *Prejudice and your child*. 2nd rev. ed. Middletown, CT: Wesleyan University Press.

Clotfelter, C. T. 2001. "Are whites still fleeing? Racial patterns and enrollment shifts in urban public schools, 1987–1996." *Journal of Policy Analysis and Management* 20:199–221.

Du Bois. W. E. B. 1935. "Does the negro need separate schools?" *The Journal of Negro Education* 4 (3): 328–35.

Hill Collins, P. 2006. *From black power to hip hop: Racism, nationalism, and feminism*. Philadelphia: Temple University Press.

The History of Jim Crow. www.jimcrowhistory.org.

Fraizer, E. F. 1965. *Black bourgeoisie*. New York: Free Press

Friedman, L., ed. 2004. Brown v. Board: *The landmark oral argument before the supreme court*. New York: The New Press.

Jackson v. Alabama, 347 U.S. 888 (1954).

Jackson v. State, 37 Ala. App. 519, 72. So. 2d, 114, cert.

Kelley, R. D. G. 1997. *Yo' mama's disfunktional: Fighting the culture wars in urban America*. Boston: Beacon Press.

King, M. L., Jr. 1986. "Letter from Birmingham jail." In *A Testament of Hope: The Essential Writings of Martin Luther King, Jr.*, ed. J. M. Washington, 289–302. New York: Harper and Row

Kluger, R. 1975. *Simple justice: The history of* Brown v. Board of Education *and black America's struggle for equality*. New York: Vintage Books.

Kozol, J. 2005. *The shame of the nation: The restoration of apartheid schooling in America*. New York: Crown Publishers

McWhorter, J. 2003. *Authentically black: Essays for the black silent majority*. New York: Gotham Books.

Myrdal, G. 1944. *An American dilemma: The negro problem and modern democracy*. New York: Harper and Brothers.

O'Connor, A. 2001. *Poverty knowledge: Social science, social policy, and the poor in twentieth-century U.S. history*. Princeton, NJ: Princeton University Press.

Orfield, G., and S. Eaton. 1997. *Dismantling desegregation: The quiet reversal of Brown v. Board of Education.* New York: The New Press.

Orfield, G., and C. Lee. 2006. *Radical Transformation and the changing nature of segregation.* Cambridge, MA: Harvard University Civil Rights Projects.

Park, R. E., and E. W. Burgess. 1967. *The city.* Chicago: University of Chicago Press.

Parliament. 1975. "Chocolate City." In *Chocolate City* (Studio album). United States: Casablanca Records.

Patterson, O. 1998. *Rituals of blood: Consequences of slavery in two American centuries.* Washington, DC: Civitas/CounterPoint.

Payne, C. M. 2004. "The whole United States is southern! *Brown v. Board of Education* and the mystification of race." *The Journal of American History* 1 (91): 83–91.

Thabit, W. 2003. *How East New York became a ghetto.* New York: New York University Press.

Wamba, N. G., and C. Ascher. 2003. "An examination of charter school equity." *Education and Urban Society* 35 (4): 462–76.

Weinberger, A. D. 1957, Autumn. "A reappraisal of the constitutionality of miscegenation statutes." *Journal of Negro Education* 4 (26): 435–46.

West, C. 2001. *Race matters.* Boston: Beacon Press.

Williams, J. 2006. *Enough: The phony leaders, dead-end movements, and culture of failure that are undermining Black America—and what we can do about it.* New York: Crown Publishers.

Wilson, S. H. 2003. *The rise of judicial management in the U.S. District Court, Southern District Court of Texas, 1955–2000.* Athens: University of Georgia Press.

Wilson, W. J. 1980. *The declining significance of race: Blacks and changing.* Chicago: University of Chicago Press.

———. 1990. *The truly disadvantaged: The inner city, the underclass, and the public.* Chicago: University of Chicago Press.

———. 1997. *When work disappears: The world of the new urban poor.* United Kingdom: Vintage Books.

———. 1999. *The bridge over the racial divide: Rising inequality and coalition politics.* Berkeley and Los Angeles: University of California Press.

———. 2006. *There goes the neighborhood: Racial, ethnic, and class tensions in four Chicago neighborhoods and their meaning for America.* New York: Knof Publishing Group.

Research for Liberation

9

Du Bois, the Chicago School, and the Development of Black Emancipatory Action Research

A. A. AKOM

LOVE AND HEALING ARE AMONGST THE MOST REVOLUTIONARY ideals available to us, and yet academics and activists across the African Diaspora have failed miserably to grapple with their sociological, psychological, and political significance (Kelley 2002). Despite over a decade of writing about racial identity and youth development I am only just beginning to see the ways in which love and healing lie at the very heart of the most radical social movements in education and beyond. I had been thinking about these issues when I was invited to take part in Ghana's fiftieth anniversary of African Independence. In many ways the opportunity to take part in Ghana's fiftieth anniversary, particularly the contemporary re-imagining of PanAfricanism, brought many of these issues to the forefront.

Kwame Nkrumah constantly warned that we would not be able to build a truly liberatory social movement without embracing "PanAfricanism." PanAfricanism for Nkrumah served at least two important sociopolitical functions. First, it was a "geopolitical concept" whereby race, African identity, and nationalism were pragmatically reconstructed in order to unify "those who shared the African continent" (Appiah 1998, 18).

Second, PanAfricanism for Nkrumah[1] represented important political, economic, cultural, and intellectual connections across the African Diaspora that were central to the cultural and economic survival of African Diasporic people. This web of interconnectedness, this ability to have a "call" on one side of the Black Atlantic and a "response" on the other, is indicative of what J. L. Matory (1999) refers to as a live "Afro-Atlantic dialogue" in which the Diaspora and Africa itself are united by a "discontinuous" and mutually influential dialogue that has continued long beyond the end of slavery" (Matory 1999, 36–44). Such Pan-African connections and collaborations ultimately have implications that extend beyond the intellectual realm and the political sphere; rather these Afro-Atlantic crossings have produced significant transformations of daily life, symbols, and knowledge production on both sides of the Atlantic (Shipley and Pierre 2007).

Perhaps because I was in Ghana, Nkrumah's PanAfricanism as a form of Afro-Atlantic dialogue became a template for this chapter. I began to think about how the collective memory of Africa has been deeply distorted by the ways in which knowledge about Black people has been collected, classified, and characterized by the West, and at times misrepresented by those who have been colonized by the West (Smith 1999). I began to think about how fictive, corporate, and scholarly depictions of Blackness often mischaracterize, exoticize, and destabilize Black people across the Diaspora. In all of these activities—including the formal production of knowledge or informal travelers tales—pathologizing Blackness has been intimately intertwined with the research process itself. As a result, "when mentioned in many indigenous contexts the term research itself stirs up silence, conjures up bad memories, raises a smile that is knowing and distrustful" (Smith 1999, 1).

The central purpose of this chapter, then, is to introduce a Black Emancipatory Action Research framework (BEAR) that will allow us to explore the implications that "racing research and researching race" have for methodological practices and knowledge production in the field of education and beyond (Twine and Warren 2003). Drawing on critical race theory (CRT); participatory action research (PAR); and queer, Critical Africentricity, and Africana womanist scholarship, the BEAR framework questions notions of objectivity and a universal foundation of knowledge by breaking down the barriers between the researched and the researcher and underscoring ethical principles such as self-determination, social justice, equity, healing, and love. With its commitment to liberation, asset-based approaches to community capacity building, and action as part of the research process, BEAR represents an orientation to inquiry that is highly consistent with Paulo Freire's critical pedagogy aimed at creating effective strategies of liberation from multiple forms of domination experienced by African Diasporic peoples.

In the rest of this chapter I briefly review BEAR's conceptual developments and underlying principles. Additionally, I examine the centrality of race in the experiences of Africans across the Diaspora. Race, in the sense of pigmentocracy, particularly a sense of "lightness or darkness," not only figures prominently in the collective identities of Black working people but substantially shapes and reshapes the entire Diaspora's conceptions of social status, class, gender, and other axes of social difference. Part of what this chapter suggest is that we need to rethink how we conduct research with Black populations and be mindful to deal with questions of Black identity from the perspective of Black people as centered, located, oriented, and grounded in African-Atlantic cultures. Key questions that this chapter addresses are: How do we integrate a theory of race into qualitative research methods? What is the role of race, gender, and intersectionality in the research process? How can a BEAR approach be used as a theoretical, methodological, and pedagogical tool to challenge racism, sexism, and classism and work toward social justice?

Du Bois and the Chicago School: The Beginning of a Researching Race Revolution

In August of 1999, I was in graduate school at the University of Pennsylvania receiving training in urban sociology and urban ethnography. One hundred years after W. E. B. Du Bois had written the *Philadelphia Negro* (1899)—one of the first works to combine urban ethnography, social history, and descriptive statistics—I was about to leave my apartment in south Philadelphia with my newborn daughter to embark on my dissertation research on forms of racial domination and colorblindness in the liberal Bay Area. At the time, I was eager to follow Du Bois's work on the problems of Black integration in America and examine how racism in the heart of liberalism, as a sociological phenomenon, was playing out in the liberal Bay Area. In Philadelphia I was living adjacent to the seventh ward, the neighborhood where Du Bois had conducted his original research, and I had been taught to revisit his principles both in classroom and in the neighborhood. Like Du Bois, on the streets of south Philadelphia I found a world filled with joblessness, drugs, vice, and crime, as well as genuine love, humor, hope, hard-working nontraditional families, positive relationships toward men, women, and children, and all kinds of social capital that is alive, well, and thriving in Black urban communities that is presently flying under the radar (Akom 2006, 2007; Sullivan 1997).

A central issue of my research in Philadelphia was to examine the ways in which Black achievement, community capacity building, and self-determination were created and enacted within poor Black communities— places Du Bois referred to as the "submerged tenth"—where academic and economic achievement (largely due to institutional and other forms of racism) were more challenging than in more well resourced neighborhoods. To no surprise, I found the seventh ward very different than when Du Bois originally described it one hundred years prior, with "urban renewal" and gentrification transforming the neighborhood from a "Black metropolis" into a yuppies' paradise. As I followed in the footsteps of Du Bois both physically and intellectually, I found myself in dialogue with other theorists of urban space such as Elijah Anderson, Mary Patillo, Mitchell Duneier, Frances Windance-Twine, Howard Winant, Yasmin Gunaratnam, and Wade Nobles—scholars interested in analyzing changing conditions of social inequality, racial transformation, and cultural difference for Black populations on both sides of the Atlantic. Additionally, I became curious about the following questions: As we enter the twenty-first century have Du Bois's insights contributed to the amelioration of conditions of social inequality for Black communities? Are Black folks today, whether in Philadelphia, Atlanta, London, California, or Ghana—or anywhere across the African Diaspora—"free from the forces Du Bois chronicled"? With these thoughts in mind I moved to California determined to examine the status of Blacks and the invisible forms of colorblind racism in the liberal Bay Area.

California Dreaming: A Critique of the Chicago School of Ethnography

When I arrived in California I was a focused graduate student who wanted to know how youth and adults in Berkeley and Oakland struggled to overcome racialized social practices as they structure local meanings of culture, class, privilege, and power in every day life. I had been trained to conduct research in the tradition of urban ethnographic field methods introduced by Du Bois and institutionalized by the Chicago School in the early part of the twentieth century. From 1892 to 1942 the University of Chicago towered over the landscape of urban sociology, training over half of the sociologists in the world by 1930 (Deegan 2001). Scholars such as Robert Park, Ernest Burgess, and R. D. McKenzie introduced the intellectual apparatus that is now commonly referred to as urban ecology while W. I. Thomas, George Herbert Mead, and John Dewey introduce Chicago symbolic interactionism (Deegan 2001; Flanagan 1993).

This homogenous group of white male scholars fundamentally shaped the discipline through their teaching methods, mentorship, and training of doctoral students who produced thousands of books and manuscripts that depicted everyday life from the standpoint of an outsider looking in. During this time, the Chicago school viewed the city as a laboratory for exploring social interaction, and over the years, several themes emerged that guided their approach to the growth and evolution of urban space (Lutters and Ackerman 1996). These include, but are not limited to, the following four themes: (1) Urban ecology—the notion that the physical environment is the expression of a rational order governed by Social Darwinist principles; (2) Social worlds—or the belief that the best way to describe complex inter or intra group patterns was to embed the research in local communities with the express purpose of learning about the people residing there; (3) Social disorganization—the theory that neighborhood poverty (among other factors) produces socially disorganized communities (Akom 2007); and (4) perhaps the most enduring legacy of the Chicago School's influence was the ways in which the sociology of race was embedded in human ecological frameworks (Anderson and Massey 2001)

Yet for all of the important contributions of the Chicago school there are some key criticisms. In particular, the invisibility of women in Chicago school research—as subjects, authors, and colleagues—was unacceptable, even for the time (Deegan 2001, 21). The invisibility of woman and the sexist practices by the Chicago school is perhaps best expressed by Deegan (2001) when she states: "Women as half the population in everyday life are severely understudied and underrepresented in the core of Chicago school ethnographies. The topic selections are also male-biased focusing on populations where males predominate: Hoboes, juvenile delinquents, the male patrons of dance halls and gang members" (21). Another important critique of the Chicago school is their lack of self-reflexivity about their own race (white) and gender (male) privilege and their place in the lives of the urban poor. As a result, even though the legacy of urban ethnography at the University of Chicago is well documented, what is less well known is that the work Du Bois represents the first true example of "American social scientific research," preceding the work of Park and Burgess and the Chicago school by at least two decades (Anderson and Massey 2001, 4). According to Anderson and Massey:

> Were it not for the short-sighted racism of Penn's faculty and administration, which refused to acknowledge the presence—let alone the accomplishments—of a Black man or to offer him a faculty appointment, the maturation of the discipline might have been advanced by two decades and be known to posterity as the Pennsylvania School of Sociology. Instead, Du Bois went on to a distinguished career as a public intellectual,

activist, and journalist, and the University of Chicago, not the University of Pennsylvania, came to dominate the field.

Key contributions of the Chicago school, initially introduced by Du Bois, include the use of multiple methods—now called triangulation. Additionally, Chicago school ethnographers often lived in the setting studied, walked the streets, worked for local agencies, kept detailed field notes, and entered the field armed with what C. W. Mills referred to as a "sociological imagination" so that as fieldwork proceeded questions concerning the social organization of the subject and their setting could be connected to larger issues of public and social policy (Anderson 2002).

Perhaps the major Achilles' heel of the Chicago school interpretation of how to conduct qualitative research was fundamental lack of recognition of the role of research in constructing the "Other" and the failure to accurately depict the institutionalized nature of social inequality when representing communities of color. The lack of a concrete power sharing approach to ethnographic research that could address my growing concern for the human rights of community experts (i.e., subjects) and the resistance, agency, and political contestation of heavily researched low-income Black populations, left me wanting for an approach that could discuss research methodology, racial and other forms of social difference, and social justice, while also understanding of the complex ways that the pursuit of knowledge is deeply embedded in larger historical, political, and hierarchical power relations. The method that emerged that began to address my concerns about equitably involving all partners in the research process, while building the communities capacity to realize its own unique strengths and goals, was participatory action research (PAR).

My Experience with Participatory Action Research: Theory, Method, and Practice

When I first arrived to California I began working at an urban school as a tutor and then a teacher for more than five years. During that time I employed Duneier *extended place method* for expanding the traditional boundaries of the neighborhood study by focusing on how schools—and other institutions of various kinds—become "race-making institutions" by normalizing race, space, and power in the micro-settings I studied (Wacquant 2002). As my understanding of community-based participatory action research evolved, I moved my fieldwork from advanced placement classrooms, into on-campus suspension venues, special education programs, neighborhoods, homes, jails, and the street. It was in this social and political context that the work of Fals Borda, Frantz Fanon, Michelle Fine, and Maria Torre became highly influential. Their theories of participatory action research (PAR) advanced the position that "valid knowledge is produced only in collaboration and in action . . . and that those studied harbor critical social knowledge and must be repositioned as subjects and architects of research" (Torre and Fine 2006, 271).

Based largely on the theory and practice of Black and Latino activist/scholars, PAR draws on feminist, queer, neo-Marxist, and critical race theories (Anzaldua 1987; Fanon 1963) in an effort to reposition marginalized populations at the center of knowledge creation, shift experiential knowledge of people of color from the margins to the center (Hall 1992), and place the tools of research into "the hands of deprived and disenfranchised people so that they can transform their lives for themselves" (Park 1993, 1).

By repositioning Black people as researchers, rather than the "researched," and enabling Black communities to interrogate and denaturalize the conditions of our oppression, PAR inspires collective empowerment and the deepening of community knowledge (Torre and Fine 2006, 271). As Hall (1992) argues:

> Participatory research: joins people together for radical social change (Maguire 1987, 29); enables oppressed groups to acquire leverage for action (Fals Borda and Rahman 1991, 4); presents people as researchers in pursuit of answers to questions of daily struggle and survival (Tandon 1988, 7); breaks down the distinction between the researches and the researched (Gavneta 1988, 19); acts as a flow-through mechanism between indigenous and western science (Colorado 1988, 63) and returns to the people the legitimacy of the knowledge they are capable of producing. (Fals Borda and Rahman 1991, 15)

Indeed, PAR's greatest attribute is perhaps its potential to democratize the research process as it intersects with race, class, gender, language, religion, sexual orientation, special needs, and other axes of social difference. As summarized by Hall (1981), Fals Borda (1979), and Minkler (2004) the fundamental principals of PAR are as follows:

- The research originates within the community itself
- It is participatory
- It is cooperative, engaging community members and researchers in a joint process in which people in the community have control of the research process

- It is a co-learning process
- The researcher's goal is to fundamentally improve the lives of those involved through structural transformation
- The focus of PAR is on oppressed groups whose issues include access to institutional resources, marginalization, exploitation, racism, sexism, religious discrimination, homophobia, etc.
- PAR plays a role in enabling by strengthening people's awareness of their own capabilities and involves systems of local community capacity building
- The people themselves are researchers as are those involved who have specialized research training
- It achieves a balance between research and action

As suggested above, PAR has enormous potential as a tool of resistance against interlocking systems of oppression. Yet, at present PAR is only a partial solution to the historical tendency to "abuse" and "exploit" people of color in the research process because it is too often romanticized as an all-empowering alternative to traditional research, regardless of the research question or the communities' interests (Wallace 2005). Moreover, much of what is being called PAR isn't. What was once being called consultations with community organizations is now being called participatory. Finally, I realized that PAR needs some redefinition. Rather than asking how can we get communities to participate in research we could be asking how can we get researchers to participate with communities? (Wallace 2005).

In an effort to build and expand upon PAR and bring a holistic awareness of the struggles involved in moving from theory to practice I have drawn on the work of Linda Tuhiwai Smith (1999) to create Black Emancipatory Action Research (BEAR), which ask researchers to consider the following self-reflexive questions before starting a project in marginalized communities: Whose research is it? Who owns it? Whose interest does it serve? Who will benefit from it? Who has designed its questions and framed its scope? Who will carry it out? Who will write it up? How will its results be disseminated? What are the barriers to participation? How meaningful will the participation be at each stage? What are the limitations to this project? How flexible is this project? What are the possible negative impacts of this project? Is the researcher's spirit clear? Does she or he have a good heart? What baggage is she or he carrying? Is the research useful to our community? Can it get the environmental pollution out of our community? Can it actually do anything right here right now that can help us grow?

Introducing Black Emancipatory
Action Research (BEAR)

Black emancipatory action research (BEAR) is a theory of praxis aimed at creating strategies of liberation from intersecting forms of oppression experienced by people of African descent across the Diaspora. Since BEAR has roots in critical Africentricity and Africana womanist scholarship, it deals with the question of race, gender, and other forms of identity from the perspective of Black cultures being centered, located, and grounded in an African-Atlantic culture in which the Diaspora and Africa are united by continuous, hybridized, and mutually influential cultures that have existed long before slavery (See T'Shaka 2004). In this manner, BEAR encompasses a theoretical and philosophical perspective derived from an understanding of precolonial African experiences as well as the collective lived experiences of Black people across the Diaspora.

From a research perspective BEAR suggest that researchers examine data from the standpoint of Black people as subjects and human agents rather than objects in a European frame of reference (Mkabela 2005, 359). While committed to racial and cultural consciousness, the aim of BEAR is to be sensitive to the structural role that race, culture, gender, class (i.e., poverty), and other axes of social difference play in actual social context and to investigate these social phenomena from the standpoint of the subjects' perspective through participation in their everyday lives (Bogdan and Biklen 1992). Although explicitly committed to race consciousness, one of the goals of BEAR is to have relevance in the context of the multicultural realities of Africa, Latin America, Asia, the United States, Europe, and an increasing globalized world, and move toward a pluralistic research orientation where all racial, culture, and gendered centers are respected.

Thus, for the purpose of a BEAR framework the racial designation of Black is both a national/racial concept and a spiritual concept and as such transcends skin color (Gardell 1996). As a result, Latino/a, Native Americans, Asians, Pacific Islanders, and other people of color are all "Black" at this level of meaning (Gardell 1996). Where BEAR departs from Afrocentric research methods is that "Afrocentricity," according to Asante, "is not color-conscious, it is not a matter of color but of culture that matters in the orientation to centeredness" (Asante 1995, 3). Whereas in the BEAR methodological approach, borrowing and extending critical race methodology: (a) foregrounds race and racism in all aspects of the research process while challenging separate discourses on race, class, gender, religion, nationality, sexual orientation, and special needs, by illustrating how these forms of oppression interlock creating a system of oppression (Hill-Collins 1990); (b) challenges traditional research paradigms and theories used to explain the experiences of Black people; (c) utilized an asset building approach to systems of oppression by focusing on problems as well as transformative solutions and community capacity building; (d) focuses on the experiential knowledge of Black people as sources of strength; (e) uses an interdisciplinary knowledge base of Africana studies, ethnic studies, women's studies, sociology, psychology, history, humanities, and the law to better understand the experiences of Black people (Yosso and Solorzano 2002, 24). In the following section I further explain the key issues that define the BEAR paradigm.

Articulating a Black Emancipatory Action Research Agenda

It is important to articulate a BEAR agenda by defining race and racism. For the purposes of this chapter, Tatum's (1997) four-tiered framework of institutionalized, ideological, interpersonal, and internalized racism is useful for confronting race as a central axis of power and privilege that has a profound effect on Black peoples' everyday lives.[2] According to Tatum, institutional racism is defined as the "cultural and *institutional* images and messages that affirm the assumed superiority of whites, and the assumed inferiority of people of color" (6).[3] Manning Marable (1992) adds to Tatum's definition of racism by defining it as a "system of ignorance, exploitation, and power used to oppress African Americans, Latinos, Asians, Pacific Americans, American Indians and other people on the basis of ethnicity, culture, mannerism and color" (5). "Marable's definition of racism is important not only because it shifts the discourse on race and racism from a Black-white discourse to one that includes multiple faces, voices, and experiences, but also because it begins to move the discussion of race to phenotype and skin-color privilege" (Yosso and Solorzano 2002, 24). In the following section Tatum's and Marable's definition of racism serve as guides as I begin to critically examine the four major theoretical foundations that define the BEAR paradigm: These include (1) the social construction of race; (2) intersectionality and the social construction of knowledge; (3) the development of critical consciousness; (4) love, healing, and a commitment to social justice.

The Social Construction of Race

Informing the BEAR research orientation is the view that race is a social construction, a function of how particular racial groups are valued or devalued by society. Specifically, BEAR draws on critical race theory (CRT) as an epistemological and methodological tool to evaluate racism and to analyze the formation of an ideology that supports and reproduce persistent racial injustices and social inequalities in the world of education and beyond (Ladson-Billings 1999; Tate 1997). A key assumption of CRT is that racism is a permanent feature of globalization that rests on a structural foundation, what Bonilla-Silva (2003) has termed the "racial structure" of a society (37). Since different racial groups receive different social rewards, they each develop different material (and conflicting) interests. Where BEAR deviates from CRT is in the belief that racism is permanent. In the BEAR framework race goes through "relentless deconstruction and reconstruction" (Hayman 1995, 70) and these, like other aspects of identity, are sociopolitical constructs that change and evolve over time. What the BEAR framework and CRT share in common is the

> Insistence that justice cannot be merely theoretical. Furthermore, it must be informed by and realized in lived experiences, and while the struggle for racial justice may offer no prospects for immediate or ultimate success, the struggle has to be continuous. (Hayman 1995, 70)

Intersectionality and the Social Construction of Knowledge

Although race and racism are at the center of a BEAR research orientation, the BEAR framework also views race at the intersection of other forms of oppression such as class, gender, religion, nationality, sexual orientation, immigration status, surname, phenotype, accent, and special needs, by illustrating how these forms of oppression interlock creating a system of oppression (Hill-Collins 1990). Thus, informed by the intercentricity of racialized oppression, BEAR challenges traditional claims toward objectivity, meritocracy, colorblindness, and neutrality and argues that traditional research methods often mask the self-interest, power, and privilege of dominant groups (Solorzano 1997). In an effort to challenge traditional research paradigms, texts, and theories used to explain the experiences of people of color, the BEAR framework seeks to expose "deficit-informed research and methods that silence and distort the experiences of people of color" and instead focuses on an asset-building approach that views their racialized, gendered, and classed experiences as a source of strength (Ginwright and Cammarota 2006; Yosso and Solorzano 2002, 26).

The Development of Critical Consciousness

By encouraging a deep participation of the community in every aspect of the research process, including design, development, and dissemination, BEAR enables everyday people to deconstruct the material and ideological conditions that oppress them and to transform the underlying causes into opportunities for community building, policy change, and knowledge production. Paulo Freire termed this method of social inquiry as pedagogy of the oppressed—a social praxis where we learn to perceive social, political, and economic contradictions, and to take action against the oppressive elements of reality. At the core of Freire's work was the belief that transformative education for the poor and disempowered begins with the creation of pedagogic spaces where marginalized people are enabled to gain a consciousness of how their own experiences have been shaped by larger social institutions. Through a counter-hegemonic research orientation that focuses on race, culture, and resistance; womanism, sexism, and sexuality (Gordon 2000; Hill-Collins 2005; Hudson-Weems 2000); and counter narratives (Akom 2008; Solorzano and Delgado-Bernal 2001), communities of color are able to provide alternate explanations of social inequality as well as gain a critical perspective of their world.

Love and a Commitment to Social Justice

The indigenous and modern world of Africa have much to offer the developing world, in terms of ways to combat bitterness and cynicism by more deeply understanding, embracing, and practicing concepts such as love, healing, ritual, and community. Healing is central to Black community development because of the historical trauma white supremacy has and continues to inflict upon our communities as well as the interpersonal and internalized ways we have and continue to inflict trauma upon ourselves. Love is "the will to extend one's self for the purpose of nurturing one's own or another's spiritual growth" (Peck 1978, 69). Yet with the notable exception of Vincent Harding, few Black social scientists since W. E. B. Du Bois have been bold enough to assert a connection between the spirit and spiritual world of African Diasporic peoples and the realm of socio-political struggle (Kelley 1993). Du Bois in Black Reconstruction had the audacity to boldly include freed people's narratives of divine intervention in the struggle for liberation and emancipation from white supremacy and, in doing so, gave future researchers insight into how spaces of marginalization were at the same time spaces hope, healing, resistance, and community building.

It follows that a BEAR agenda is focused strategically on the goal of self-determination of Black people. Self-determination, love, and healing when embedded in research agendas become something more than socio-political goals, rather they offer a liberatory and transformative response to racial, gender, and class oppression, across a wide range of social, political, psychological, and economic terrains (Matsuda 1995; Smith 1999).

Figure 9.1 is a simple representation of a BEAR agenda. Following J. L. Matory's live "Afro-Atlantic dialogue" in which the Diaspora and Africa itself are united by a "discontinuous" and mutually influential dialogue that has continued long beyond the end of slavery, the chart uses the Yoruba metaphor of a river. The Yoruba religion is perhaps the largest African-born religion in the world (Awolalu 1996). Born in the soil of West Africa (mainly in Nigeria and Benin) yet practiced all over the world, especially in the Caribbean (Haiti, Trinidad) and Latin America (Colombia, Venezuela), the Yoruba cosmology has given birth to several African-Atlantic religions such as Santeria in Cuba and Candomble in

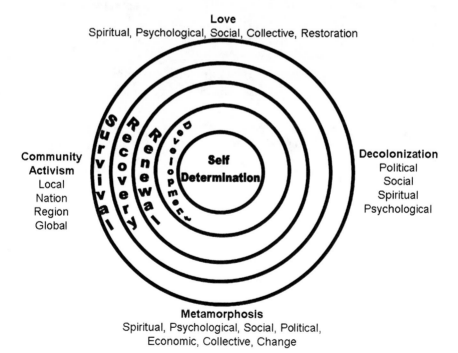

Figure 9.1.   Representation of a BEAR Agenda
This figure is adapted from Linda Tuhiwai Smith, *Decolonizing Methodologies: Research and Indigenous Peoples* (London and New York: Zed Books, 1999). Copyright © 1997 by Linda Tuhiwai Smith. Reproduced by permission of Zed Books, London and New York.

Brazil (Awolalu 1996). The Philosophy of Yoruba is that all human beings have Ayanmo (manifest destiny) to become one in spirit with Olódùmarè (the divine creator and source of all energy). Each person in Ayé (the physical realm) uses thought or action energies to impact the community of all other living things including the Earth, and so to move toward destiny. As a result of the power of action and thought in Yoruba cosmology, one's destiny is in one's hands.

For Yoruba practitioners a significant deity of the river is Osun (or Oxum, Oshun). Although there are multiple directions that can be taken, the chart takes the Yoruba equivalent to the four points of light. The number four is extremely consequential in Yoruba culture, which emphasizes four directions or corners of the world (Fatunmbi 2005). In Yoruba culture it is believed that there are four gates from the outer world to the earth. The four directions named here—love/healing, decolonization, metamorphosis, and community activism—are not goals in themselves but rather represent processes that can be incorporated into research practices, models, and orientations (Smith 1999, 116). The four major currents are represented in the chart as: survival, recovery/renewal, development, and self-determination. These are nonlinear conditions and states of being through which Black communities across the Diaspora are moving.

Overall the BEAR agenda is broad in scope and ambitious in its goals. There are many elements that make this agenda very different from a typical Western research agenda, as well as some elements that we share in common. The most important differences can be found in key words such as: love, healing, decolonization, spiritual transformation, recovery, and renewal. These terms appear to be at odds with a great deal of Western research terminology because they appear to be politically and spiritually motivated rather than neutral and objective (Smith 1999, 117). However, a BEAR framework rejects notions of "neutral" or "objective" research in an effort to conduct engaged research which privileges epistemologies of people of color. In sum, although the four pillars of BEAR are not collectively new, they represent a challenge to existing models of research that uphold deficit racialized notions of people of color (Yosso and Solorzano 2002, 27).

Conclusion

The purpose of creating a new research orientation is not to completely dismiss the old ones, but instead to create a methodological orientation that links theories and understandings about race, class, and gender to actual practice and actions for racial justice and social change. I contend that the BEAR approach begins an important conversation that moves us past the Black-white paradigm, while establishing connections from theory to practice to activism. By employing a BEAR methodological approach a research environment is established that creates the conditions for researchers to examine the moral and ethnic dilemmas of being "outsiders" while challenging their own intrinsic assumptions about learning to talk about navigating race and other intersectionalities of difference (Smith-Maddox and Solorzano 2002, 80).

It is very difficult to change the internalized beliefs, perspectives, and worldviews that researchers bring into Black communities. Yet, BEAR maintains that an emphasis on learning on how to talk about race and racism is not only possible but essential if we hope to use research methods as a practice of freedom. The methodological orientation outlined in the preceding pages emphasizes self-actualization and self-determination in an effort to promote community well-being. Vietnamese monk Thich Nhat Hanh reminds us that the practice of a researcher, teacher, or healer should be directed toward self-reflection first because if the research is at dis-ease it can have a potentially harmful effects on the entire community (hooks 1994). In the United States it is very rare to talk about research and healing in the same breath. And it is even more rare to suggest that researchers, teachers, and healers have a responsibility to be self-actualized individuals and help communities to achieve their own goals (hooks 1994). Deployment of PAR, BEAR, and other action-centered approaches rather than containment will require researches to reexamine their epistemological, ontological, axiological, and cosmological orientations and understand the values and everyday practices of communities of color as well as the racial, cultural, and language differences we present. Failure to do so will limit their ability to use this knowledge to meet the challenges and opportunities of an increasingly diverse and globalized world. I am hopeful that future researchers will continue to uphold the idea of research as a practice of freedom and use engaged research to empower marginalized communities.

Notes

1. In this sense, Nkrumah as a spatial theorist was one of the first Pan Africanists to articulate important differences between "traditional" PanAfricanism and "continental" Pan Africanism—linking the latter to the idea that "Africa was for Africans"—with the specific intention of realigning colonial constructions of nation-state, culture, and economy falsely constructed during the Berlin Conference.

2. For more on the four-tiered framework of institutionalized, ideological, interpersonal, and internalized racism, see Jones (2000) and Tatum (1997).

3. The word in italics, institutional, was added by the author.

Works Cited

Akom, A. A. 2006. "The racial dimensions of social capital: Toward a new understanding of youth empowerment and community organizing in America's urban core." In *Beyond resistance: Youth activism and community change*, ed. Shawn Ginwright, Pedro Noguera, and Julio Cammarota, 81–92. New York: Routledge.

———. 2007. "Cities as battlefields: Understanding how the Nation of Islam impacts civic engagement, environmental racism, and community development in a low-income neighborhood." *International Journal of Qualitative Studies in Education* 209:711–30.

———. 2008. "Critical race theory meets participatory action research: Creating a community of youth as public intellectuals." In *Handbook for social justice*, ed. William Ayers, Therese Quinn, and David Stovall. New York: Teacher College Press.

Anderson, Elijah. 2002. "The ideologically driven critique." *American Journal of Sociology* 107:1533–50.

Anderson, Elijah, and Douglas S. Massey. 2001. *Problem of the century: Racial stratification in the United States*. New York: Russell Sage Foundation.

Anzaldua, Gloria. 1987. *Borderlands/La Frontera: The new Mestiza*. San Francisco: Aunt Lute Press.

Appiah, Kwame Anthony Akroma-Ampim Kusi. 1998. Pan-Africanism. In *Routledge encyclopedia of philosophy*, ed. Edward Craig. London: Routledge. Retrieved December 14, 2007, from www.rep.routledge.com/articleZ018.

Asante, Molefi Kete. 1995. *Afrocentricity: The theory of social change*. Retrieved on December 14, 2006, from www.asante.net/articles/guadalupe-asante.html.

Awolalu, J. Omosade. 1996. *Yoruba beliefs and sacrificial rites*. New York: Athelia Henrietta Press.

Bogdan, Robert C., and Sari K. Biklen. 1992. *Qualitative research for education: An introduction to theory and method*. Boston: Allyn and Bacon.

Bonilla-Silva, Eduardo. 2003. *Racism without racist: Color-blind racism and the persistency of racial inequality in the United States*. Lanham, MD: Roman & Littlefield.

Colorado, Pam. 1988. "Bridging native and Western science." *Convergence* 21:49–68.

Deegan, Mary Jo. 2001. "The Chicago school of ethnography." In *Handbook of ethnography*, ed. Paul Atkison, Amanda Coffey, Sara Delamont, John Lofland, and Lyn Lofland, 11–25. London: Sage Publication.

Du Bois, W. E. B. 1899. *The Philadelphia negro: A social study*. Philadelphia: University of Pennsylvania Press.

Fals Borda, Orlando. 1979. "Investigating the reality in order to transform it: The Colombian experience." *Dialectical Anthropology* 4:33–55.

Fals Borda, Orlando, and Muhammad A. Rahman. 1991. *Action and knowledge: Breaking the monopoly of participatory action research.* New York: Apex Press.

Fanon, Franz. 1963. *Wretched of the earth.* New York: Grove Press.

Fatunmbi, Awo Falokun. 2005. *Inner peace: The Yoruba concept of Ori.* New York: Athelia Henrietta Press.

Flanagan, William G. 1993. *Contemporary urban sociology.* London: Cambridge University Press.

Freire, Paulo. 1970. *Pedagogy of the oppressed.* New York: Continuum.

Gardell, Mattias. 1996. *In the name of Elijah Muhammad: Louis Farrakhan and the Nation of Islam.* Durham, NC: Duke University.

Gaventa, John. 1988. "Participatory research in North America." *Convergence* 21:19–27.

Ginwright, Shawn, and Julio Cammarota. 2006. Introduction. In *Beyond resistance: Youth activism and community change,* ed. Shawn Ginwright, Pedro Noguera, and Julio Cammarota, xiii–xxu. New York: Routledge.

Gordon, Vivian V. 2000. "Black women, feminism and black studies." In *Out of the revolution: The development of Africana studies,* ed. Dolores P. Aldridge and Carlene Young, 165–76. New York: Lexington Books.

Hall, Budd L. 1981. "Participatory research, popular knowledge and power: A personal reflection." *Convergence* 14:6–19.

———. 1992. "From margin to center? The development and purpose of participatory research." *The American Sociologist* 23:15–28.

Hayman, Robert L. 1995. "The color of tradition: Critical race theory and postmodern constitutional traditionalism." *Harvard Civil Rights and Civil Liberties Law Review* 30:57–108.

Hill-Collins, Patricia. 1990. *Black feminist thought: Knowledge, consciousness and politics of empowerment.* New York: Routledge.

———. 2005. *Black sexual politics: African Americans, gender, and new racism.* New York: Routledge.

hooks, bell. 1994. *Teaching to transgress: Education as a practice of freedom.* New York: Routledge.

Hudson-Weems, Clenora. 2000. "Africana womanism: An overview." In *Out of the revolution: The development of Africana studies,* ed. Dolores P. Aldridge and Carlene Young, 205–17. New York: Lexington Books.

Jones, Camara P. 2000. "Levels of racism: A theoretical framework and a Gardener's Tale." *American Journal of Public Health* 90:1212–15.

Kelley, Robin D. G. 1993. "'We are not what we seem': Rethinking black working-class opposition in the Jim Crow south." *The Journal of American History* 80:75–112.

———. 2002. *Freedom dreams: The black radical imagination.* New York: The Free Press.

Ladson-Billing, Gloria. 1999. "Preparing teachers for diversity." In *Teaching as the learning profession*, ed. Linda Darling-Hammond and Gary Sykes, 86–123. San Francisco: Jossey-Bass.

Lutters, Wayne G., and Mark S. Ackerman. 1996. *An introduction to the Chicago School of Sociology*. Unpublished manuscript.

Maguire, Patricia. 1987. *Doing participatory research: A feminist approach*. Amherst, MA: The Center International Education, School of Education, University of Massachusetts.

Marable, Manning. 1992. *Black America*. Westfield, NY: Open Media.

Matory, J. Lorand. 1999. "Afro-Atlantic culture: On the live dialogue between Africa and the Americas." In *Africana: The Encyclopedia of the African and African American Experience*, ed. Kwame A. Appiah and Henry L. Gates, 36–44. New York: Basic Civitas Books.

Matsuda, Mari. 1995. "Looking to the bottom: Critical legal studies and reparations." In *Critical race theory: The key writings that formed the movement*, ed. Kimberly Crenshaw, Neil Gotanda, Gary Peller, and Kendall Thomas, 63–79. New York: The New Press.

Minkler, Meredith. 2004. "Ethical challenges for the 'outside' researcher in community-based participatory research." *Health Education & Behavior* 31:684–97.

Mkabela, Queeneth. 2005. "Using the Afrocentric method in researching indigenous." *The Qualitative Report* 10:178–89.

Park, Peter. 1993. "What is participatory research? A theoretical and methodological perspective." In *Voices of change: Participatory research in the United States and Canada*, ed. Peter Park, Mary Brydon-Miller, Budd L. Hall, and Ted Jackson, 1–19. London: Bergin & Garvey.

Peck, Scott. 1978. *The road less traveled*. New York: Simon & Schuster

Shipley, Jesse W., and J. Jemima Pierre. 2007. "The intellectual and pragmatic legacy of Du Bois's Pan-Africanism in contemporary Ghana." in *Re-cognizing W. E. B. Du Bois in the twenty-first century: Essays on W. E. B. Du Bois (Voices of the African Diaspora)*, ed. Mary Keller and Chester J. Fontenot Jr., 91–117. Macon, GA: Mercer University Press.

Smith, Linda Tuhiwai. 1999. *Decolonizing methodologies: Research and indigenous people*. New York: Zed Books Ltd.

Smith-Maddox, Renee, and David G. Solorzano. 2002. "Using critical race theory, Paulo Freire's problem-posing method, and case study research to confront race and racism in education." *Qualitative Inquiry* 8:66–84.

Solorzano, David G. 1997. "Images and words that wound: Critical race theory, racial stereotyping, and teacher education." *Teacher Education Quarterly* 24:5–19.

Solorzano, David G., and Dolores Delgado-Bernal. 2001. "Examining transformational resistance through a critical race and latcrit theory framework: Chicana and Chicano students in an urban context." *Urban Education* 36:308–42.

Sullivan, Lisa. 1997. "Hip-hop nation: The underdeveloped social capital of black urban America." *National Civic Review* 86:235–44.

Tandon, Rajesh. 1988. "Social transformation and participatory research." *Convergence* 21:5–18.

Tate, William. 1997. "Critical race theory and education: History, theory, and implications." *Review of Research in Education* 22:195–247.

Tatum, Beverly D. 1997. *Why are all the black kids sitting together in the cafeteria? And other conversation about race*. New York: Basic Books.

Torre, Maria. E., and Michelle Fine. 2006. "Researching and resisting: Democratic policy research by and for youth." In *Beyond resistance: Youth activism and community change*, ed. Shawn Ginwright, Pedro Noguera, and Julio Cammarota, 269–85. New York: Routledge.

T'Shaka, Oba. 2004. *The integration trap; The generation gap*. Oakland: Pan Africanism Publisher.

Twine, France W., and Jonathan W. Warren, eds. 2003. *Racing research, researching race: methodological dilemmas in critical race studies*. New York: New York University Press.

Wacquant, Loic. 2002. "From slavery to mass incarceration." *New Left Review* 13:41–60.

Wallace, Bruce. 2005. "Participatory action research can be complicated." *Perspectives*, May, 16–17.

Yosso, Tarra, and David G. Solorzano. 2002. "Critical race methodology: Counter-storytelling as an analytical framework for education research." *Qualitative Inquiry* 8:23–44.

Index

Harding, Vincent, 143, 204
Harlem Renaissance, 18
Harrington, Michael, 142
Hemming, Sally, 17
"hermeneutical posture of suspicion,"
    70
Herskovits, Melville, 124
Higginbotham, Evelyn Brooks, 57
Highlander Folk School, 141
Hilliard, Asa, 79, 81
hooks, bell, 80, 82, 84, 86
Horton, Myles, 141
Houston, Charles, 166, 168, 171; legal
    instruction approach of, 169
Howard Law School, 167–70
Howard University, 37, 38
Huggins, Erika, 154
Hunt's Merchants' Magazine, 16
hypersegregated nation, 163–66, 186,
    187n3

industrial educational programs:
    Burroughs on, 57; classical versus,
    54–58; Cooper on, 56; pragmatic
    views on, 55–56
"The Influence of Climate upon
    Longevity," 16
integration solution, 173–75; Bell on,
    177–78; *Brown v. Board of Education*
    and, 170–73; class/caste system
    and, 175; communism and, 176,
    181; equal educational opportunity
    from, 179–80; failure of, 178;
    racial balance and, 177–78; racial
    segregation and, 175–77; separate
    but equal and, 172–73; SNCC for,
    138
Intercommunal Youth Institute (IYI):
    direct-experience learning at, 153–
    54; progressive pedagogy of, 153;
    student encouragement at, 152–53;
    student portrayal of, 151. *See also*
    Oakland Community School

interest convergence theory: Bell on,
    180; compromise/consensus of,
    180–81
IYI. *See* Intercommunal Youth
    Institute

Jamison, Theodore, 127, 130
Jefferson, Thomas: Black inferiority
    argument of, 17; educational system
    proposed by, 28–29, 43n3
Jenkins, Martin David, 97
Jennings, Regina, 149
Jim Crow, 49, 51, 52, 96, 140, 144,
    165, 167, 172, 177, 181, 185,
    187n7
Johnson, Mordecai, 168
Jonathan Livingston Seagull, 155

Kant, Immanuel, 17
Katherine Dunham: Dancing a Life
    (Ashenbrenner), 127
Kelley, Robin D. G., 169
Kennedy, John F., 126
Kincheloe, Joe, 75, 76, 80, 83, 86
King, Martin Luther, Jr., 126, 157,
    183
Kluger, Richard, 168–69, 172
Ku Klux Klan, 169

Ladson-Billings, Gloria, 74, 75, 83,
    86
Lane, Lunsford, 4
Laney, Lucy Craft, 52
Langston, John Mercer, x;
    achievements of, 27, 35;
    acknowledgment, lack of, 43;
    as congressman, 39–40; court
    register on, 31, 43n5; early years
    of, 30–34; education of, 32,
    40–41, 44n7; family history of, 31,
    43–44n6; Freedmen's Bureau and,
    35; on his parents, 31; Howard
    University and, 38; for national

About the Editors and Contributors

Editors

Noel S. Anderson is an associate professor in the Department of Political Science at Brooklyn College of City University of New York. He received his Ph.D. from New York University. His scholarly research focuses on urban politics and education, education policy, and comparative issues in education policy (South Africa/United States). He is the coauthor of *Our Schools Suck: Students Talk Back to a Segregated Nation on the Failure of Urban Education* (2009).

Haroon Kharem is an associate professor in the School of Education at Brooklyn College of City University of New York. He received his Ph.D. from the Pennsylvania State University. His scholarly research focuses on race and education and African American history. He is the author of *Curriculum of Repression: Pedagogy of Racial History in the United States* (2006).

Contributors

A. A. Akom is an assistant professor of urban sociology and Africana studies and codirector of educational equity at the Cesar Chavez Institute at San Francisco State University. He received his Ph.D. from the University of Pennsylvania. His research interests are urban ethnography, urban sociology, racial identity formation, and youth culture. His scholarly work has appeared in numerous academic journals, edited texts, and periodicals.

Ojeya Cruz Banks is a dance anthropologist and choreographer in the dance studies program and directs Dance Lab at the University of Otago in Dunedin, New Zealand. She received her Ph.D. from the University of Arizona. Her dance research has been conducted in Uganda, Zanzibar, Mali, Guinea, Cuba, and several other countries.

Eric A. Hurley is an assistant professor in the Departments of Psychology and Black Studies at Pomona College. He received his Ph.D. from Howard University. His research interests are minority education, stereotype threat, and Black psychology. He has published in numerous academic journals.

Karen A. Johnson is an assistant professor in the Department of Education, Culture, and Society at the University of Utah. She received her Ph.D. from the University of California, Los Angeles. Her research interests are cultural studies/historical foundations of education, multicultural education, and Black feminist theory. She is the author of *Uplifting the Women and the Race: The Educational Philosophies and Social Activism of Anna Julia Cooper and Nannie Helen Burroughs* (2000).

Judith E. King-Calnek teaches anthropology, theory of knowledge, and history at the United Nations International School. She received her Ph.D. from Columbia University–Teachers College.

Daniel Perlstein is an associate professor at UC Berkeley's Graduate School of Education. He received his Ph.D. from Stanford University. His work focuses on the interplay of democratic aspirations and social inequality in American schools. He is the author of *Justice, Justice: School Politics and the Eclipse of Liberalism* (2004).

Sabrina N. Ross is a visiting assistant professor in women's and gender studies and African American studies at the University of North Carolina at Greensboro. She earned her Ph.D. from the University of North Carolina at Greensboro. Her research areas include race/ethnic and gender identities, Black feminist and womanist philosophies, and philosophies of education. She is the coeditor of *The Institution of Education* (2006).